Applied Econometrics Association Series

General Editors: **Jean H. P. Paelinck**, Emeritus Professor, Erasmus University, Rotterdam; and **Henri Serbat**, University of Paris 2.

The vital importance of econometrics for understanding economic phenomena is increasingly recognized in every field of economics.

The discipline is based on 'scientific processes which aim to identify, explain and forecast economic phenomena using formalised tools to produce, measure, structure and model the information' (Gerard Duru and Henri Serbat, 1991).

The Applied Econometrics Association, established in 1974, seeks to develop the use of econometric tools by producing regular updates on the state of the art and the progress made in each specific field, and so to further the transformation of unconnected facts into pertinent information for the use in analysis and decision-making.

The series was conceived to form a set of working references for advanced students and researchers in each specific field, as well as a guide to development across the discipline more broadly.

This exchange of knowledge will be continued permanently by the opening of a debate-site on the Internet [http://www.aea.Fed-Eco.org].

Titles include:

Françoise Bourdon and Jean Bourdon (*editors*)
WAGE ECONOMETRICS AND MODELLING

Fabrizio Carlevaro and Jean-Baptiste Lesourt (*editors*)
MEASURING AND ACCOUNTING ENVIRONMENTAL NUISANCES AND SERVICES

Arthur Getis, Jesús Mur and Henry G. Zoller (*editors*)
SPATIAL ECONOMETRICS AND SPATIAL STATISTICS

Siv S. Gustafsson and Danièle E. Meulders (*editors*)
GENDER AND THE LABOUR MARKET
Econometric Evidence of Obstacles to Achieving Gender Equality

Hans Heijke and Joan Muysken (*editors*)
EDUCATION AND TRAINING IN A KNOWLEDGE-BASED ECONOMY

Pavlos Karadeloglou (*editor*)
EXCHANGE-RATE POLICY IN EUROPE

Sandrine Lardic and Valérie Mignon (*editors*)
RECENT DEVELOPMENTS ON EXCHANGE RATES

Danièle Meulders, Robert Plasman and Francois Rycz (*editors*)
MINIMUM WAGES, LOW PAY AND UNEMPLOYMENT

Carine Peeters and Bruno van Pottelsberghe de la Potterie (*editors*)
ECONOMIC AND MANAGEMENT PERSPECTIVES ON INTELLECTUAL PROPERTY RIGHTS

Emile Quinet and Roger Vickerman (*editors*)
THE ECONOMETRICS OF MAJOR TRANSPORT INFRASTRUCTURES

Philippe Thalmann and Milad Zarin-Nejadan (*editors*)
CONSTRUCTION AND REAL ESTATE DYNAMICS

Applied Econometrics Association
Series Standing Order ISBN 978-0-333-71460-7
(*outside North America only*)

You can receive future titles in this series as they are published by placing a standing order. Please contact your bookseller or, in case of difficulty, write to us at the address below with your name and address, the title of the series and the ISBN quoted above.

Customer Services Department, Macmillan Distribution Ltd, Houndmills, Basingstoke, Hampshire RG21 6XS, England

Economic and Management Perspectives on Intellectual Property Rights

Edited by

Carine Peeters

and

Bruno van Pottelsberghe de la Potterie

palgrave
macmillan

Softcover reprint of the hardcover 1st edition 2006 978-1-4039-4963-9

First published in 2006 by
PALGRAVE MACMILLAN
Houndmills, Basingstoke, Hampshire RG21 6XS and
175 Fifth Avenue, New York, N.Y. 10010
Companies and representatives throughout the world.

PALGRAVE MACMILLAN is the global academic imprint of the Palgrave Macmillan division of St. Martin's Press, LLC and of Palgrave Macmillan Ltd. Macmillan® is a registered trademark in the United States, United Kingdom and other countries. Palgrave is a registered trademark in the European Union and other countries.

ISBN 978-1-349-52589-8 ISBN 978-0-230-50474-5 (eBook)
DOI 10.1057/9780230504745

This book is printed on paper suitable for recycling and made from fully managed and sustained forest sources.

A catalogue record for this book is available from the British Library.

A catalog record for this book is available from the Library of Congress.

10 9 8 7 6 5 4 3 2 1
15 14 13 12 11 10 09 08 07 06

Transferred to digital printing in 2007.

Contents

Part II Knowledge Transfer and Intellectual Property Systems

Part III Innovation Management and Intellectual Property Rights

List of Tables

List of Figures

Notes on the Contributors

Stefano Breschi is Associate Professor of Applied Economics at Bocconi University and Deputy Director of CESPRI (Bocconi University, Milan). He earned his PhD in economics from the University of Pavia with a dissertation on the geography of innovation. Since then his research interests have extended to the geographical aspects of knowledge diffusion and network analysis and the new economics of science. He has published in *Economic Journal, Research Policy, Economics of Innovation and New Technology, Industrial and Corporate Change* and the *Annales d'Economie et Statistique*.

Michele Cincera is Associate Professor at the Free University of Brussels (ULB) and has been affiliated to the Centre d'Economie Regionale et de la Technologie at DULBEA since 1993. He is also a Research Fellow of the Centre for Economic Policy Research. His research interests embrace the quantitative assessment at the micro-level of innovative activities, their determinants and their socio-economic impacts, the analysis of National Innovation Systems, and the development of new S&T indicators.

Arnoud De Meyer is Akzo Nobel Fellow in Strategic Management and Professor of Technology Management at INSEAD, Paris. Formerly Associate Dean for the MBA programme, Director General of the INSEAD Euro-Asia centre and Dean of the Asia Campus, he is now Deputy Dean of INSEAD, in charge of Operations External Relations. Arnoud De Meyer has a doctoral degree in management from the State University of Ghent (Belgium). He was Visiting Professor at Keio Business School (Tokyo), Waseda University (Tokyo) and the University of Kiel (Germany). He has also taught at the University of Gent (Belgium). Professor De Meyer's main research interests are in manufacturing and technology strategy and the management of R&D.

Sam Garg is Research Fellow at IWSEAD, Singapore. He is co-author (with Arnoud De Meyer) of Inspire to Innovate.

Christine Greenhalgh is Director of Economic Research at the Oxford Intellectual Property Research Centre and Tutor in Economics, St Peter's College. Her research includes the economics of intellectual property and technological change, with a special interest in the employment and skills consequences of such change.

Dietmar Harhoff is Professor of Business Administration at the Ludwig-Maximilian University (LMU), Munich. He is the Director of the Institute of Innovation Research, Technology Management and Entrepreneurship and a Co-Director of the ODEON Center for Entrepreneurship at LMU. From 1985 to 1987 he was a McCloy Scholar at Harvard University and concluded his PhD studies at MIT in 1991 with a dissertation on research incentives and voluntary information revelation. In 1998 he joined LMU's School of Management in his current position. Dietmar Harhoff's research focuses on issues in innovation and entrepreneurship research, industrial economics and technology management, and has been published in a large number of book and journal articles.

Sung Jin Kang is an Assistant Professor at the Department of Economics, Korea University. He received a PhD from Stanford University in 1999. His publications relate to Q-convergence with interquartile ranges, the *Journal of Economic Dynamics and Control* (2005). His current research topics are technology spillover through FDI and patents and their impacts on productivity.

Francesco Lissoni is Associate Professor of Applied Economics at the University of Brescia, Deputy Director of CESPRI (Bocconi University, Milan) and coordinator of the European Summer School on Industrial Dynamics. He earned his PhD in economics from the University of Manchester with a dissertation on adoption of new technologies. Since then his research interests have extended to the geographical aspects of knowledge diffusion, university technology transfer and the new economics of science. He has published in *research policy, economics of innovation and new technology, industrial and corporate change*, the *Cambridge Journal of Economics* and the *Annales d'Economie et Statistique*.

Fabio Montobbio is Associate Professor of Political Economy at the University of Insubria, Varese, and Senior Researcher at CESPRI (Bocconi University, Milan). His PhD from the University of Manchester was on technological spillovers and structural change. His research interests are patent economics, the measurement of knowledge spillovers, the economics of science and sectoral patterns of innovation and structural change. He has published in *World Development*, the *Cambridge Journal* of *Economics*, the *Journal of Evolutionary Economics*, and *Structural Change and Economic Dynamics*.

Sadao Nagaoka is the Director (Professor) of the Institute of Innovation Research of Hitotsubashi University in Japan. He has a PhD in economics and an MS in management from the Massachusetts Institute of Technology. He worked in the Ministry of International Trade and Industry and the World Bank before joining the Hitotsubashi University.

Carine Peeters is Research Fellow at Duke University. She obtained her PhD from the Solvay Business School, Université Libre de Bruxelles. Her research focuses on innovation capabilities, patenting behaviour and performance of firms. She is now Research Fellow at the Fuqua School of Business, Duke University, where she works on a research project on offshoring of white-collar jobs by US and EU firms.

Robert Pitkethly is Lecturer in Management Studies at the Said Business School, Fellow and Tutor in Management at St Peter's College, Oxford, and a Senior Research Associate of the Oxford Intellectual Property Research Centre. He holds degrees in chemistry, business administration, and Japanese studies and has qualified and worked as a UK and European patent attorney and management consultant.

Mark Rogers is Senior Research Fellow at the Oxford Intellectual Property Research Centre and Tutor in Economics at Harris Manchester College. His research interests include empirical research on economic growth and industrial organization, with a focus on innovation, knowledge and intellectual property.

Astrid Romain is Research Fellow at the Solvay Business School and in the Department of Applied Economics (DULBEA) at Université Libre de Bruxelles. Her research interests embrace the venture capital, technology-based small firms and entrepreneurship. She is doing a PhD at the Solvay Business School on the empirical analysis of high-tech entrepreneurship.

Hwan Joo Seo is Assistant Professor in the Department of Economics at the Sangji University in South Korea. He received his PhD from EFESS in 1998. His current research interests concern services innovations and the role of IPR in the innovation process.

Bruno van Pottelsberghe de la Potterie is Vice-president of the Solvay Business School (ULB), and Director of its MBA Programmes. As holder of the Solvay SA Chair of Innovation he teaches courses on the economics and management of innovation and intellectual property. His research and publications are articulated around five main themes: the effectiveness of S&T policies, the internationalization of R&D activities, innovation competencies in large firms, the factors fostering entrepreneurship, and the economics and management of intellectual property. Before joining the teaching staff of the ULB, Bruno van Pottelsberghe worked for two years at the OECD (Department of Science, Technology and Industry). He has been visiting researcher at the Columbia Business School and at the Research Institute of the METI (Tokyo) and Visiting Professor at the Institute of Innovation Research of Hitotsubashi University (Tokyo) and at the Stellenbosch Business School (Cape Town).

Introduction: Advanced Research Findings and Fields for Further Research in Economics and Management of Intellectual Property

Bruno van Pottelsberghe de la Potterie
and Carine Peeters

The role of intellectual property (IP), and more precisely the role of patents, is increasingly considered as a major issue for managers and policy-makers. At the firm level, patents are used as a legal protection means for innovative products and processes, and as a strategic tool in technological negotiations. At the country level, the patent system aims at fostering research efforts and innovation, and ultimately economic growth.

The effectiveness of IP systems, and their role in the innovation process is, however, not unanimously recognized, and is far from being well understood. The objective of this book is to shed some light on the effectiveness of patents in stimulating innovation and growth. It is composed of ten chapters that focus on a specific issue of the relationship between IPRs and innovation. The chapters originate from selected papers presented at the AEA Conference on Innovation and Intellectual Property, held in Singapore on INSEAD Campus, in July 2004.

Beside their contribution to the existing literature on intellectual property and innovation, the ten chapters are multidisciplinary in their research methodologies, units of analysis and levels of implications, and international in their scope and content. The various quantitative methods used in the studies range from survey data analysis to econometric techniques and advanced indicators. They are applied at individual, firm, sector and country levels to derive implications in terms of both management of IP and public policy. The international dimension of the book is best assessed by looking at the panel of authors and the various regions they address. Actually, the authors of the ten chapters

Table I.1 Disciplines and geographical scope of the ten chapters

Chapters	Regions studied	Survey data	Quantitative methods	Managerial implications	Policy implications	Analytical level
1	Europe		x	x		Firm/Sector
2	UK		x		x	Firm
3	UK	x		x	x	VCs
4	Italy		x		x	Inventors
5	Belgium		x		x	Sector/Macro
6	Global		x		x	Macro
7	Asia	x		x		Firm
8	Global		x	x		Macro/Firm
9	Belgium	x	x	x		Firm
10	Global		x		x	Macro

originate from eight different countries, from Hitotsubashi University in Japan to Oxford University in the UK and Duke University in the US. Their papers focus either on specific countries or regions, or use panel data including several countries. The geographical scope, research methodology, management versus public policy implications, and analytical level of the various studies are summarized in Table I.1.

The variety of all contributions makes it *a priori* difficult to provide a synthetic overview of the ten chapters. However, a closer look reveals that the different contributions complement each other to a much larger extent than would appear at first sight.

One major field of investigation in this book concerns the effectiveness of patents and the patent systems in stimulating innovation and growth. The contribution of Kang and Seo (Chapter 6) suggests that IPRs are positively and significantly related to innovation once other complementary aspects of the environment are taken into account, such as the stage of economic development, industrial structure, trade regime and institutional environment. This idea is extensively illustrated by De Meyer and Garg in the case of Asian countries (Chapter 7). The authors show that education, training, market data, IP enforcement and managerial practices constitute a different context to innovation in Asia than in the Western world. The issue put forward by Kang and Seo is further discussed by Greenhalgh and Rogers (Chapter 2), who show that the market valuation of patents depends on the type of patents considered (UK or EPO) and on the level of competition within the industrial sector. Pitkethly (Chapter 3) also argues that the patent system should not be extended to business methods inventions, as business methods patents are not valued by venture capitalists. In this respect, the macroeconomic study of Romain and van Pottelsberghe (Chapter 10) confirms that high technological opportunities, as witnessed by a high number of triadic patents, do attract higher levels of venture capital.

A second broad field of investigation regards the innovation process and its relationship with patents. Relying on the observation that intellectual property rights are increasingly important in determining a firm's value, Harhoff (Chapter 1) provides an original behavioural analysis of oppositions filed against EPO patents and discusses how organizational capabilities in patent documentation and IP management can determine the successful opposition of rivals' patents. Nagaoka (Chapter 8) suggests that it is possible to measure the speed, focus, science base and quality of the innovation process with patent data. He demonstrates that speed, focus and the reliance on scientific knowledge translate into quantity and quality of patent applications. Concerning the business–science relationship, Breschi *et al.* (Chapter 4) find that the majority of Italian academic inventions are patented by business partners. This collaborative process seems to further stimulate the scientific productivity of academic inventors, as they seem to be more productive in terms of publications than their colleagues who are not involved in patenting. Peeters and van Pottelsberghe (Chapter 9) provide further evidence that various dimensions of an innovation strategy affect the patenting portfolio of firms. The propensity to collaborate with universities through contract research has a particularly strong and positive effect. The idea that academic research plays an increasingly important role in business innovation is validated by Cincera (Chapter 5) who shows that the R&D activities of MNEs are directed towards the host country's revealed technological advantage. The presence of such foreign R&D centres is found to reduce the importance of brain drain.

In what follows the main findings of each of the ten contributions are summarized. For each chapter we attempt to highlight the most remarkable arguments and conclusions, and make suggestions in terms of interesting issues for further research.

Firms Differ Significantly in Their Ability to Handle Patent Oppositions (Chapter 1)

Given the increasingly important role of intellectual property in building and maintaining corporate value, firms are likely to fight hard in the battle for patent rights. Dietmar Harhoff analyses several aspects of this 'battleground' and attempts to shed some light on three particular issues. The first one concerns the extent of oppositions filed against patents granted by the EPO. The second one relates to the determinants of this opposition activity. And the third one has to do with the success factors in undertaking patent oppositions and in defending against such attacks.

The author relies on opposition data for all patents granted by the EPO between 1980 and 1995 in two main industrial sectors: cosmetics and detergents. The following results emerge from the empirical analysis:

- A total of 7.9 per cent of patents granted by the EPO between 1980 and 1995 have been opposed. About one third of opposed patents were revoked, another third was amended, and only 27 per cent of oppositions were rejected. This indicates that the EPO opposition mechanism has a strong corrector effect.
- Opposition is more likely to occur for highly valuable patents and is more frequent in more uncertain technical and market fields. Conversely, opposition is less likely in the case of firms with large patent portfolios and less frequent for independent inventors than corporate applicants.
- Some companies (e.g., Henkel) attack more frequently than other firms do, and there is no notable reduction in its opposition success that would point to a trade-off between frequency and success of opposition.
- Firms differ significantly in their ability to handle opposition to their patents. Some firms seem also better at opposition than others. The latter might be explained by differences in organizational capabilities related to patent documentation and IP management.

Further work into what particular organizational capabilities enable firms to be more successful than others in patent opposition would extend the present study in a very interesting way. In that respect, it would be relevant to investigate more deeply the pros and cons of developing large in-house documentation centres versus using end-user tools rendered largely accessible through the Internet and commercial patent databases. Timing issues in the probability, extent and success of filing patent oppositions might also open valuable areas for further research.

EPO Patents and a Low Level of Competition Improve Market Valuation (Chapter 2)

Christine Greenhalgh and Mark Rogers study the market value of intellectual property activities and investigate how the degree of competition influences such valuations. Firms may use the IP system to temper competition, raising the value of their innovations. As a result, the level of competition, as well as the nature and efficiency of the IP system, will determine the expected value of innovations. The chapter seeks to shed some light on these issues by analysing the stock market value of R&D and IP on a sample of UK firms.

The empirical analysis relies on a new panel dataset (from the Oxford Intellectual Property Research Centre Database) on R&D and IP activities of UK production firms covering the period 1989 to 1999. The authors extend the traditional approach to analysing the market value of innovative firms in a number of ways. First, they investigate whether the market valuation of firm-level innovation varies across sectors and firms. Second, in contrast to previous studies, the analysis includes the role of both trade mark activity and UK and European Patent Office patent activity. Third, the authors build two alternative proxies of the firms' competitive environment. At the sector level they use profit persistence analysis to capture the extent of competition, a new approach in the literature on market value. At the firm level they use market share, a traditional proxy for market power and an inverse proxy for competition.

Several interesting results emerge from their empirical analyses. They can be summarized as follows:

- Using Pavitt's typology of sectors, which is based on differences in the process of technological change, large differences appear in the market valuation of R&D and IP activity across sectors.
- On average, higher R&D, EPO patenting and UK trade marking (relative to firm size) all tend to increase market value, but UK patenting does not have a straightforward impact. Although UK patenting is more prevalent than EPO patenting for UK-based firms (it is expensive to extend a patent internationally), EPO filings seem to be a better indicator of value.
- A higher market share improves the valuation of UK patent activity (although the strength and significance of such an effect varies across sectors).
- The results support Schumpeter much more than Arrow concerning the hypothetical relationship between market structure and innovation. The market valuation of R&D is indeed higher in sectors with relatively low competitive pressure.

Chapter 2 opens various avenues for further research. Among these, it would be of particular interest to take into account the international activities of the firms included in the sample. Indeed, taking into consideration foreign sales performances might significantly affect both the measurement of market shares and the statistical relationship between market valuation and patenting activity. Another research opportunity is suggested by the authors. It consists in taking into account the spillover effects induced by the R&D activities of the science-based sector, and test whether such spillovers would affect the complex relationship between the market valuation of R&D and the competition level of a sector.

Business Methods Patents are Not Valued by Venture Capitalists (Chapter 3)

Robert Pitkethly opens his chapter with a historical review of the controversial role of patent systems. The controversy concerns in particular the effectiveness of IP systems as a policy tool used to foster investments in innovation. The author refers to Penrose's statement that uncertainty about the consequences of a patent system counsels against implementing one where none exists, as well as against abolishing any existing system. According to Robert Pitkethly, this argument which is often used in discussions on the scope of individual patents can further be applied to debates on the creation of new fields of patent protection where none have existed previously.

One such recent debate concerns the granting of patents for business methods. Currently, 'methods of doing business' are excluded from patentability under European and UK Patent Law. There are no corresponding restrictions in the Patent Law of the United States and patents are being granted on business methods. Drawing on a UK-based survey the chapter discusses implications of granting business method patents (BMPs). Rather than merely revisiting past debates, changes in patent law and the IP environment give reason enough to raise old questions in the light of new circumstances.

The effectiveness of patents as incentives to invest in R&D does after all not only depend on what the patent system can and does provide but also, at least to some extent, on what investors believe or perceive that it provides. This research investigates the effect of possession by companies seeking venture capital (VC) funding of IPRs, and in particular patents and BMPs, on the willingness of VC investors to invest in them. It is particularly informative about the benefits patents, and BMPs especially, might or might not provide to society.

The empirical implementation of the research relies on a survey addressed to executives who directly or indirectly participate in VC investment decisions or advise those who do. The main objective of the survey was to assess whether the possession of intellectual property rights by companies seeking investment affects VC investment decisions:

- The data show quite clearly that IPRs can increase the attractiveness of an investment opportunity in the eyes of venture capital executives and those advising business angels.
- However, this attractiveness-enhancing effect differs significantly across sectors, and not just as a result of different legal environments.
- Patent applications in the chemical/pharmaceutical and biotechnology sector do substantially increase investment attractiveness.
- The overwhelming response seems to be that business method patents (BMPs) would have at most some, but in general very little, effect on investment decisions.
- These findings have implications for both firm IP management and national IP policy regarding patents, and business method patents in particular.

The quotes from two survey respondents provide some clear explanations as to why BMPs would not attract venture capitalists. One of them underlines 'tacit knowledge' as the most valuable form of intellectual property. The other one emphasizes much higher priorities than BMPs, such as market opportunities and a skilled team of sales, marketing and support people.

In view of his research findings about VC investment incentives and several considerations regarding the other potential benefits of BMPs, Robert Pitkethly concludes that their costs are almost inevitably going to outweigh their benefits.

Further investigation would be welcome in this promising area of research. First, such cost/benefit analysis should be performed more frequently and extended to other technological areas, such as the software industry, to cite only one. In addition, it would be legitimate to wonder whether the venture capitalist's perception is not biased by their view of the current patent system. In this respect, a similar analysis for the US VC industry – where BMPs are allowed and frequently used – would be informative. Finally, this research focuses on later-stage investment incentives, while patent systems are designed to stimulate inventions. It would therefore also be interesting to survey the perceptions of the inventors of new business methods.

Academic Patenting Seems to Improve Publication Performance (Chapter 4)

Stefano Breschi, Francesco Lissoni and Fabio Montobbio address the issue of university patenting and its impact on the scientific activity of academic researchers. The relationship between patenting and publishing may be negative for two main reasons. First, there may be a 'publication delay' effect and/or a 'basic-applied trade-off'. Publication delays may be induced by the novelty step requirement in patent legislations: ideas that enter the common pool of knowledge through a published output are not new. In other words, academic researchers that aim to (or must) file a patent should keep their inventions secret as long as the patent application has not been filed. Second, the diversion of a researcher's attention from basic research to more applied targets may result in lower rates of publications in international scientific journals. This can exert non-negligible effects if patenting is non-occasional and if it results from business-oriented research.

The authors also provide three arguments as to why there might be no such publishing–patenting trade-off: the 'resource effect', the 'productivity-fixed effect' and the 'augmented Matthew effect'. These arguments suggest that patenting by scientists would contribute further to raise contract research (i.e., increase the level of academic research), and that patents and publications are both part of a research quality indicator and a researcher's reward and incentive system (visibility, reputation, access to further resources, financial incentives).

The issue is addressed empirically with data at the individual level. The number of scientific publications of a sample of 296 academic inventors is compared to a sample of 296 matched controls, with patenting as a treatment variable. A new longitudinal dataset of 592 Italian professors is used to compare matched pairs of patenting and non-patenting individuals. The authors enquire whether a trade-off is caused by publication delays or a shift from basic to applied research, or whether a 'resource effect' occurs, by which academic inventors access superior resources as long as they take care of IPRs over their research results.

The empirical work exploits two data sources. One contains information on Italian 'academic inventors' (available in patent data). The other is based upon the *ad hoc* collection of publication data on both these 'academic inventors' and a sample of 'non-inventor' colleagues, from the on-line version of ISI's *Science Citation Index*.

The econometric analysis leads to the following results:

- Academic inventors are highly productive scientists, even more productive than their non-inventor controls.
- The difference is particularly relevant for persistent inventors, namely those scientists who patent more than once over a long time period.
- Patents have a significantly positive impact in terms of increased number of publications within the scientist's academic career. Holding other variables constant, being an inventor improves scientific productivity by about 14 per cent.
- It is, however, not possible to exclude the existence of some 'publication delay effect'.

An important institutional specificity of the Italian case is that 75 per cent of patents signed by at least one academic inventor belong to business companies. These patents are often the result of research contracts, by which the business company retains all the intellectual property rights over the research results. The above findings suggest, therefore, that contract research may generate a positive 'resource' effect on the academic inventors' publication rate, in particular when it expands over long time periods.

The conclusions of the three authors open several fields for further research. One important research question relates to national academic systems. One might wonder to what extent these results would hold in the case of academic patents applied for by universities (as opposed to business firms). Indeed, the patenting process requires a lot of time, resources and competences, which might affect an academic inventor's behaviour. The methodology developed in Chapter 4 could be used to validate the positive publishing–patenting relationship in other countries than Italy. As suggested by the authors, another issue would be to investigate whether by patenting their research results, academic inventors reduce the accessibility of their inventions to other scientists, hence reducing the pace of innovation.

R&D Activities of Foreign MNEs Seem to Reduce the Risk of Brain Drain (Chapter 5)

Michele Cincera opens his chapter with striking evidence put forward by the European Commission about brain drain flows among industrial economies. For instance, about 75 per cent of EU-born US doctorate recipients who graduated between 1991 and 2000 had no specific plans to return to the EU. The most important reasons which keep EU-born scientists and engineers abroad relate to the quality of work, better prospects and projects, and easier access to leading technologies.

The purpose of this chapter is to shed some light on one aspect of this international mobility of factors by examining the interactions between the emigration of highly skilled workers and the presence of subsidiaries of foreign MNEs in a small open economy like Belgium. Based on European and US patent statistics, the author performs an empirical analysis of R&D activities carried out by foreign MNEs in Belgium over the last two decades. He investigates the role of demand-pull and technology-push determinants of the MNE's decision to delocalize its R&D in a host country as well as the impact of these activities on brain drain of Belgian R&D personnel. The empirical analysis leads to four main observations:

- The scientific fields where Belgium holds comparative advantage with respect to the OECD are characterized by a strong presence of foreign firms.
- The relatively low value of patents applied for by foreign subsidiaries suggests that the main objective of MNEs' R&D units may be the transfer and adaptation of existing knowledge to the host country (i.e., Belgium).
- Higher R&D internationalization is associated with lower rates of emigration of highly educated workers across countries. In other words, the importance of brain drain is smaller in highly internationalized countries.
- There seems to be a positive 'brain gain' (higher number of new inventors in patents applied for by foreign subsidiaries and MNEs as compared to domestic firms) associated with the presence of foreign MNEs.

These results suggest that MNEs invest in R&D in Belgium mainly in order to gain access to the local science base. The presence of these companies positively affects the demand for highly skilled workers and hence reduces the importance of brain drain. Important policy implications are suggested by the author, especially regarding policies aiming at increased openness and attraction of foreign R&D laboratories.

This chapter induces several fields for further research. One of them would be to validate these results with data on other small open economies like Sweden, Finland and Switzerland. Another interesting analysis would be to assess the extent to which foreign MNEs enter into collaborative R&D with local firms and especially with local universities.

Stronger Intellectual Property Rights Do Not Always Lead to More Innovation (Chapter 6)

There is an ongoing debate on whether stronger IPRs encourage or retard innovative activities. W. D. Nordhaus initiated the economic analysis of patent systems, showing that granting innovators temporary monopoly power for the exploitation of their inventions enhances R&D efforts and innovative activities. However, recent empirical and theoretical analyses put forward more mitigated, and sometimes opposite, conclusions.

Professors Sung Jin Kang and Hwan Joo Seo study this issue empirically over a large number of countries. Their contribution aims at testing whether the strengthening of intellectual property rights would effectively stimulate innovation. The authors argue that such empirical exercise must be performed by taking into account complementary factors such as industrial structure, social capability and trade regime.

The quantitative analysis, which relies on a long-run panel dataset of about 110 countries, draws the following conclusions:

- There is no evidence that stronger IPRs alone boost innovation, as measured by the number of patent applications.
- IPRs are positively and significantly related to innovation once other complementary aspects of the environment for innovation are taken into account, such as the stage of economic development, industrial structure, trade regime and institutional environment.
- Even when complementary conditions are taken into account, some countries are negatively affected by stronger IPRs.

These results suggest that the effectiveness of IPRs in fostering innovation varies across countries according to national economic and institutional contexts. For example, only countries with a per capita GDP above about US$ 9,000 seem to gain from the strengthening of IPRs. The authors conclude with a discussion of the potential implications of their results for current international policy debates regarding TRIPs (Trade Related Intellectual Property).

This issue is indeed of critical importance for less developed economies. Further research would be required to shed more light on the debate. A first avenue for future empirical investigation would be to use another indicator of innovation effort than patent data. IPR regimes are designed to spur innovation. In this respect, the number of researchers or R&D outlays might be appropriate to assess the effectiveness of IPR regimes. Another field of research would be to assess what component(s) of an IP policy design (e.g., scope, length, quality, enforcement etc.) plays the most important role in stimulating innovation.

Asian Firms have Specific Perceptions and Competences as Regards the Innovation Process (Chapter 7)

The starting point of the chapter by Arnoud De Meyer and Sam Garg originates from Asian managers' view regarding the management of innovation. These managers argue that the application of the lessons learned in the Western world may well be different in Asia. The argument is not that the lessons do not apply, but rather that the specific circumstances in East Asia are such that their implementation would be radically different.

The study presented in Chapter 7 aims at understanding how the implementation of innovation management concepts is indeed different in Asia. The research methodology consisted first in collecting data on 30 innovative firms or innovative clusters in order to specify a large number of hypotheses about innovation management in Asia. In a second step the authors developed a questionnaire that was sent to 336 senior managers in East and South Asia. Numerous observations are derived from this study. The most compelling ones can be summarized as follows:

- On top of the shortage in training, companies in Asia are confronted with a lack of quality of training.
- Asian financial markets miss the sophistication and the willingness to invest in innovation.
- The mindset of many managers in Asia drives them towards cost-reduction strategies, as opposed to the creation of new value.
- The average Asian company has a limited understanding of, or experience with, marketing. Brand building is often neglected and there is an absolute lack of reliable market data.
- The regulatory environment favourable to innovators and entrepreneurship is often lacking: innovators need good IPR protection and in particular the enforcement of these rights.
- Local governments tend to be conservative in their procurements and do not favour local innovators over well-established international brands.

A set of factors are specific to Asia and influence the implementation of innovation management practices developed in the Western world. It is worth mentioning that not all companies/respondents evaluate the factors specific to Asia in the same way. A typology of four groups of companies/respondents is put forward by the authors: the innovation starters, the tradition fighters, the poor in knowledge resources, and the stuck in the muck. The chapter extensively documents the different types of support required by the four groups. This discussion should help policy-makers and educators in the field of management to customize their action to each of their specific targets.

From this chapter it seems that our understanding of the innovation process in Asia would particularly benefit from two main fields for further research. The first one would be to conduct a similar survey in Europe, Japan and the US in order to test whether the above results are really specific to Asia. Another interesting field of investigation would be to measure the extent to which the four typologies correlate with the financial performance of surveyed firms.

Speed, Science Linkage and Focus Affect R&D Performance (Chapter 8)

Sadao Nagaoka examines how the speed, science linkage and focus of corporate R&D as well as new entry matter as determinants of R&D performance in the IT (information technology) sector. He discusses the recent R&D performance of US, Japanese and European firms from this perspective. The author relies on the number of forward patent citations per patent and the number of patents as proxies for the quality and for the quantity of innovation respectively. He uses these measures as indicators of the performance of R&D.

The two measures show that, in the 1990s, the R&D performance of US firms in the IT sector improved significantly relative to the rest of the world. Several hypotheses may explain this improvement. One is better management practices and organization of US firms (more emphasis on speed). Second, many US firms may have chosen a vertical disintegration strategy. The third reason is the increasing dependence of the IT industry innovation on scientific research. Fourth, a more entrepreneurial culture would translate into the entry of more new technology firms. The 1990s were indeed characterized by a sharp increase in the contribution of small firms to aggregate R&D outlays in the US.

Sadao Nagaoka attempts to assess quantitatively the significance and the contribution of the above four factors as determinants of R&D

performance. The speed of the innovation process is measured by the time lag between a patent and its underlying patent literature. The frequency of references made by a patent to scientific journals would provide a measure of the propensity of firms to exploit scientific knowledge. The degree of concentration of the patent portfolio of a firm is used to measure the extent to which a firm has a focused research agenda. New entrants are defined as firms that are major patentees in the most recent period (1998–2002) but do not have patents granted in the previous periods.

There is clear evidence that in IT areas patenting performance of US firms compared to Japanese firms has improved in both quantity and quality. The econometric analysis provided in Chapter 8 attempts better to understand the determinants of this improved performance. The results can be summarized as follows:

- There is a positive effect of speed on research productivity. That is, higher speed of R&D measured by citation lag improves R&D performance in terms of both the quality and the number of patents granted.
- There is a positive effect of science linkage on research productivity. That is, a stronger science base, as measured by citations to the scientific literature, improves the R&D performance of a firm in terms of both quality and number of patents granted.
- A focused research agenda tends to improve patent quality in the IT core sector, but does not lead to a higher quantity of patents. A firm that patents in a single technology domain has a patent quality indicator 11 per cent higher than a firm that patents in two technology domains.
- New entrants have higher patent quality than incumbents, only part of which can be explained by an average higher speed and stronger science linkage.

The above findings suggest that the higher performance of US firms is due to their increased R&D speed, intensification of science linkage and a substantially higher rate of new entries. This result is consistent with the idea that the increase in patenting in the US has been driven by changes in the management of innovation by US firms, which brought a real burst in innovation.

The methodology developed by Sadao Nagaoka is a good example of how quantitative analyses can be used to assess the management of R&D. Three avenues for future research can be raised to improve or validate this methodology. First, it would clearly be interesting to extend the analysis to other sectors or technologies. Second, the robustness of the indicators presented by the author could be further tested. One important issue is whether the reliance on the United States Patents and Trademarks Office (USPTO) data might bias the results, through a potential 'home effect'. Indeed, new entrants generally lack resources to apply for patents abroad. The significance of the bias could be assessed through the use of EPO (European Patent Office) or JPO (Japanese Patent Office) data. Third, the number of forward patent citations and the lag to the first citation are two major indicators included in the empirical analysis. It would be of particular interest to separate self from non-self patent citations, to test whether the speed of innovation and its quality are determined mainly 'internally' to the firm or 'externally' as a result of strong inter-firm knowledge spillovers.

A Firm's Patenting Behaviour Strongly Depends on its Innovation Strategy (Chapter 9)

In Chapter 9, Carine Peeters and Bruno van Pottelsberghe investigate several factors that determine the patenting behaviour of firms. The theoretical model the authors rely on suggests that the patenting behaviour of firms is influenced by three types of factors: firm and sector specific variables, characteristics of the innovation strategy, and barriers to innovation and to the use of the patent system.

A central issue in the study is to assess the role played by different types of innovation strategies. Four main dimensions of an innovation strategy are taken into account. The first one differentiates R&D active from non-R&D active firms. The second one relates to the kind of R&D activities undertaken and, more particularly, the relative importance of basic and applied research on the one hand and development work on the other hand. The third one reflects the propensity of firms to enter into research partnerships with business and scientific institutions. The last dimension accounts for the orientation of the innovation strategy towards the development of new products, new processes, or both.

The database used in the empirical study is built through a survey of 148 firms operating in Belgium in 2001. The patent behaviour of these firms is proxied by two variables reflecting the existence and size of their patent portfolio. Four main findings should be highlighted:

- First, even though it sharply reduces the significance of traditional firm and sector specific variables, introducing characteristics of the innovation strategy pursued by firms improves the general quality of the model.

- Second, entering into research partnerships with scientific institutions or competitors has a strong positive effect of the patenting behaviour of firms. This stresses that collaborative research induces a need for strong intellectual property protection.
- The importance of science-based research in determining the patenting behaviour of firms is witnessed by the positive and significant coefficient of both the share of basic and applied research in the total R&D budget, and the propensity to collaborate with universities, research institutes and public labs.
- A complex innovation strategy targeting high levels of both product and process innovation is associated with patent portfolios of intermediate size. Product innovators have the largest patent portfolios and process innovators the smallest, not significantly different from non-innovators.

This study opens the way to several avenues for further research. First, the empirical analysis could be improved by taking into account the quality of the patent portfolio (with the number of forward citations) along with the quantity of active patents. It would also be worthwhile validating the results using larger databases of firms, ideally in different countries or regions. Finally, as suggested by the authors, being able to differentiate patent portfolios as mere indicator of innovation performance from patent portfolios as strategic tools to leverage in technological negotiations or to use in building strong technological positions vis-à-vis competitors, would constitute a quantum leap in the current state of research on patenting behaviour.

Technological Opportunity Attracts More Venture Capital (Chapter 10)

Despite the wide recognition of venture capital funds as key players in the national innovation system, there are important differences across countries in the relative amounts of VC. It is, for instance, relatively high in the US and Canada but very low in Japan.

The central hypothesis tested by Astrid Romain and Bruno van Pottelsberghe is that, besides the determinants previously tested in the literature, two broad sets of factors unheard of in the existing empirical research might also contribute to explain heterogeneity of VC intensity across countries. These factors relate to the entrepreneurial environment and to technological opportunity – intellectual property rights in particular. A theoretical model that takes into account the factors that affect the demand and supply of VC is developed. These factors include the growth of GDP, short-term and long-term interest rates, several indicators of technological opportunity (business R&D expenditures growth rate, level of business R&D capital stock, and number of triadic patents), and indicators of entrepreneurial environment.

The model is tested using a panel dataset composed of 16 countries over an 11 year period. Empirical results can be summarized as follows:

- Interest rates have a significant impact on VC intensity. Whereas short-term and long-term interest rates influence positively the relative level of VC via a strong demand-side effect, the difference between long-term and short-term interest rates has the opposite impact, revealing a stronger supply-side effect.
- VC is pro-cyclical. It follows an evolution similar to the GDP growth rate. In periods of high growth, the flow of venture capital outperforms the GDP growth rate, and vice versa.
- Indicators of technological opportunity, such as the available stock of knowledge and the number of high value patents (triadic patents), positively influence a country's investment in VC.
- The positive effect of the stock of knowledge is strongly reinforced in countries with a very high rate of entrepreneurship.

One important policy implication that emerges from these results is that in order to stimulate VC activity in a country, demand-side factors have to be taken into account. The most important factors affecting the demand of VC are the stock of knowledge, the innovative output proxied by the number of highly valued (triadic) patents, and the interest rates. The level of entrepreneurship does play an important role as well.

This empirical study of the determinants of venture capital could be improved in several ways that constitute interesting avenues for future research. A first and simple upgrade would be to reiterate similar estimates over a longer time-span that would go beyond the year 2000. Indeed, after the turn of the century a significant drop has occurred in the level of VC in most industrialized countries. It would be interesting to test the robustness of the results in this respect. Another improvement would be to include data on IPOs and stock market performance, as they reflect the effectiveness of capital markets.

This introductory chapter has highlighted that, besides significantly contributing to the current stream of research, the ten chapters of this book open fascinating avenues for future research in the field of the economics and management of innovation and intellectual property, at the individual, firm, sector and country level, in various regions of the world, and with implications for policy-makers, business practitioners, research scholars and educators.

The research question of whether and how intellectual property ultimately fosters innovation and economic growth is definitely far from being obsolete. Through their contributions to this book, professors and research scholars from leading institutions throughout the world have pushed one step farther the frontiers of our understanding of this issue. It is our greatest hope that, as it has been for us as editors, this book will prove a valuable and inspiring experience to the readers and a fruitful source of ideas for research scholars.

Part I

Patent Value

1
The Battle for Patent Rights

Dietmar Harhoff

1.1 Introduction

Many scholars have pointed to the fact that intangible assets have become very important determinants of corporate value (see, for example, Lev, 2001). Book and market valuations of corporations have seen a steady de-coupling since the early 1980s. Over the same period, intellectual property and in particular patent rights have become important resources for building and maintaining corporate value. It is therefore not surprising that firms fight hard for intellectual property. This chapter turns to an arena in which the battle for patent rights is being pursued with great vigour – the opposition proceedings at the European Patent Office (EPO). In 2003, 2,634 oppositions were filed against patents granted by the EPO.[1] Typically, the opponents are rivals of the patent-holder who seek to have the patent revoked or narrowed. Given the extent of these attacks, it is surprising that the institution has not found more attention to date. This chapter addresses a number of aspects of this particular battleground for intellectual property and describes some results obtained by studying opposition proceedings in particular industries. I attempt to shed some light on three questions:

1. What is the extent of opposition?
2. What are the main determinants of opposition activity?
3. What determines the success of undertaking and of defending against such attacks at the firm level?

There are a number of reasons why a study of opposition activity can contribute to interesting and important insights. First, the institution of opposition *per se* is an important one. Opposition serves as a hygiene element in the system of the European Patent Office. Given the complexity of patent examination – the central task undertaken by modern patent offices – it is not surprising that errors occur, and that some patents receive protection that is too extensive. Without correction, such errors would lead to a loss of economic welfare. Opposition occurs frequently – historically, about 7.9 per cent of all patents granted by the EPO between 1980 and 1995 have been attacked. Thus, opposition selects important patents, for which a correct delineation of the patent right is particularly relevant. Moreover, patents that have successfully withstood opposition are likely to be legally more robust than other, uncontested patent rights. And finally, if a patent is revoked, society is likely to gain from the fact that costly litigation will not be undertaken for this patent (see Graham *et al.*, 2003). For the purpose of this chapter, there is another, even more interesting aspect – opposition data allow us to address two simple, yet important questions: who is bashing whom? And why? Opposition activity generates data that let us observe rivalry directly, rather than inferring it by assuming that firms who are assigned a common industry classification are competing with each other. In the empirical strategy and industrial economics literatures, researchers typically have to revert to the latter strategy, unless they are willing to collect qualitative information on the nature of competition. While there may be other sources from which rivalry can be observed *directly* – such as a listing of firms participating in auctions for supply contracts – opposition gives us a unique research lens. Moreover, the relatively high frequency of opposition events constitutes an advantage over litigation data and helps to establish statistically more robust results.

In the remainder of this chapter, I first describe the institutional setting for the chosen analysis. In particular, I will briefly describe the institutional framework for opposition at the European Patent Office (section 1.2). I will also present data on the overall extent and outcomes of opposition. In section 1.3, I present some simple theoretical considerations that allow us to derive a first set of predictions as to when opposition will occur. In section 1.4, I first summarize multivariate results from other studies and then take a look at the interaction of applicants in two particular industries, using cross-tabulations of oppositions by opponent (the attacking party) and patent-holder to identify particularly intensive rivalry relationships. Section 1.5 then turns to case study evidence suggesting that organizational capabilities may be decisive in using the instrument of opposition successfully. Section 1.6 concludes and summarizes the implications of the research undertaken to date.

1.2 Patent Opposition at the EPO

Institutional background

I briefly summarize the most essential characteristics of the opposition procedure in this section. A more detailed description of the institutional setting at the EPO is presented in Hall and Harhoff (2004). Opposition allows any third party to object to a patent granting decision made by the EPO. The opposition has to be filed within nine months after the grant date. The cost of opposition ranges between 15,000€ and 25,000€ for each party – in comparison to litigation in US or European courts, opposition is therefore a relatively inexpensive way of challenging a rival's patent. In the opposition proceedings, three EPO examiners, among them the examiner responsible for the patent granting decision, re-examine the patent in the light of the opponent's arguments. The opposition division may decide to reject the opposition, to revoke the patent or to amend the claims of the patent. The latter outcome amounts to a restriction and narrowing of the patent right. In a small number of cases, the opposition proceedings are closed because either the patent-holder allows the patent to lapse or because the opponent no longer pursues the case. However, once initiated by the opponent, opposed and opposing parties cannot expect to settle 'out of court' as the EPO is entitled to proceed with the case on its own motion. In such a case, the patent may be revoked even if the opponent is no longer seeking to remove the patent right, for example, after having obtained a licence. Both parties have the right to appeal the outcome of the opposition proceedings in an appeal, which is dealt with by the Technical Board of Appeal of the EPO.

Overall incidence of opposition and appeal

Table 1.1 summarizes the frequency of opposition for all patent grants occurring between 1980 and 1995. A total of 7.9 per cent of all patents granted in this period were opposed, and roughly one third of these opposition cases were then appealed. The median duration is about 1.9 years for opposition and 2.1 years for appeal cases. Getting to legal certainty for patents filed at the EPO is certainly a lengthy process: the average duration of examination is 4.3 years,[2] and for contested patents, another 4.0 years are needed to sort out the opposition and appeal cases. Across aggregate technical areas, there is little variation in opposition and appeal rates; moreover, the median durations do not vary strongly, with the exception of cases involving chemistry patents for which the appeal stage takes somewhat longer than in other technical areas (2.6 years at the median).

Table 1.1 Frequency and duration of EPO opposition and appeal proceedings by technical area (grant years 1980–95)

Main technical area	Incidence of opposition (%)	Median duration of opposition (years)	Incidence of appeals (%)	Median duration of appeal (years)
Electrical engineering	5.3	2.1	27.0	1.8
Instruments	7.1	2.0	34.7	1.9
Chemistry	9.1	2.1	32.3	2.6
Process engineering	9.7	1.7	32.5	2.3
Mechanical engineering	7.7	1.7	30.5	1.9
Consumption and construction	7.2	1.7	32.3	2.0
All technical areas	7.9	1.9	31.7	2.1

Note: The nine-month filing period for oppositions is not included in the duration of opposition. The incidence of appeal is computed as a share of all opposed patents

Source: Based on EPO data from http://www.epoline.org.

Table 1.2 Outcomes of opposition and appeal proceedings by technical area (grant years 1980–90)

Main technical area	Outcome (final instance)			
	Patent revoked (%)	Opposition rejected (%)	Patent amended (%)	Opposition closed (%)
Electrical engineering	37.8	27.4	30.7	4.1
Instruments	34.8	27.9	32.2	5.1
Chemistry	36.1	24.5	35.2	4.2
Process engineering	33.5	28.3	30.8	7.4
Mechanical engineering	32.4	30.3	32.3	5.1
Consumption and construction	31.0	30.4	31.0	7.7
All technical areas	34.7	27.4	32.7	5.3

Source: See Table 1.1.

The opposition and appeal mechanism is remarkable because it overturns a significant percentage of the preceding examination decisions. The outcome distribution is summarized in Table 1.2, again by main technical area. The table documents the final outcome after a possible appeal proceeding. Roughly one third of the patents (34.7 per cent) are revoked, and roughly another third (32.7 per cent) are maintained in amended form with narrowed breadth. Only 27.4 per cent of all cases lead to a rejection of the opposition. These results indicate that the EPO opposition mechanism corrects a large number of errors from earlier examination decisions.

In 5.3 per cent of all oppositions, the case is closed without yielding any of the three outcomes discussed so far. Closure can result from withdrawal of the opposition by the opponent, or from the patent-holder letting the patent lapse by not paying the renewal fees. Hence, this outcome reflects either cases that were successful from the attacker's point of view (the patent lapsed into the public domain), or cases that were successes for the patent holder (the opposition was dropped).

1.3 Theoretical Considerations

When is opposition likely to occur? To simplify matters, consider a world in which parties have access to the same information. A model of this type is used in Harhoff and Reitzig (2004) to study the likelihood of opposition for biotechnology and pharmaceutical patents. The opponent and the patent-holder may have diverging subjective assessments of the outcome of the case, but information is distributed symmetrically and the value of the patent is known. To qualify for opposition, any case must satisfy the condition that the expected value for the opponent will dominate the expected cost of opposition. Let V be the gain to the opponent if the patent is revoked, p the expected probability of success, and c the opponent's cost of opposition. In order to make opposition feasible from the opponent's perspective, the expected gain from opposition has to exceed the opponent's cost. For all patents that fulfil the condition $pV > c$, an attack is profitable.

But even if the attack is feasible in this sense, the parties may still want to settle if a cooperative arrangement is more profitable. Such settlements can be risky in the context of opposition, since another opposing party may still file an opposition without the first opponent's knowledge. There is indeed room for surprises, since most oppositions are filed within the last few days of the opposition period. Once an opposition has been filed, the European Patent Office can pursue the opposition case even if the parties involved have achieved some kind of understanding. One would therefore assume that settlement negotiations take place prior to the filing of the opposition – if at all.[3]

The model in Harhoff and Reitzig (2004) can be used to develop the following predictions: the more valuable the patent is to the patent-holder, and the more valuable a revocation is to the potential opponent, the greater is the likelihood of opposition. Thus, opposition will screen out particularly important patents. This prediction is in line with results from an earlier study (see Harhoff *et al.*, 2003) which showed that patents which had survived opposition were roughly ten times more valuable than other, unopposed patents. Another important (not surprising) prediction from the above model is that opposition becomes more likely as the costs of opposition proceedings decrease in comparison to the costs of settlement, and as the perceived likelihood of winning a case increases. Other predictions – not derived from the model described before – concern the impact of asymmetric information. The presence of asymmetrically distributed information will generally lead to more cases being filed rather than settled prior to the expiration of the opposition filing deadline.

With these basic considerations in mind, we can now turn to the question that is of considerable interest to any researcher in the field of strategy – whether opposition allows firms to develop heterogeneous capabilities. We have to ask whether some players in the patent system may want to use the opposition instrument more frequently than others, and why such heterogeneity could emerge. Is this behaviour a reflection of strategic motivation, for example to establish a reputation for toughness, or are frequent users of opposition simply more refined and skilful in handling patent information?[4]

To explore the implications of such forms of specialization, suppose there are N rival patents in the industry that could conceivably be attacked by an opponent. The patents have been ranked according to the likelihood of having them revoked in opposition. For the N-th patent, the revocation probability is zero, while it is positive for all other patents. Figure 1.1. depicts this likelihood of having the n-th patent revoked as a function of the rank and of the type of opponent. I assume that high quality opponents have a uniformly higher likelihood of getting the n-th patent revoked than less capable opponents. The advantages of the high quality opponent may be due to investments in patent documentation or search capabilities. An opponent will attack patents until the return from attacking the next-strongest patent is no longer sufficiently large to cover the cost of opposition. Let me assume that for the marginal patent attacked, the condition $pV > c$ or $p > c/V$ holds while it no longer holds for the next patent in the ranking.

In Figure 1.1, the parameters c and V are assumed to be constant and identical for the two types of opponents. As is evident from the figure, the high quality opponent will attack more patents (case B) than the low quality one (case A).

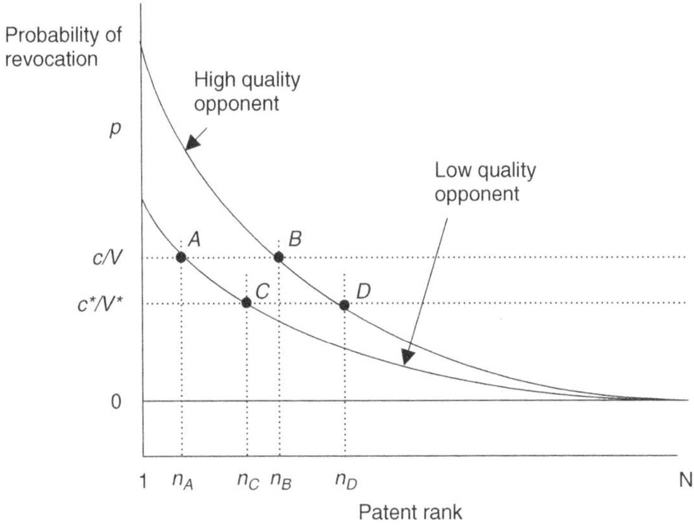

Figure 1.1 Opposition decisions as a function of patent value and cost of opposition

With higher values of V or with lower costs of opposition (both captured by the second horizontal line c^*/V^* where $c^* < c$ and $V^* > V$) the opponents will choose to attack more patents than in the previous situation. For example, to an opponent who considers additional strategic benefits, such as deterrence of future entry or generating a reputation for toughness, V^* will be greater than V. In this case, even the low success type may file relatively many oppositions, as there is an additional benefit which makes filing the additional oppositions worthwhile. Pursuing oppositions for such strategic purposes would lead to relatively low success rates together with comparatively frequent use of opposition. The same comment would apply to an opponent who has relatively low cost of opposition. Such an opponent type would also be characterized by relatively frequent opposition and low opposition success.

To summarize, observing a relatively high propensity to oppose patents in conjunction with a high success rate can be taken as evidence supporting the hypothesis that an opponent has developed a strong capability of getting rivals' patents revoked. In combination with low success rates, frequent opposition would tend to point to strategic behaviour or low cost of opposition.[5] However, it turns out that the empirical picture developed in the next section is unambiguous and broadly consistent with the notion of heterogeneous opposition capabilities.

1.4 Empirical Results on the Determinants of Opposition Activity

Determinants of opposition incidence

Before discussing differences in the behaviour of potential opponents, I summarize the results of multivariate tests of the general hypotheses discussed in the previous sections. By now, there is a fairly stable set of empirical results on the determinants of opposition. These results largely confirm the discussed hypotheses. In particular, the following empirical results have been established (see Harhoff, 2005): (i) particularly valuable patents are selected with higher likelihood than less valuable ones; (ii) patents in fields with technical and market uncertainty are attacked more frequently than patents in more established fields; (iii) patents of applicants with large portfolios appear to enjoy a somewhat lower likelihood of attacks; and (iv) patents of independent inventors are attacked *less*, not more frequently than corporate patent applicants.

The first result confirms that opposition at the EPO has a screening property: particularly valuable patents are more likely to be opposed than low-value ones. The second result points to the fact that any analysis of opposition activity has to control for idiosyncratic contextual conditions, such as uncertainty. The third result is consistent with the notion that some screening of cases and settlement prior to the filing of cases may be going on – in such negotiations, players with large patent portfolios would be able to license patents from their portfolio to achieve some kind of agreement. The last result suggests that independent inventors – probably a group of applicants facing financial constraints – are attacked less frequently than other types of applicants.

Patent rivalry in two selected industries

The above results address the research questions addressed in this chapter from the perspective of the patent-holder. I now turn to an exploration of the interaction between patent-holders and opponents. Some industries are characterized by a particularly high incidence of opposition and appeal. In this subsection, I take a look at two particular fields – cosmetics and detergents. To identify possible patterns of interaction, I neglect the time dimension and consider all patent grants in cosmetics and detergents that were issued between 1980 and March 2002.

I tabulate the frequency of opposition by patent-holder and opponent together with statistics summarizing the revocation rate among the patent-holder's opposed patents and the revocation rate among patents opposed by a particular opponent. Table 1.3 displays the results in the field of cosmetics. The results are taken from a recent study jointly undertaken with Bronwyn Hall (see Harhoff and Hall, 2004). Table 1.4 displays the corresponding results for the field of detergents.

The tables list the number of patents received by the patent-holder vertically, and the number of oppositions filed against these patents (by opponent) horizontally. Note that there can be multiple opponents for any given patent. The unit of analyis in the cross-tabulation part is therefore an opposition filed by the opponent against a patent of the patent-holder.[6] The opposition frequency in cosmetics is high – there are 840 attacks on some of the 3,114 patents. A total of 576 patents (18.5 per cent) are challenged, often by multiple opponents. L'Oréal is the leading patent holder with 738 patents granted by the EPO between 1980 and March 2002, and the company is the target of 248 oppositions. 38.3 per cent of the attacked L'Oréal patents are revoked. L'Oréal has filed only 53 oppositions, mostly against Unilever and P&G, and 65.5 per cent of these attacks (opposition filings) are successful in that the attacked patent is revoked. The overall pattern is one of aggressive patent application and of a parsimonious opposition strategy with above-average success.[7] But L'Oréal is clearly not the firm using the instrument of opposition most frequently. Out of the 840 oppositions filed against cosmetics patents, 264 filings (31.4 per cent) came from Henkel. Henkel filed more oppositions than it received patent grants – its share of patents is only 4.9 per cent of the industry total. Moreover, few oppositions were filed against Henkel (20), and only one fifth of the cases led to a revocation of the patent. The average rate of revocation due to Henkel's opposition filings is 59.9 per cent. These data suggest that Henkel is very successful both in defending own patents against opposition challenges and in attacking the patents of rivals. In the light of the earlier discussion we can say that the intense opposition activity has not led to any degradation in Henkel's opposition success. This suggests that Henkel may have developed strong specialization advantages in opposition in the field of cosmetics.

Table 1.3 also shows that a small number of cosmetics firms account for a very large share of patent grants and opposition cases. The top four firms own 43.3 per cent of all patent grants; they also account (largely due to Henkel's activities) for 45.2 per cent of total opposition filings.

Table 1.3 Patenting and opposition activity in cosmetics

Patent-holder name	Patents	Revocation rate of own patents (%)	Opponent name									Oppositions received
			L'Oréal	Unilever	P&G	Henkel	KAO	Wella	Colgate	Goldwell	Other	
L'Oréal	738	38.3	0	2	11	79	0	33	0	47	76	248
Unilever	273	55.6	13	0	5	34	0	4	6	21	19	102
P&G	183	65.9	15	8	0	34	0	2	7	15	24	105
Henkel	154	20.0	2	1	1	0	0	1	0	6	9	20
KAO	148	25.9	5	2	2	26	0	5	0	0	10	50
Wella	104	31.3	2	0	0	2	0	1	0	6	10	21
Colgate	55	71.4	0	1	5	3	0	0	0	2	2	13
Goldwell	53	30.0	1	0	0	7	0	5	0	0	3	16
Other	1,406	47.6	15	10	15	79	0	19	5	30	92	265
Total	3,114	45.5	53	24	39	264	0	70	18	127	245	840
		Revocation rate of attacked patents (%)	65.5	52.9	48.2	59.9	n.a.	48.2	100. 0	56.1	42.6	53.3

Note: Patents granted between 1 January 1980 and 28 March 2002 with main IPC A61K7 (international patent classification for 'cosmetics and perfumes').

Table 1.4 Patenting and opposition activity in detergents

Patent-holder name	Patents	Revocation rate of own patents (%)	Opponent name							Oppositions received
			Unilever	P&G	Henkel	Colgate	KAO	BASF	Other	
Unilever	627	46.2	0	123	134	8	1	2	56	324
P&G	609	38.6	104	0	96	0	1	1	45	247
Henkel	405	50.0	26	40	0	0	1	2	42	111
Colgate	71	72.7	4	5	11	0	0	0	1	21
KAO	69	41.7	4	6	3	2	0	0	8	23
BASF	56	28.6	1	1	2	0	0	0	8	12
Clorox	52	42.9	5	8	0	0	0	0	4	17
Dow	42	100.0	1	0	1	0	0	2	1	5
Other	871	40.8	40	45	70	2	1	0	93	251
Total	2,802	43.9	185	228	317	12	4	7	258	1,011
		Revocation rate of attacked patents (%)	49.3	48.9	47.9	63.6	100.0	60.0	55.1	50.7

Note: Patents granted between 1 January 1980 and 28 March 2002 with main IPC C11D (international patent classification for 'detergents').

In detergents (see Table 1.4), a similar picture emerges. The top three firms in this field – Unilever, P&G and Henkel – account for 1,641 patents, 58.6 per cent of the industry total of 2,802 patents. The concentration of IP ownership is even higher in detergents than it is in cosmetics. The incidence of opposition is also higher than in cosmetics: a surprising 26.3 per cent (738) of all patents are attacked in opposition. The share of oppositions filed by the top three firms is 72.2 per cent (730 filings) of the overall number of 1,011 oppositions filed. The top three firms are also the most likely receivers of oppositions: Unilever, P&G and Henkel are the target of 67.5 per cent (681) of the 1,011 opposition filings. Note also that nearly 44 per cent of the attacked patents are revoked. The extent of patent office error-correction is anything but marginal in this industry.

In order to summarize the performance of patent-holders and opponents in a more concise way, Table 1.5 lists a number of indicators for Unilever, L'Oréal, P&G and Henkel in the respective fields of cosmetics and detergents. I first compute the number of oppositions that a firm has filed against rivals' patents divided by the number of the firm's own patents – a measure of how frequent opposition by a particular firm occurs, relative to the size of the opponent's own patent portfolio. The intuitive notion underlying this indicator is that with each additional patent a firm owns, the patent-holder is likely to run into some conflict with existing or future patents pursued by rivals. Variation in this measure (listed in column (1) of the table) should therefore capture an opponent's aggressiveness quite well. The second measure (column (2)) is a success measure corresponding to the first measure of opposition frequency: the share of rival patents that were revoked after an opposition had been filed against them. These figures are taken directly from the bottom lines in Table 1.3 and Table 1.4.

The numbers in column (3) are computed as the number of opposition filings received, divided by the number of own patents. Hence, this measure captures to what extent the firm has become a target of opposition. Finally, column (4) summarizes the share of the firm's patents that were revoked (conditional on opposition) as already given in Table 1.4 and Table 1.5.

This summary demonstrates that firms differ remarkably in how successfully they handle opposition challenges. In both technical fields, Henkel is using the instrument of opposition frequently (see the first column in Table 1.5). In cosmetics, Henkel attacks almost twice as many patents as it owns. In detergents, the ratio of oppositions filed to own patents is close to one. No other firm uses opposition so frequently.

Table 1.5 Summary of opposition performance measures in cosmetics and detergents

Company/ Technical field	Oppositions filed against rivals/Own patents (1)	Share of rivals' patents revoked after opposition (2)	Opposition filings received/Own patents (3)	Share of own opposed patents with revocation (4)
L'Oréal/Cosmetics	0.07	65.5	0.34	38.3
Henkel/Cosmetics	1.71	59.9	0.13	20.0
Henkel/Detergents	0.78	47.9	0.27	50.0
Unilever/Cosmetics	0.09	52.9	0.37	52.9
Unilever/Detergents	0.30	49.3	0.52	49.3
P&G/Cosmetics	0.21	48.2	0.57	48.2
P&G/Detergents	0.37	48.9	0.41	48.9

Source: Data in Tables 1.3 and 1.4.

The high frequency of challenges initiated by Henkel does not lead to a considerable trade-off with the company's success in opposition. In cosmetics, Henkel enjoys above-average success in the form of rivals' patents being revoked (see column 2). Note that L'Oréal has the highest success in getting rivals' patents revoked – but given the small number of oppositions filed by L'Oréal, this appears to be due to a strong selection effect in that L'Oréal only picks relatively promising cases for opposition. In detergents, the share of successful oppositions (column 2) is roughly the same for the three major players. In conclusion, Henkel attacks more frequently than other firms do, and there is no notable reduction in the company's opposition success that would point to a trade-off between frequency and success of opposition. Is there possibly also a pattern in the firms' defensive success, that is, in the results regarding opposition cases filed against own patents? The data point to such a relationship as well. First, in cosmetics an astonishingly low share of Henkel patents is attacked, and the success of the opponents is remarkably low (see column (4)). In detergents, Henkel loses about as many of its opposition cases against attackers as do P&G and Unilever. But as column (3) in Table 1.5 shows, Henkel patents are attacked less often – Henkel's effective loss of patents due to revocation is considerably smaller than for its two main rivals.

The confrontation with these figures leaves a major puzzle. The simplest economic explanation for using opposition frequently is to employ it for strategic purposes, such as to deter rivals. But that should be accompanied with a reduction in the opponent's success in having rivals' patents revoked. This is not the case in the detergent or the cosmetics industry. We can therefore exclude this explanation with some confidence. Instead, the statistical results suggest that some firms are simply better at opposition than others. But where do these advantages originate from?

1.5 Organizational Capabilities and Patent Documentation – the Internationale Dokumentationsgesellschaft für Chemie GmbH

The above paragraph showed that opposition performance differs considerably across firms, and that some firms are remarkably effective using the instrument of opposition. This section contains qualitative evidence suggesting that deeply engrained organizational capabilities in patent documentation and IP management may be a decisive determinant of opposition success. I proceed by first summarizing qualitative evidence that the premier opponent in detergents and cosmetics – Henkel – has had a long history of supporting investments in patent documentation and IP management.[8] One of these investments took a particular form – Henkel's participation in the Internationale Dokumentationsgesellschaft für Chemie GmbH (International Documentation Corporation for Chemistry), in short IDC. This venture will be the focus of this section.[9] Although the IDC does not exist any more, the documentation work performed by it has had a remarkable impact that would be worth a detailed exploration which cannot be performed here. Instead, I will provide a brief overview and leave the details to more extensive future work.

The IDC was founded in 1967 by a number of chemical companies with the primary goal of sharing the effort of documenting patent information in chemistry. The IDC's founding members were BASF, Bayer, Chemische Werke Huels, Degussa, Dynamit Nobel, Henkel, Hoechst,[10] Nederlandse Staatsmijnen, Österreichische Stickstoffwerke,[11] Ruhrchemie and Wacker-Chemie (see Hartel and Kolb, 1987, p. 11). The main motivation driving the joint effort was the member companies' dissatisfaction with the performance of patent information providers. A particular disadvantage was the lack of patent claims in the information provided by these organizations. Establishing a competitive advantage through exclusive access to the superior information contained in a new, jointly established database was an explicit objective of the new organization. The expenses involved in the creation of this database were shared by the members. The running costs were enormous: they amounted to around 30 million DM in the mid-1980s.

At the time of the IDC's foundation, Chemical Abstracts was considered to be the only organization that provided an extensive collection of abstracts of patent and other relevant literature. Although these abstracts contained images of chemical structures as well as written information, no information was available on the claims of a patent. However, the IDC was able to add claims information using a proprietary coding system and began the construction of a database that included patent claims for exclusive use by its members.

For the database to be constructed, a contractual agreement was negotiated with the Chemical Abstracts Service (CAS) and Derwent that covered the purchase of the abstracts that provided the raw input of the IDC's database, but also allowed the IDC to process the acquired information and distribute it among its members. The IDC also had access to other information sources (such as abstracts of the Patent Documentation Group) going back to 1959 (Ochsenbein, 1987, p. 92) and INPADOC (Suhr, 2000, p. 489). The abstracts were fed into the IDC's database and subsequently enriched, using a special coding system to recode the abstracts and add the claims of the individual patents.

Initially, this work was done exclusively by specialists at Hoechst who had developed the coding system, but it soon became obvious that they could not process the huge amount of patent literature on their own. Therefore, the work was distributed among various firms and offices of the IDC. While the largest share of the coding was still done at Hoechst, other firms participated as well.

While a central database was used to enter and enrich the purchased abstracts, every member company received a copy of this database to perform their research individually. These copies were updated regularly with the latest additions supplied by the specialists working with the master database. This separation of coding and research was necessary to maintain secrecy between members. Had all members done their research using the same database, the type of information accessed by a company could have communicated its business strategy to others.

Although the IDC member companies cooperated in the documentation of the state of the art, they remained competitors. Membership in the same community did not stop them from challenging each other's patents, when business operations seemed threatened. The primary competitive advantage bestowed on members of the IDC derived from superior knowledge concerning the state of the art. This had direct implicatons both for the drafting of patents (which were less likely to be attacked) and for attacking rivals' patents in opposition. More comprehensive knowledge concerning the state of the art also enabled member companies to file 'stronger', more sustainable patent applications. The IDC member firms were also able to focus their patent application activity on less developed, but promising fields. Moreover, members of the IDC had more and better information to support oppositions put forth against patents held by their competitors.

The high expenses eventually proved to be the downfall of the IDC, together with the technological change which altered the search task significantly. The rise of the Internet made on-line access to information providers affordable. Individual employees could conduct their own research at their desks via end-user-tools. This developed into a serious alternative to centralized information departments. While these developments aided the work of the IDC as well, the technological change favoured the use of end-user-tools even more. Some members of the IDC held on to their specialized central information departments that could supply a company with sophisticated reports, but others embraced the end-user approach to search.

Commercial patent database vendors, such as Derwent or CAS, were finally offering a service the quality of which had increased sufficiently to provide information similar to the IDC information. Some members of the IDC began to doubt the necessity of continuing their own in-house documenting activities. They began to wonder whether the high costs associated with the IDC were really worth the added value it provided, thinking the information available through patent database vendors would be sufficient for their purposes. As a consequence, the members became increasingly unable to agree on the extent to which new information should be processed by the IDC.

After the first members had dropped out of the joint effort, the remaining companies were still interested in the continuation of the IDC's activities, but were confronted with having to bear the entire costs themselves. Finally, in 1992, the members decided to discontinue the IDC. This decision was carried out over the course of a few years, until the venture was finally dissolved in 1997. The member list at the time of the IDC's discontinuation was reduced to BASF, Bayer, Chemie Linz, Degussa, Henkel, Hoechst and Chemische Werke Huels. For the purpose of this study, it is important to note that the former members of the IDC still maintain the exclusive right to access the IDC's database which is maintained at the FIZ Karlsruhe, a patent information service provider.

Although no information has been added to the IDC database since the mid-1990s, the database is still accessed frequently by the former members who continue to appreciate the added value provided by its contents. Interviews with industry experts have shown that the information remains particularly useful with regard to patent search in general and oppositions in particular. This is partly due to the fact that the half-life of knowledge in chemistry is quite long. The information contained in the IDC database is still considered very useful by most of the former IDC members. Extensive knowledge of the state of the art and the availability of excellent patent documentation may prevent a company from initiating new projects in a field where certain discoveries have already been made. When a member of the IDC plans to initiate a new project, IDC information may still help to assess these risks. Therefore, IDC information can contribute to identifying less developed fields as targets for new projects and patent applications. Moreover, the information contained in the IDC database supports former IDC member companies in filing oppositions against competitors by providing the necessary proof of a patent's lack of novelty or inventive step.

While it is not possible at this point to determine exactly to what extent the IDC resource has helped Henkel to become a very successful user of the opposition system, it is clear from the interview record that the IDC data had a notable impact on opposition success. Moreover, other organizational decisions, such as to maintain a strong in-house patent documentation centre, are also likely to have contributed to this result (see Haxel, 2002). A more extensive analysis will hopefully clarify these contributions with more precision.

1.6 Implications and Further Research

In this chapter, I pointed to the astonishingly intensive battles for patent rights that have been taking place within the framework of patent oppositions at the European Patent Office. Little work has been done to date to study the functions and implications of this institution. The tabulations in Table 1.3 and Table 1.4 have demonstrated that opposition data can be used as a powerful research tool for observing rivalry for patents and product markets *directly*. In the course of the analysis, it became clear that there is considerable heterogeneity in how successfully firms apply the instrument of patent opposition. In the technical fields of cosmetics and detergents, the data support the notion that some firms have developed strong specialization advantages and in-house capabilities. In this chapter, I also considered the possibility that the outstanding success of one player, Henkel, had been affected by long-standing investments in patent documentation databases and techniques. There is considerable support for this hypothesis, although the chapter does not claim to go – at this point – beyond proposing a plausible and promising explanation. More structured tests encompassing data on all of the IDC member companies will have to follow in order to show in more detail how the IDC's coding and documentation system helped member companies to gain competitive advantage. But from the interview record contained in Martin (2004), it is clear that the IDC venture had generated a powerful weapon in the battle for patents. In many ways, the IDC may be understood as an early and very successful knowledge management tool. The investments made decades ago are still affecting today's fight over patent rights.

Notes

1. See Table 7.6 in the EPO *Annual Report 2003* (EPO, 2003).
2. See Harhoff and Wagner (2004) for a detailed analysis of granting procedures at the EPO.
3. Interviews conducted with patent lawyers in Munich suggest that cases settled prior to the expiration of the opposition period could make up about 15 to 25 per cent of the cases actually filed. However, for obvious reasons no exact statistic is available.
4. Other explanations are possible as well, but I will focus on these two in this chapter.
5. Developing a structural test from this logic is not simple, as it requires that we hold constant for measurable differences in the benefit from revocation and in costs. The test pursued in section 1.4 is only a first step towards such a structural analysis.
6. There is a small number of patents with multiple patent-holders. These are treated as separate patent rights.
7. For details, see Harhoff and Hall (2004).
8. I owe many of the insights into the patent documentation practice in the chemical industry to discussions with industry experts at various companies. Discussions with Christoph Haxel were particularly helpful. See Haxel (2002) for a description of Henkel's documentation practice.
9. The history of the IDC was recently summarized in a diploma thesis written by Christopher Martin. The thesis was conducted at the Institute for Innovation Research (INNO-tec) at the University of Munich (Martin, 2004). Section 1.5 is based mainly on this source and on the interview evidence compiled therein.
10. Hoechst merged with Rhône-Poulenc in 1999 to create Aventis.
11. The Österreichische Stickstoffwerke became the Chemie Linz AG in 1973.

References

European Patent Office, *Annual Report 2003*. Munich (2003).

Graham, S., B. H. Hall, D. Harhoff and D. C. Mowery, 'Post-Issue Patent Quality Control: A Comparative Study of US Patent Re-Examinations and European Patent Oppositions', in W. M. Cohen and S. A. Merrill (eds), *Patents in the*

Knowledge-Based Economy (Washington, DC: The National Academies Press, 2003), 74–119.

Hall, B. H. and D. Harhoff, 'Post Grant Review Systems at the US Patent Office – Design Parameters and Expected Impact', *Berkeley Law Technology Journal*, 19 (2004), 989–1016.

Harhoff, D., 'Incidence, Duration and Outcomes of Opposition and Appeal Cases at the European Patent Office', CEPR discussion paper (London: Centre for Economic Policy Research, 2005).

Harhoff, D. and B. H. Hall, 'Intellectual Property Strategy in the Global Cosmetics Industry', unpublished discussion paper (Munich: Munich School of Management, 2004).

Harhoff, D. and M. Reitzig, 'Determinants of Opposition against EPO Patent Grants – The Case of Biotechnology and Pharmaceuticals', *International Journal of Industrial Organization*, 22 (2004), 443–80.

Harhoff, D., F. M. Scherer and K. Vopel, 'Exploring the Tail of the Patent Value Distribution', in O. Granstrand (ed.), *Economics, Law and Intellectual Property: Seeking strategies for research and teaching in a developing field* (Boston/Dordrecht/London: Kluwer Academic Publisher, 2003), 279–309.

Harhoff, D. and S. Wagner, 'Modelling the Duration of Patent Examination at the European Patent Office', unpublished discussion paper (Munich: Munich School of Management, 2004).

Hartel, H. and A. Kolb (eds), *IDC Chronik 1967–1987* (Sulzbach, 1987).

Haxel, C., 'Patent information at Henkel: from documentation and information to collaborative information commerce', *World Patent Information*, 24 (2002), 25–30.

Lev, B., *Intangibles – Management, Measurement and Reporting* (Washington, DC: Brookings Institution Press, 2001).

Martin, C., 'Competitive Advantages Through Cooperation in Patent Documentation – An Empirical Analysis of Oppositions in the Chemical Industry', unpublished diploma Thesis (Munich: Munich School of Management, 2004).

Ochsenbein, P. 'The Patent Documentation Group (PDG)', *World Patent Information*, 9 (1987), 92–5.

Suhr, C., 'Patentliteratur und Ihre Nutzung', Expert-Verlag (2000), Germany.

2
Intellectual Property, Competition and the Value of UK Firms

Christine Greenhalgh and Mark Rogers

2.1 Introduction

This chapter analyses the market value of intellectual property (IP) activities of a sample of UK firms and how the extent of competition influences such valuations. To motivate what follows, consider a firm operating in a single, well-defined market. Suppose the firm makes an innovation which has a maximal value V^* (as assessed by some hypothetical, all-knowing economist). Competition between firms will erode this value, as rival firms seek to copy, imitate or invent around the innovation. The firm may use the IP system to temper this competition, raising the value of innovation. It is clear that the extent of competition, as well as the nature and efficiency of the IP system, will determine the expected value of the innovation (i.e., $V^* - z$ where z is a positive number reflecting the combined effect of competition and the IP system). This chapter seeks to throw some light on these issues by analysing how the stock market values R&D and IP.

The analysis in this chapter uses a new panel dataset on the R&D and IP activity of UK production firms covering the period 1989 to 1999. The chapter extends the standard approaches to analysing the market value of innovative firms in a number of ways. First, we analyse whether the market's valuation of firm-level innovation varies across sectors and firms. In order to do this we use the classification system in Pavitt (1984), which analyses patterns of technical change. Pavitt put forward a taxonomy based on differences in the process of innovation, rather than a product-based industrial classification, and it seems entirely appropriate to analyse the market value of innovation using this taxonomy. Second, in contrast to previous studies, the analysis includes the role of trade mark activity and UK and European Patent Office patent activity.[1] Third, we use two alternative proxies for competition. At the sectoral level we use profit persistence analysis to capture the extent of competition, something new to the market value literature. At the firm level we use market share, a traditional proxy for market power and an inverse proxy for competition.

The structure of the paper follows these objectives. The next section outlines the nature of the data and Pavitt's typology. In particular, and in agreement with Pavitt's observations, we find substantial differences across sectors in the extent and composition of innovative activity. The third section presents some initial results using the market value approach. The main result is that the market valuation of R&D, patents and trade marks do vary substantially across Pavitt sectors. A further finding is that the stock market appears to place no significant valuation on firms obtaining UK patents, although there is a positive premium for patents from the European Patent Office. The fourth section deals with the role of competition using two different proxies. At the sectoral level we use profit persistence analysis, arguing that this is a superior means of gauging competitive conditions. The analysis indicates that the sectors with the highest levels of competition also have the lowest market valuation for R&D. At the firm level, we focus the analysis on whether the market value of IP varies with market share. The findings indicate that the market value of UK patents tends to rise with market share. The final section concludes.

2.2 Data Overview

The OIPRC database

The Oxford Intellectual Property Research Centre database covers firms in the production, construction, utilities and commerce sectors, which reported their financial accounts in the UK Company Analysis (Extel Financial, 1996, and Thomson, 2001). The financial data include the usual items, such as sales, profits and also R&D expenditure, as well as the share price (at end of accounting period), if the company was publicly quoted. The firm-level data are matched to three forms of IP: patents published via the UK, patents published via the European Patent Offices (which designated the UK *inter alia*), and trade mark applications via the UK office. These IP data are obtained from a range of sources (European Patent Office, 1996, 2001, 2002; Patent Office, 1986–95, 1997, 2002; Search Systems Ltd, 1996; and Marquesa Search System, 2002). Importantly, the IP data are matched to parent firm names and all wholly owned subsidiaries (using 'Who Owns Whom' from Dun and Bradstreet International, 1994, 2001).[2]

Pavitt's sectoral typology

As indicated in the introduction, a new approach in our analysis is to use the sectoral typology in Pavitt (1984). Pavitt introduced an industrial classification based on technological trajectories, which has subsequently been used extensively in the analysis of innovation. Firms were considered to be in one of four categories: supplier dominated, production intensive (scale intensive), production intensive (specialist suppliers) and science based. The motivation for this typology comes from the observation that the process of technological change varies substantially across firms and industries. In Pavitt's original typology the first category included several types of manufacturing together with non-manufacturing firms, whose technological trajectories were supplier-dominated. Given their rather different natures in respect of R&D and patenting, in what follows we have distinguished between manufacturing and other supplier-dominated firms to create five sectors. Table 2.1 shows the five technological sectors and some simple summary statistics (which are defined in the note to the table). The table shows two different measures of patent activity: UK patents and EPO patents. Firms can choose to patent by means of separate applications to each national patent office, or they can take the route of applying for patent coverage in several European jurisdictions with one application to the European Patent Office. There are different costs and varying likelihoods of obtaining patent coverage via these routes, so firms may have chosen either route for a variety of reasons, including, of course, the number of markets to be targeted for sales.

Table 2.1 shows that Pavitt sectors (3) and (4) have the highest proportion of firms reporting R&D expenditure, nearly twice that of sectors (2) and (5) and more than three times the level of sector (1). Trade mark activity is more common than patenting; it is present in one-third to one half of firms in every sector and shows less variation across sectors than patenting. Note also that UK patenting is more prevalent than EPO patents, by a factor of around two in sectors (1) and (5), but by a smaller factor between 1.5 and 1.3 for the production intensive and science-based sectors. As with R&D, patenting activity is higher in sectors (3) and (4).

The model

This section summarizes the standard model of market value and its relationship with R&D and intellectual property activity. Most previous

Table 2.1 Pavitt technological sectors

Pavitt category	Number of firms	Median firm sales (million £)	R&D active*	UK patent active*	EPO patent active*	UK trade mark active*
(1) Supplier dominated, manufacturing and mining	571	80	0.181	0.217	0.120	0.335
(2) Production intensive, scale intensive	424	109	0.365	0.329	0.213	0.501
(3) Production intensive, specialized suppliers	233	70	0.630	0.413	0.301	0.428
(4) Science-based	291	116	0.621	0.442	0.341	0.516
(5) Supplier dominated, non-manufacturing**	682	66	0.327	0.161	0.086	0.434

Notes: The table is based on 16,257 observations over the period 1989–99. * R&D (IP) active means the proportion of firm-year observations where the reported accounts contain R&D (IP). The Pavitt sectors are defined as follows:

Pavitt (1): Traditional manufacturing. Generally small firms with weak in-house R&D and engineering capabilities. Innovations come from suppliers of equipment or materials (US SIC codes 12, 13, 15, 16, 22, 23, 24, 25, 26, 27, 30, 31)

Pavitt (2): Large firms producing standard materials or durable goods, including cars (US SIC codes 20, 21, 32, 33, 34, 37)

Pavitt (3): Machinery and instruments. Tend to be smaller firms which are technologically specialized (US SIC codes 35, 38, 39)

Pavitt (4): Electronics, electrical and chemicals. Often large firms. Technology from in-house R&D but based on basic science from elsewhere (US SIC codes 28, 29, 36)

Pavitt (5): Users of technology, whose innovations mainly come from suppliers of equipment or materials (US SIC code 40 and above)

The concordance between the two-digit SIC (US) available in the data and Pavitt's categories is based on Vossen (1998) and Dewick *et al.* (2002). ** This includes some firms in distribution, utilities, business services, etc., which are in OIPRC database; in Pavitt's original 1984 taxonomy these were included with manufacturing firms in category (1).

empirical studies use an empirical specification based on Griliches (1981) who assumed that the market value (V) of the firm is given by

$$V = q(A + \gamma K)^{\sigma} \tag{1}$$

where A is the book value of total assets of the firm, K is the stock of intangible assets not included in the balance sheet, q is the 'current market valuation coefficient' of the firm's assets, σ allows for the possibility of non-constant returns to scale, and γ is the ratio of shadow values of intangible assets and tangible assets $\left(\text{i.e., } \frac{\partial V}{\partial K} \Big/ \frac{\partial V}{\partial A}\right)$. Most authors take natural logarithms of (1) and, using the approximation ln $(1 + \varepsilon) \approx \varepsilon$, rearrange (1) to yield:

$$\ln V = \ln q + \sigma \ln A + \sigma\gamma \frac{K}{A} \tag{2}$$

A major issue facing empirical studies is how to proxy *K*. This paper follows previous studies in using flow data on R&D expenditure (*R*), UK patent publications (*UKP*), EPO patent publications (*EPOP*) and trade mark applications (*TM*) as proxies for such capital. Note that since we are using flow variables to proxy stock variables, our coefficient estimates cannot be related directly to (2). Instead, the coefficient estimates on these flow variables are best thought of as an estimate of the (average) market valuation of such activity. The main interest is in comparing these valuations across sectors and firms. These issues mean that the estimation equation is:

$$\ln V_{it} = \alpha_j + \alpha_t + \sigma \ln A + \sigma\gamma n \frac{R_{it}}{A_{it}} + \alpha_1 \frac{UKP_{it}}{A_{it}} + \alpha_2 \frac{EPOP_{it}}{A_{it}}$$

$$+ \alpha_3 \frac{TM_{it}}{A_{it}} + \eta X + u_{it} \tag{3}$$

where *i* indexes a firm and *t* a year, and α_j and α_t are sets of industry and year dummies. Note that (3) allows ln$q$ from (2) to vary across industries and over time (i.e., $\ln q = \alpha_j + \alpha_t$), to allow for variations in the 'current market valuation coefficient'. As in other studies, other control variables are also included (*X*), including sales growth, the debt to equity ratio and the book value of intangible assets.[3] This basic specification is later augmented with the market share of the firm to investigate the role of competition in the determination of market value in the presence of intangible assets.

Market value regressions

A variety of estimators can be used to analyse (3). The panel nature of data means we can estimate a fixed or random effect model (which means replacing α_j with firm-specific fixed effects in (3)). A drawback of these methods is that the presence of measurement error in the data can lead to coefficients being biased downwards. A related issue concerns the presence of influential observations within the data. In particular, since some – especially smaller – firms have volatile IP activity, this tends to cause considerable inter-temporal variation in the R&D and IP variables. Preliminary regression analysis indicated that a few observations can affect the coefficients dramatically, especially those of the IP-based variables. For this reason, Table 2.2 shows the results from using a robust regression procedure, which uses an algorithm to eliminate overly influential observations.[4] Further discussion and analysis of these issues, and results from OLS and panel estimators for the data used here, are contained in Greenhalgh and Rogers (2004).

The table shows regressions for the full sample and for each Pavitt sector. Looking only at the full sample regression in the first column, the major results are as follows. R&D has a significant and positive coefficient. The coefficient on the UK patenting variable is *negative* and significant, whereas EPO patenting and UK trade marking have a positive partial correlation with market value. One possibility for the unexpected result for UK patents may be multicollinearity. However, re-estimating the model omitting the EPO and UK trade marks variables, and also then omitting R&D, only causes the UK patent variable to be insignificantly different from zero (rather than negative). In contrast, entering only the EPO variable, or only the trade mark variable, makes the estimated coefficients slightly larger and more significant. Thus, for the full sample regressions, a major result is that firms that are active in UK patenting do not command any share market premium.

Table 2.2 also shows the regression results on the different Pavitt sectors. Focusing on the coefficient on the R&D variable, although it is always significant, the magnitude varies substantially across Pavitt's technology sectors. Perhaps unexpectedly, the lowest coefficient on R&D is for sector (4), which is seen as benefiting from university science, while the highest magnitude is for sector (5). The coefficients on the IP variables also vary dramatically across sectors. Again, the results were checked by entering only one IP variable at a time, and then by omitting the R&D variable (in case multicollinearity in the sector-specific regressions is clouding results). The results of these separate regressions indicate broad support for Table 2.2. The only important difference is that the EPO patent variable is positive (4.2) and significant (at 1 per cent level) if it is entered as a sole proxy for K/A in Pavitt sector (4). Apart from this finding it is, perhaps, surprising that the science-based sector shows no significant market premia for IP.

Other coefficients estimated in Table 2.2 are also of interest. The coefficients on sales growth suggest firms with faster growth have higher market valuations. The results for the book value of intangible to total assets ratio are generally positive, but the debt to equity ratio is generally

Table 2.2 Market value regressions, by Pavitt category

	Full sample	Supplier-dominated manufacturing (Pavitt 1)	Production intensive (scale) (Pavitt 2)	Production intensive (specialist) (Pavitt 3)	Science-based (Pavitt 4)	Supplier-dominated non-manufacturing (Pavitt 5)
ln of total assets	1.036	0.927	1.055	1.065	1.063	0.982
	(129.66)***	(39.86)***	(74.32)***	(52.06)***	(57.13)***	(60.37)***
R&D expend/total assets	4.532	5.026	8.302	8.313	3.995	14.425
	(13.60)***	(1.89)*	(4.94)***	(8.73)***	(9.20)***	(6.92)***
UK patent/total assets (mill)	−0.646	−3.147	−0.864	−0.208	−3.035	−9.077
	(2.15)**	(3.05)***	(1.84)*	(0.27)	(4.52)***	(7.49)***
EPO patent/total assets (mill)	2.186	12.450	1.903	2.144	0.352	17.445
	(5.66)***	(4.79)***	(1.52)	(2.92)***	(0.64)	(1.81)*
Trade mark/total assets (mill)	0.382	−0.268	0.603	0.500	0.216	−0.520
	(2.94)***	(0.70)	(2.03)**	(1.65)*	(1.05)	(0.98)
Growth in sales (t, t − 1)	0.737	0.493	0.431	0.917	0.690	0.158
	(12.82)***	(2.93)***	(3.33)***	(6.48)***	(7.59)***	(1.23)
Debt/shareholders' equity	−0.003	−0.004	−0.001	−0.046	0.001	−0.033
	(1.07)	(0.14)	(0.44)	(5.14)***	(0.07)	(0.79)
Intangible assets/total assets	1.122	1.031	1.291	1.250	0.726	−1.379
	(5.35)***	(1.55)	(3.17)***	(1.64)	(2.13)**	(3.16)***
Constant	−1.410	−1.241	−1.178	−2.765	−0.998	−0.027
	(2.90)***	(2.37)**	(3.31)***	(5.38)***	(1.98)**	(0.05)
Observations	2472	348	600	596	617	311
Number of firms	347	55	79	81	82	50
R-squared	0.92	0.95	0.94	0.87	0.93	0.98
Industry dummies (prob.)	0.00	0.00	0.00	0.00	0.00	0.00
Year dummies (prob.)	0.00	0.00	0.00	0.00	0.01	0.00
Test of H_0: $\sigma = 1$	0.00	0.00	0.00	0.00	0.00	0.27

Notes: The dependent variable is ln of market value (mv), where 'mv' is defined as shares outstanding (average in year) × price (end accounting period) plus creditors and debt less current assets (see Chung and Pruitt, 1994). The sample period is 1989–99. Estimator is robust least squares estimator (see text). * significant at 10%; ** significant at 5%; *** significant at 1%. The industry and year dummies rows show the probability of a type 2 error in rejecting the hypotheses that all industry (year) dummies are equal. A Chow test, using OLS estimations, on whether the sub-samples can be pooled yields a F-statistic of 7.5 (rejecting the null hypothesis that the samples can be pooled at the 1% level).

rather insignificant. The book value of intangible assets reflects the accounting values of goodwill, and possibly patents and brands, obtained via takeovers.[5] The major result from Table 2.2 is that the market's valuation of different measures of innovation varies substantially across sectors. In subsequent sections we investigate whether variations in competitive conditions can explain some of these differences. The other important result from Table 2.2 is that the market valuation of patenting via the UK Patent Office seems to generate no market premium. One explanation for this result is that, on average, firms choose UK patents when the value of the innovation is lower, hence justifying registration in fewer national jurisdictions. Evidence in favour of this view is contained in Greenhalgh and Longland (2002), who investigated the impact on firm-level net output of both UK and EPO patents. They found a consistently stronger impact of EPO than of UK patents in terms of both the size and duration of their impact on productivity, confirming the idea of qualitative differences in the two patents that are recognized by the market. Even so, it is surprising that UK patenting never receives a positive coefficient.

An alternative view is that the stock market is myopic in respect of UK patents. We can test whether the stock market reacts to UK patenting after a lag of one or more years. However, including variables for UK patent activity in t − 1 and t − 2 years, alongside the current patent activity variable, we find only in sector (3) is there a (net) positive coefficient (the t − 2 coefficient is 1.9 and is significant at the 10 per cent level). In contrast, a parallel analysis of EPO patenting shows that the coefficients on current and t − 1 patent activity are sometimes significant.

Another possible explanation is that different types of firms choose to file for UK patents as opposed to EPO patents (and that the stock market recognizes that these firms are, for whatever reason, unable to generate value from UK patents). Overall, this appears difficult to justify: of the 2,472 observations in the regression sample, 1,294 have a UK patent and of these 812 (63 per cent) also filed for an EPO patent in the same year. Thus, there are a substantial number of firms that file for both UK patents and EPO patents. A further test of this issue is to conduct regression analysis only on those firms with EPO patents. Undertaking such analysis again seems to show that the UK patents of these firms generate no share market premia. In conclusion, there is little evidence that UK patents receive any current or future share market premium. The implication is that there may be a quality effect whereby better patents are filed through the EPO.

2.3 Competitive Conditions

One of the most fundamental concepts in economics is competition and, in particular, how rivalry between firms may create socially optimal outcomes. A stylized Schumpeterian view is that large firms, which have monopoly power, have both the financial resources and the incentives to undertake investment in innovation. The corollary is that society must accept static monopoly welfare losses in order to gain increased investment in innovation and, ultimately, dynamic welfare gains. In contrast, Arrow (1962) put forward a model where, under certain assumptions, there is a higher incentive to innovate for a perfectly competitive market than a monopoly. A key assumption for Arrow's result is that there are 'perfect' intellectual property rights in the sense that the innovator can license the innovation at full market value.[6]

Below we assess the competition conditions in each Pavitt sector. If the Arrow view is correct we should observe higher market value in sectors with greater competition (although clearly this relies on firms being able to use the IP system effectively). In contrast, if the Schumpeterian view is correct the market value of R&D should fall with the intensity of competition.

We have explored various industry- and firm-level proxies for competitive conditions. Traditional proxies for competition include measures of concentration, market share, barriers to entry and profitability. All of these have various drawbacks, although all can contribute something to the difficult task of measuring competitive conditions. Here we introduce a new methodology into market value studies by using an analysis of the persistence of profit shocks as an indicator of the intensity of competition at the sectoral level. Although this method has a well-established literature in its own right, there are no previous studies that attempt to integrate it into an analysis of the market value of innovative activities. The strength of the approach is that it permits a dynamic assessment of the actual competitive process in the spirit of the contestable markets theory, which has argued that actual market share is a poor guide to competitive conditions, as what matters is whether there are potential market entrants able to enter and exit easily (Baumol, 1982).

Profit persistence and market valuation

The profit persistence literature is based on the assumption that all firms will experience profit shocks and that the degree of competition from other firms determines how long this shock will persist (e.g., Mueller and Cubbin, 1990; Waring, 1996; Glen *et al.*, 2001). For example, a positive profit shock due to the launch of a successful new product may be short-lived if other firms compete effectively. The average degree of profit persistence for a group of firms can be estimated using:

$$\pi_{it} = \phi_i + \beta\pi_{it-1} + \varepsilon_{it} \qquad [4]$$

where π_{it} is firm i's profit margin in year t, ϕ_i is a firm fixed effect, β represents the persistence to a profit shock and ε_{it} is the standard error term. In these studies a β-coefficient close to zero implies little persistence and, therefore, suggests a competitive environment (i.e., any positive profit shock due, say, to an innovation, is rapidly competed away by rivals). In contrast, when $\beta > 0$, profit shocks persist and the implication is that the competitive process is less strong. The advantage of profit persistence studies is that the β-coefficient should encapsulate all aspects of competition, whether from rivals within the same domestic industry, overseas firms, or from the threat of new firm entry.

Equation [4] can be used to analyse profit persistence at the industry, sector or economy level. Using the ratio of net profit before tax to total sales as the measure for π, we compute the value of β for each Pavitt sector (over the period 1989–99).[7] Table 2.3 shows these β-coefficients, with the sectors arranged from high to low β-coefficients, which means from low to high competitive conditions.[8] Table 2.3 also shows the coefficients on the R&D variables from Table 2.2. We can see that the coefficient on R&D falls as competitive intensity increases. These results are consistent with the idea that rents are rapidly competed away. Table 2.3 suggests, therefore, support for the Schumpeterian view of competition and innovation.

What is also striking is that the lowest profit persistence and the lowest return to R&D, is seen in Pavitt 4, the science-based manufacturing sector, which draws on university and other science for its innovation and exhibits the highest incidence of IP-active firms (Table 2.1). However, as discussed above, the analysis finds little evidence that firms that use IP gain any share market premia. Another way of interpreting these results is to consider the lack of profit persistence and low returns to patents in sector (4) as reflecting R&D spillovers. Thus, firms in the science-based sector may undertake extensive R&D, but much of its value spills over to other firms (indeed undertaking R&D increases a firm's ability to absorb others' knowledge, Cohen and Levinthal, 1989).

Table 2.3 Competitive conditions and the return to R&D, by Pavitt sector

Sector	**Supplier-dominated non-manufacturing (Pavitt 5)**	**Production intensive (specialist) (Pavitt 3)**	**Production intensive (scale) (Pavitt 2)**	**Supplier-dominated manufacturing (Pavitt 1)**	**Science-based (Pavitt 4)**
	lowest		*competitive intensity*		*highest*
Profit persistence (β-coefficient)	0.52	0.51	0.47	0.36	0.27
Coefficient on R&D (Table 2.2)	14.425	8.313	8.302	5.026	3.995

Market share and the value of innovative activities

While the strong link between competitive conditions and returns to R&D at the Pavitt sector level is of interest, it is unrealistic to assume that firm-level differences in market power do not exist. In fact, the existing literature on the valuation of innovation focuses on whether a firm's market share is important. The standard assumption is that a larger market share implies less competitive pressure. Blundell *et al.* (1999), using a sub-set of the SPRU (Science Policy Research Unit) dataset of major innovations (innovations matched to 340 listed manufacturing firms 1972–82), found that higher market share raises the market valuation of an innovation.[9] In contrast, Toivanen *et al.* (2002) find that there is no significant interaction between market share and R&D activity (they use a previous version of the data used here that ended in 1995).[10] In this section we provide additional insight into this debate in three ways. First, the data used here runs to 1999, making it much more up-to-date than Blundell *et al.* (1999) and adding four years to Toivanen *et al.* (2002). Second, the analysis uses the Pavitt sectors, which have been shown above to be important. Third, unlike Toivanen *et al.* (2002) we also test for any interaction effects between market share and IP activity in addition to R&D activity (i.e., we do not solely focus on the interaction between R&D and market share). This issue is central to the question of whether firms with low market shares can use the IP system to appropriate the benefits of innovation.

Although not the centre of focus here, we have investigated the relationship between R&D, market share and stock market value (see Greenhalgh and Rogers, 2004). The results show that the relationship varies across sectors. In particular, market share and R&D intensity are significant strong complements in the 'science-based' sector (4). Thus it seems that market share is deemed most valuable, *ceteris paribus*, within the sector with the lowest average levels of returns to R&D and patenting activity.

Table 2.4 documents the coefficients from three sets of market value regressions that explore the interaction between market value and intellectual property for each IP asset in turn. The table only shows the coefficients on market share, the interaction term and the relevant IP variable in order to save space (the full regression specification is the same as in Table 2.2). The table shows that the coefficient on market share varies across sectors. In the production intensive (specialist) and non-manufacturing sectors, a higher market share tends to be associated with lower market value, but in other sectors there is an insignificant or positive association. The main focus here is on the interaction terms and, of these, the interaction term between UK patent activity and

Table 2.4 Market share and IP activity

	Full sample	Supplier-dominated manufacturing (Pavitt 1)	Production intensive (scale) (Pavitt 2)	Production intensive (specialist) (Pavitt 3)	Science-based (Pavitt 4)	Supplier-dominated non-manufacturing (Pavitt 5)
UK patent/total assets (mill)	−1.238 (3.63)***	−3.277 (2.90)***	−1.314 (2.51)***	−1.262 (1.42)	−5.003 (6.65)**	−43.277 (11.2)***
Market share (4-digit) (ratio)	−0.087 (2.01)**	0.136 (1.40)	0.015 (0.20)	−0.345 (3.00)***	0.009 (0.10)	−0.213 (1.93)***
(UK patents/assets)* Market share	4.323 (3.81)***	3.407 (0.83)	5.130 (2.44)**	4.263 (2.31)**	23.646 (6.20)***	43.340 (6.15)***
EPO patent/total assets (mill)	2.494 (5.39)***	10.275 (3.29)***	1.654 (1.16)	1.282 (1.35)	3.316 (4.91)***	−4.987 (0.33)
Market share (4-digit) (ratio)	−0.021 (0.50)	0.165 (1.63)	0.063 (0.80)	−0.257 (2.35)**	0.171 (1.82)*	−0.213 (1.97)**
(EPO patents/assets)* Market share	−1.385 (1.40)	1.579 (0.24)	2.465 (0.50)	3.841 (1.26)	−2.741 (2.27)**	59.772 (1.90)*
Trade mark/total assets (mill)	0.221 (1.52)	−0.073 (0.11)	−0.1 (0.24)	0.341 (1.07)	0.183 (0.82)	−0.975 (1.41)
Market share (4-digit) (ratio)	−0.064 (1.48)	0.192 (1.83)*	−0.001 (0.01)	−0.322 (2.73)***	0.195 (2.08)**	−0.206 (1.84)*
(Trade marks/assets)* Market share	1.088 (2.18)**	−0.406 (0.24)	2.268 (2.15)**	1.614 (1.90)*	1.258 (0.86)	4.416 (1.22)

Notes: The dependent variable is ln of market value. Other explanatory variables are included in regressions (as per Table 2.2), but results not shown. Coefficients are from robust regression estimator with *t*-statistics in parentheses. * significant at 10%; ** significant at 5%; *** significant at 1%.

market share is the most interesting. The coefficient is positive and significant in the full sample and in four of the five sectors. A positive coefficient indicates that higher market share tends to increase the association between UK patent activity and market value.

To interpret these results consider, for example, Pavitt sector (2). There is a *negative* coefficient on patent activity but a positive coefficient on the interaction term (the coefficient on market share itself is not significant). For a firm in this sector with median market share (0.55), these coefficients imply a net coefficient on 'UK patent/total assets' of 1.51. Another way of viewing the result is to consider the threshold level of market share where UK patenting just starts to have a positive effect. For sector (2) (production intensive – scale) the threshold level of market share is 0.25 (around 38 per cent of firms in this sector have market shares less than 0.25). For Pavitt sector (4) (science-based) the equivalent market share threshold level is 0.21 (around 43 per cent of firms in this sector have market shares below this level).

The UK patent results show more evidence of interaction effects than the EPO patent or trade mark measures. For the full sample, the EPO patenting results show that market share has no significant role, although in Pavitt sector (4) higher market share tends to reduce the market valuation of EPO patenting, while in Pavitt 5 the reverse is true. For UK trade marking, the coefficients on the interaction term are generally positive and sometimes significant, indicating that firms with higher market share tend to command a higher market valuation on their trade-marking activity.

2.4 Conclusions

This chapter has analysed the market valuation of the R&D and IP activities of quoted UK firms using a new dataset for the period 1989–99. The ultimate interest in such analysis is a greater understanding of firm performance and financial market performance, which in turn provides background for policy discussions. A major theme of the chapter is that existing market value studies tend to assume that the returns to innovative activities are equal across diverse firms and industries. The analysis follows Pavitt (1984) in arguing that the nature of technological change and innovative activity varies substantially across firms. If this is the case then one might expect that the market valuation of innovative activity would also vary. We find that differentiating our sample firms using Pavitt's technology typology is extremely worthwhile. Using Pavitt's sectoral typology, which is based on differences in the process of technological change, we analyse whether the market valuation varies across these sectors, finding large differences in the market valuation of R&D and IP activity across sectors. This result is robust to further analysis containing lagged values of R&D and IP, which suggests that the stock market evaluates new R&D and IP within the year of its occurrence. Overall, we find that the lowest market valuation of R&D to tangible assets is in the Pavitt 4 'science-based' sector, which is also a sector where R&D activity is common and R&D intensity relatively high (around 62 per cent of firms report R&D expenditures). This sector also has the highest proportion of firms applying for UK patents, trade marks and EPO patents, suggesting that firms actively use the IP system to try to increase appropriability.

The chapter also finds an important result with respect to UK patenting. The analysis shows that while, on average, higher R&D, EPO patenting and UK trade marking (relative to firm size) all tend to increase market value, UK patenting does not have a straightforward impact.

These findings are consistent with the observed behaviour of these firms; analysis of trends in IP per firm show a significant fall in patenting via the UK Patent Office, a small increase in EPO patenting, and a rapid increase in trade marks, particularly since the early 1990s (Greenhalgh *et al.*, 2003). For firms wishing to enhance their stock market value, the basic results suggest that patenting via the UK Patent Office will have little impact, but UK financial markets do recognize applications via the European Patent Office and also UK trade marks.

To attempt to explain variations across sectors in market valuations, the main contribution of this chapter is to study the effects of competition. At a basic level we might expect higher levels of competition within a sector to lower market valuations, *ceteris paribus*. To investigate this issue we use a profit persistence methodology to assess competitive conditions. The results show that the 'science-based' sector is the most competitive and also has the lowest market valuation on R&D. At the other extreme, the 'supplier-dominated (non-manufacturing)' sector reaped the highest market valuation of R&D within a market structure exhibiting high profit persistence (i.e., low competitive pressure).

We also examine the role of firm-level factors in explaining sectoral differences in market valuations to R&D and IP assets by using market share as a proxy (inverse) for competitive pressure. For the full sample of firms, the results suggest a negative, but not significant, role for market share; however, when we analyse by Pavitt sectors we find a diverse pattern of results. We extend the analysis to allow for the interaction of market share and R&D. This analysis suggests that only in the 'science-based' sector does higher market share raise the valuation of R&D. The magnitude of the effect appears economically important: the coefficient estimates imply a 10 per cent increase in market share is associated with a 20 per cent increase in the market valuation of R&D activity.

This chapter also conducts analysis on the link between market share and IP activity. If the IP system were working effectively for all firms – regardless of market power – we would expect to find no evidence of any link. However, for UK patent activity we find a positive effect of market share: higher market share raises the valuation of UK patent activity (although the strength and significance of such an effect varies across Pavitt sectors). Since the direct effect of UK patenting is often negative, this suggests the presence of a threshold market share. For example, in the Pavitt 4 sector the results indicate that the market share threshold level is around 0.21: only when market share rises above this level does UK patenting appear to attract a stock market premium.

The above findings offer much food for thought for the regulatory authorities concerned with competition (the Office of Fair Trading and the Competition Commission). Broadly, our results give much more support for Schumpeter than for Arrow on the relationship between market structure and innovation: the market valuation of R&D is higher in sectors with relatively low competitive pressure. Clearly, the results do not imply that lowering competitive pressure would always raise the valuation of R&D; only that this occurs within the range of competition observed in the data.[11] Our findings are of considerable relevance too for all the government agencies engaged in re-shaping industrial policy following the Lambert Review of Business–University Collaboration (HM Treasury, 2003). Our findings suggest that a possible reason for the slow rate of exploitation of scientific discovery in the UK may be an overly competitive science-based sector. A caveat on this concerns the underlying rate of innovation and productivity achieved by the science-based sector. It is possible that high competition and low valuation of R&D generate high rates of productivity growth due to spillovers. This question can only be directly addressed by further microeconomic analysis of firm-level data, something we intend to pursue in future research.

Acknowledgements

The database developed for analysis in this paper was derived by Mark Longland at the Oxford Intellectual Property Research Centre (OIPRC), St Peter's College, working with the authors and with an earlier collaborator, Professor Derek Bosworth. Funding was received at various times from the ESRC, the Leverhulme Trust and the UK Patent Office. The current development of the database to include more service sector firms, which are so far only partly covered in the database, is taking place with the support of ESRC award RES-334-25-0002 under the Evolution of Business Knowledge Programme. We are grateful to St Peter's College for accommodation and administrative support for this research.

Notes

1. Few existing studies use such data. Exceptions include analysis on an older version of these data by Greenhalgh and Longland (2002) and, for trade marks, on Australian data by Bosworth and Rogers (2001).
2. Further information on the construction of the dataset is in Greenhalgh and Longland (2001, Appendix Notes); and Greenhalgh *et al.* (2003, Technical Appendix).
3. For a review of market value studies and this methodology see Hall (2000).
4. More specifically, the procedure is: (1) calculate Cook's D for each observation from OLS, (2) observations with values greater than one are given zero weight,

(3) re-run regression, (4) calculate $M = med(|e_i - med(e_i)|)$, where e_i is the residual, (5) any observation with an absolute residual greater than 2M receives a downweight of $2M/|e_i|$ (called Huber weights), (6) repeat procedure until maximum change in weights drops below 0.01 (called 'convergence'), (7) based on final regression in step 6, repeat procedure using 'biweights', which are downweights given by $[1 - (7e_i/M)^2]^2$, until convergence. The procedure is described in more detail, with appropriate references, in STATA 7.0 reference manual under 'rreg' (www.stata.com).

5. Further analysis was conducted omitting the book value of intangible assets from the set of explanatory variables. The results suggest its inclusion does not substantially affect the other coefficients.
6. Subsequent theoretical work has developed these ideas. For example, Kamien and Schwartz (1976) find that as rivalry increases, R&D per firm may initially rise but will, ultimately, fall as rivalry becomes intense. Loury (1979) considers the firm's decision to invest in R&D when a patent race is underway, finding that more competitors reduce R&D per firm. More recently, Boone (2001) models firms as bidding for process innovations and finds that changing the level of competition has ambiguous effects on technical progress. Scherer and Ross (1990) are associated with the idea that the relationship between competition and innovation may be non-monotonic (specifically, 'hill-shaped'), something which has received recent empirical interest (Aghion *et al.*, 2002).
7. The regressions were conducted on a balanced panel of all firms present in the dataset (1989–98). To avoid problems of influential observations firms with profitability margins below −0.2 and above 0.5 were excluded (a similar condition is imposed by Waring, 1996).
8. Previous UK studies on profit persistence are limited. Geroski and Jacquemin (1988) find a β of 0.49 for a sample of 51 UK firms (1949–77), while Benito (2001) finds βs of between 0.45 and 0.54 for the period 1975–98. Benito does look at differences across sectors, although these are based on industrial classifications, not Pavitt sectors as here. Econometrically, there is a difficulty in estimating dynamic panel models (i.e., [3]) in that there is an asymptotic (downwards) bias in β. Nickell (1981) provides a formula to correct this bias (see his equation 18). However, if we use this formula all the coefficients rise in a similar proportion and the rank order is unaffected. Since our interest is in the rank order across Pavitt sectors, we do not focus on this issue in the main text.
9. They also note that the impact of market share does appear to vary across industries; however, they generally do not allow all coefficients to vary across industries, except for looking solely at the pharmaceuticals industry.
10. To be more accurate, Toivanen *et al.* (2002) state, 'The market share variable (MS) and the interaction [with R&D/assets] variable (MSRD) are insignificant throughout [the panel data estimates], confirming the results of the cross-sectional estimates' (p. 57). However, in their Table 3, one panel regression is presented which shows MSRD with a negative and significant coefficient (at 1 per cent level).
11. In contrast, current UK government policy appears to assume that the link between competition and performance is straightforward and monotonic. For example, HM Treasury (2001, p. 19) states, 'Competition is at the heart of

the Government's strategy to close the productivity gap. Vigorous competition between firms leads to increased innovation and greater efficiency – and in turn to increased productivity growth.' The evidence presented above suggests that the competition and performance relationship is much more complex than this.

References

Aghion, P., N. Bloom, R. Blundell, R. Griffith and P. Howitt, 'Competition and Innovation', IFS Working Paper 02/04 (2002).

Arrow, K., 'Economic Welfare and the Allocation of Resources for Invention', in R. R. Nelson (ed.), *The Rate and Direction of Inventive Activity* (Princeton: Princeton University Press, 1962), 609–25.

Baumol, W.-J., 'Contestable Markets: An Uprising in the Theory of Industry Structure', *American Economic Review*, 72(1) (1982), 1–15.

Benito, A., ' "Oscillate Wildly": Asymmetries and Persistence in Company-Level Profitability', Bank of England Working Paper 132 (2001).

Blundell, R., R. Griffith and J. van-Reenen, 'Market Share, Market Value and Innovation in a Panel of British Manufacturing Firms', *Review of Economic Studies*, 66(3) (1999), 529–54.

Boone, J., 'Intensity of Competition and the Incentive to Innovate', *International Journal of Industrial Organization*, 19(5) (2001), 705–26.

Bosworth, D. and M. Rogers, 'Market Value, R&D and Intellectual Property: An Empirical Analysis of Large Australian Firms', *Economic Record*, 77(239) (2001), 323–37.

Chung, K. and S. Pruitt, 'A Simple Approximation of Tobin's Q', *Financial Management*, 23(3) (1994), 70–4.

Cohen, W. M. and D. Levinthal, 'Innovation and Learning: The Two Faces of R&D', *Economic Journal*, 99 (1989), 569–96.

Dewick, P., K. Green and M. Miozzo, 'Technological Change, Industry Structure and the Environment', mimeo, Manchester School of Management, UMIST (2002).

Dun and Bradstreet International, 'Who Owns Whom – Worldwide Corporate Structures', 4th quarter CD-ROM (1994).

Dun and Bradstreet International, 'Who Owns Whom D&B Linkages', 4th quarter CD-ROM (2001).

European Patent Office, 'Espace Bulletin' (1996, 2001, 2002) Vol. 1996/05, Vol. 2001/001, Vol. 2002/002, CD-ROMs.

Extel Financial, 'Company Analysis' (1996) on-line database.

Geroski, P. A. and A. Jacquemin, 'The Persistence of Profits: A European Comparison', *Economic Journal*, 98(391) (1988), 375–89.

Glen, J., K. Lee and A. Singh, 'Persistence of Profitability and Competition in Emerging Markets', *Economic Letters*, 72 (2001), 247–53.

Greenhalgh, C. and M. Longland, 'Intellectual Property in UK Firms: Creating Intangible Assets and Distributing the Benefits via Wages and Jobs', *Oxford Bulletin of Economics and Statistics*, 63(671–96) (2001).

Greenhalgh, C. and M. Longland, 'Running to Stand Still? – Intellectual Property and Value Added in Innovating Firms', mimeo, Oxford Intellectual Property Research Centre (2002).

Greenhalgh, C., M. Longland and D. Bosworth, 'Trends and Distribution of Intellectual Property: UK and European Patents and UK Trade and Service Marks 1986–2000', mimeo, Oxford Intellectual Property Research Centre (2003).

Greenhalgh, C. and M. Rogers, 'The Value of Innovation: The Interaction of Competition, R&D and IP', Department of Economics, Oxford University Working Paper 192 (2004).

Griliches, Z., 'Market Value, R&D, and Patents', *Economic Letters*, 7 (1981), 183–7.

Hall, B. H., 'Innovation and Market Value', in R. Barrell, G. Mason and M. O'Mahoney (eds), *Productivity, Innovation and Economic Performance* (Cambridge: Cambridge University Press, 2000), 177–98.

HM Treasury, 'Productivity in the UK: Enterprise and the Productivity Challenge', HMSO (2001).

HM Treasury, 'Lambert Review of Business–University Collaboration – Final Report', HMSO (2003).

Kamien, M. I. and N. L. Schwartz, 'On the Degree of Rivalry for Maximum Innovative Activity', *Quarterly Journal of Economics*, 90(2) (1976), 245–60.

Loury, G., 'Market, Structure and Innovation', *Quarterly Journal of Economics*, August (1979), 396–410.

Marquesa Search Systems Ltd, 'Marquesa – UK Trade Marks (a)' (2002), CD-ROM, March.

Mueller, D. C. and J. Cubbin, *The Dynamics of Company Profits: An International Comparison* (Cambridge: Cambridge University Press, 1990), viii, 216.

Nickell, S. J., 'Biases in Dynamic Models with Fixed Effects', *Econometrica*, 49(6) (1981), 1417–26.

Nickell, S. J., 'Competition and Corporate Performance', *Journal of Political Economy*, 104(4) (1996), 724–46.

Patent Office, 'Espace UK: United Kingdom Patent Applications' (1986–95), CD-ROM.

Patent Office, 'Espace Access-Europe' (1997, 2002), Vol. 1997 (December), Vol. 2002 (September).

Pavitt, K., 'Sectoral Patterns of Technical Change', *Research Policy*, 13 (1984), 343–73.

Scherer, F. M. and D. Ross, *Industrial Market Structure and Economic Performance* (Boston: Houghton Mifflin, 1990).

Search Systems Ltd, 'Marquesa UK Trade Marks (a)' (1996), CD-ROM, October.

Thomson, 'Company Analysis', 2001: on-line data.

Toivanen, O., P. Stoneman and D. Bosworth, 'Innovation and the Market Value of UK Firms', *Oxford Bulletin of Economics and Statistics*, 64(1) (2002), 39–60.

Vossen, R., 'R&D, Firm Size and Branch of Industry: Policy Implications', Report 98B43, SOM Research Institute, University of Groningen (1998).

Waring, G. F., 'Industry Differences in the Persistence of Firm-Specific Returns', *American Economic Review*, 86(5) (1996), 1253–65.

3
Business Method Patents and Venture Capital Investment Decisions

Robert H. Pitkethly

3.1 Introduction

Patent systems as providers of incentives to invest

The intellectual property (IP) system of any country plays a significant but in some senses uncertain role in the range of policy measures that might be used to encourage investment in innovation. Fritz Machlup (1958) is often cited to support the view that uncertainty about patents' effects counsels against both implementing and abolishing patent systems. Edith Penrose (1951) writing seven years earlier pointed this out in her study of the international patent system, saying: 'If national patent laws did not exist, it would be difficult to make a conclusive case for introducing them; but the fact that they do exist shifts the burden of proof and it is equally difficult to make a really conclusive case for abolishing them.' Penrose made this comment when referring to the nineteenth century debate about patents and Machlup and Penrose's prior discussion of the nineteenth century patent controversy (1950) dealt in large part with the debate about abolition. However, they also commented in that article that 'little, if anything, has been said for or against the patent system in the twentieth century that was not said equally well in the nineteenth'. That statement applies equally to the twenty-first century. However, rather than merely revisiting past debates, changes in patent law and the IP environment give reason enough to raise old questions in the light of new circumstances.

The debate about entirely abolishing patent systems is now one which is more a theoretical than a practical debate. A more persistent issue though, concerns the boundaries of patent systems. At a micro level patent lawyers are paid to argue about the boundaries of their clients' or opponents' patent claims and debate the implications of incremental changes in the breadth of interpretation of patent claims. At a macro and legislative level, however, debate also concerns not just how to interpret patent claims but where the boundaries of patentability should be drawn and thus what claims should be allowed to define as patentable. The problem is that whilst at the micro level opponents and patentees may be equally matched in the debate, at the macro level opposing forces comprise on the one hand the impersonal public good and on the other hand interested parties; which in the case of patent systems would seem to comprise almost all those who understand the system. This, added to the difficulty of repealing laws favouring vested interests, has resulted in the real risk of the R in IPR standing for 'ratchet' rather than 'right'.[1] Consequently, every proposed increase in the scope of patent protection to some extent requires the debate about whether a patent system should exist or not to be revisited with just as much importance attached to it as in the nineteenth century. This is not to say that it is inevitably wrong to increase the scope of protection, merely that caution and a willingness to make the case for any change are needed before taking what may be, in practice, irreversible steps.

At the same time recent emphasis by industry on IP as a firm resource that needs exploitation can lead to a heavier emphasis being put on promoting the firm's as opposed to the societal interests involved. It can be all too easy for those using patent systems to forget that the important issue is, in effect, whether the donkey moves forward rather than how many carrots it eats – whether the social ends of the system and not just the private benefits used as a means to those ends are reached. As Besen and Raskind (1991) have said, the objective of IP is 'to create incentives that maximize the difference between the value of the IP that is created and used and the social cost of its creation, including the cost of administering the system'.

There are studies such as that by Taylor and Silberston (1973) and Pitkethly (2001) on how patents are managed within companies and on the provision of incentives to researchers to encourage filing of patent applications (Pitkethly, 1995), something of increased interest lately given recent court cases regarding employee inventor rewards in Japan. However, on the more general issue of whether patents provide an incentive to firms to invest in R&D the evidence and discussion seems to be largely at a macro level and to show at best a weak link. Jaffe (2000), for example, observes that increases in R&D spending cannot be ascribed to changes in US law. Branstetter and Sakakibara (1999) found only modest changes in response to a strengthening of Japanese patent law.

One does, of course, need to distinguish between propensity to patent and propensity to invent or invest in R&D. Kortum and Lerner (1999) suggest that increased use of the patent system in the US following the introduction of the Court of Appeals for the Federal Circuit (CAFC) and consequent strengthening of US patent law was not so much a case of cause and effect on propensity to patent, as reflection of an increase in technological opportunities. At the same time evidence from a similar period in the 1980s and early 1990s when the influence of stronger US patents and stronger enforcement of patents by US companies was being felt in Japan, showed that there was a surge in the ratio of Japanese patents filed per inventor in Japan superimposed on a general upward trend in filings, which suggests that increased propensity to patent may on occasions be inextricably mixed with other factors, such as increased investment in and or productivity of R&D.

This all suggests that it can be a difficult task to disentangle the issue of whether patents provide incentives to invest from other motivations for using the patent system that companies and inventors might have. The effect in Japan of a momentary perception that patent quantity was important, which eventually gave way to a drive for quality also emphasizes that perceptions also play an important role in the effectiveness of patents as incentives. Considering how patents are perceived by venture capitalists is not necessarily the thin end of a post-modernist wedge being inserted into the patent debate but a critical issue in their operation, just as perceptions and expectations play critical roles in many other management issues. The effectiveness of patents as incentives to invest in R&D does, after all, depend not just on what the patent system can and does provide but also, at least in part, on what investors think or perceive that it provides.

There may therefore be some advantage to be gained in trying to isolate the issue of incentives to invest in R&D by studying investment decisions made by venture capital (VC) executives and their attitudes to ownership of IPRs and patents in particular since VC investment decisions usually involve investment in some form of R&D and provide an easily identifiable investment decision where ownership or not of patents may be a material factor in the decision.

Business method patents

Computerized and on-line business processes are growing rapidly internationally. Currently 'methods of doing business' are excluded from patentability under European and UK patent law.[2] There are no corresponding exceptions in the patent law of the United States and after a recent landmark case (State Street Bank[3]) patents are being granted on business methods in the US which are unlikely to be granted in the UK or Europe.

As outlined above, when the expansion or broadening of the scope of patentability is being considered then it should be subject to some of the same considerations as would be involved in establishing an entire patent system. Patents' role as a means of encouraging investment in R&D is something that is mentioned frequently in theoretical justifications of patent systems. In the case of this research investigating the effect of possession of IPRs, and in particular patents and BMPs, by companies seeking VC funding on the attitude of VC investors' willingness to invest in them would be particularly informative about the benefits patents and particularly BMPs might or might not provide to society in the way of encouraging further investment in such businesses and more broadly about the relationship between patents and IPRs and investment in R&D-based businesses in general.

Venture capital and IPRs

There are some studies which include work on VC and innovation (Kortum and Lerner, 2000) and on the attitude of VC executives to investing in technically based businesses (Murray and Lott, 1995). A recent study which looks at the specific interaction between VC and IP is that by Petersson (2002) dealing with 20 Swedish and Danish VC companies. Another paper by Lockett *et al.* (2002), which updated Murray and Lott's earlier work, found that lack of intellectual property protection was a key reason why technology based ventures were refused funding compared to non-technology-based ones. Whilst addressing some of the issues this chapter discusses, the two aforementioned papers did not deal directly with the issue of business method patents.

This chapter therefore studies whether those in the UK who contribute directly or indirectly to VC investment decisions or advise those who do are influenced by whether firms wishing to attract investment possess IPRs and especially patents and patent applications. It also investigates whether the influence of any patents would depend on the technical or non-technical nature of any innovation concerned and whether non-technical business method patents, if allowed, would differ in the incentives to invest that they might offer. The means used to investigate these questions comprised a survey addressed to those who currently contribute directly or indirectly to VC investment decisions or advise those who do; it asked whether the possession of intellectual property rights by companies seeking investment affected their investment decisions.

3.2 Methodology

Survey instrument

The survey was run using a web-based questionnaire form served from an Apple G4 computer equipped with a Dragon Web Surveys Filemaker database. Potential respondents were contacted by being sent an e-mail which included an invitation to complete the survey by clicking on a web link embedded in the e-mail. As an alternative, respondents could click on an another link which led to a different page on the OIPRC[4] website allowing them to download a fax-back ready questionnaire form that they could print out, complete and return by fax, e-mail or ordinary post. The present survey used two identical but separate web pages to allow replies from venture capital firm executives and business angel-related firm executives to be kept separate. The web-based nature of the survey meant that the respondents not only completed the form but also carried out the data entry. Reply data could thus be downloaded directly from the server for analysis using SPSS without any risk of data transcription errors. The present survey led to 123 completed questionnaires of which 107 (87 per cent) were returned using the web page. Sixteen other replies were received via other means (12 by fax, three by e-mail and one by post), either due to respondent choice or because of technical problems encountered by the respondent.

Sampling

Respondents were obtained from the from the British Venture Capital Association list of members (2001), others from the British Venture Capital Association list of sources of business angel capital (2001) and others from the UK national business angels network directory (http://www.bestmatch.co.uk/home/), the latter two of which list companies which provide links between business angels and companies seeking finance. Twenty-six (21.1 per cent) of the respondents were from the latter group of business angel-related companies, whilst 97 (78.9 per cent) were from venture capital companies.

The reason for including companies which advise on business angel finance was that it was thought likely that venture capital firms might not cover the start-up stages of finance and might concentrate more on later-stage investments. It was therefore hoped that by including business angel-related firms in the same survey but in such a way that the two sets of replies could be distinguished and compared (a separate but identical website was used for each), the potential pool of potential respondents could be increased. There was thought to be a risk that the business angel-related respondents might not, in fact, be involved in VC investment decisions and consequently, whilst the survey was conducted using separate but identical websites to enable the replies to be distinguished into the two groups, both groups were asked if they did currently contribute directly or indirectly to VC investment decisions or advised those who did.

Using the above directories, individual e-mail addresses for 1,220 VC investment executives or business angel-related firm executives were identified either directly from the directories or indirectly via the company websites listed in the directories. E-mails were sent to all of these. One thousand, one hundred and ninety-one of these e-mails were sent successfully, only twenty-nine being revealed on sending as incorrect and unsendable. A further 146 failed after delivery and were returned as undeliverable by the intended recipients' mail server. In total 1,045 (86 per cent) were sent and received successfully by the intended recipients. From these 1,045 requests 123 completed replies were received giving an effective response rate of 11.8 per cent. The response rate achieved, whilst it could have been greater, compares favourably with other methods of administering surveys in the UK.

Non-response

Fifteen e-mails were received reporting problems with accessing the website, though it is likely that these were due to problems with the respondent's computer rather than the server, bearing in mind the number of successful uses of the server by other respondents. Whilst there may have been others who failed to be able to access the site at all for technical reasons it is thought that this was unlikely. Looking at the web server log it can be seen that in total 173 people successfully accessed the server. Of these, 107 respondents successfully completed questionnaires.

Tests for non-response bias

To try and test for non-response bias in the replies, since the total funds invested and the average investment made by the company the respondent worked for were available for the BVCA-listed venture capital firms, the distributions of such values for respondent and non-respondents were compared. A *t*-test showed that the means for such values were lower in both cases for respondents compared to non-respondents but the differences were not significant at the 5 per cent level. Whilst similar data were not available for the business angel-related companies, the similarity in business makes it a reasonable assumption that the difference, if any, between respondents and non-respondents for such companies is unlikely to be significant either.

Anonymity

The initial section of the questionnaire gave respondents an opportunity but not an obligation to give their name and address. Eighteen respondents of the 123 who replied chose not to give a name or address. It should be noted that the above analysis for non-response bias excludes the 18 cases involving anonymous replies since it was not possible to assign figures for mean average investment or mean total funds invested from the BVCA data. However, inspection of the distribution of levels of finance dealt with by the anonymous respondents' companies and those of named respondents listed in their respective responses showed little apparent difference, so combined with their small number their omission is unlikely to have significantly altered the above analysis.

Response times

The participation request e-mail was sent out on the evening of Monday, 9 September 2002. Monday evenings were selected as being potentially the best date to send out survey requests in order to avoid commercial spam on Sunday night and the rush of e-mail at the beginning of the week whilst leaving almost a full week for respondents to consider replying. Of the 107 replies received via the web server, 65 (61 per cent) were received within the first day, 94 (88 per cent) by the end of the first week and all by 16 October 2002 or within about a month. The few latter replies were mostly said to be the result of respondents having been out of their office or on holiday.

Comments and interview requests

At the conclusion of the questionnaire respondents were asked to write any further comments they might have on the issues surveyed, to confirm their e-mail address if they wished to receive a copy of the report of the research and to give their telephone number if they would be prepared to be interviewed by telephone in the future. Of the 123 useable replies 29 (24 per cent) added brief comments, some of which are reported below.

3.3 Data Collection

Respondent characteristics

Investment decisions

The aim of the survey was to establish the opinions of those in the UK who currently contribute directly or indirectly to VC investment decisions or advise those who do. To check on this respondents were asked whether they currently contributed directly or indirectly to VC investment decisions or advised those who do. From the 123 replies, ten respondents answered no, or in one case did not reply. In order to be absolutely certain to confine the research findings to those who currently contribute directly or indirectly to VC investment decisions or advise those who do, the analysis from this point onwards was confined to the 113 replies where this was the case.

Levels of finance

Respondents were asked (Table 3.1) which levels of finance they were involved with. This question allowed for multiple replies.

Obviously many companies dealt with more than one level of finance and as can be seen most dealt primarily with funding between £100,000 and £50 million, with few companies specializing in only seed finance or only higher level MBO/MBI finance. Dividing the companies into mutually exclusive groups it can be seen that only 13 per cent of companies spanned a range of different levels of finance which was neither exclusively

Table 3.1 Levels of finance

Which levels of finance are you involved with? (Check all that apply with Y.)

	No.	(VC:BA)	%
a) up to £100,000	20	(12:8)	17.7
b) from £100,001 to £500,000	38	(21:17)	33.6
c) from £500,001 to £1,000,000	41	(24:17)	36.3
d) from £1,000,001 to £10,000,000	71	(58:13)	62.8
e) from £10,000,001 to £50,000,000	31	(29:2)	27.4
f) above £50,000,000	22	(21:1)	19.5
Only low level (only a, b or c)	19	(13:6)	16.8
Only medium (only b, c, d or e)	56	(48:8)	49.6
Only high (only e or f)	23	(23:0)	20.4
Other combinations	15	(10:5)	13.3
Total	113	(94:19)	100.0

Table 3.2 Stages of finance

Which stages of finance are you involved with? (Check all that apply with Y.)

	No.	(VC:BA)	%
a) Seed	42	(27:15)	37.2
b) Start-up	69	(50:19)	61.1
c) Expansion	89	(70:18)	78.8
d) MBO/MBI/Other	63	(51:11)	55.8
Only Seed or Start-up	10	(9:1)	8.8
Only MBO/MBI/Other	13	(13:0)	11.5
Other combinations	90	(72:18)	79.6
Total	113	(94:19)	100.0

low, medium or high level. As might be expected, the business angel-related firms tended to be concentrated on lower levels of financing.

Stages of finance

Questions were also asked about the stages of finance involved (Table 3.2). Again multiple responses were possible and most companies concerned dealt with more than one stage as well as more than one level of finance.

Whilst many companies dealt with more than one stage of financing, few were involved exclusively in seed/start-up or MBO/MBI forms of finance and most provided finance for a range of stages of investment. Though business angel-related companies tended to focus on earlier stage finance there was almost no specialization on only seed or start-up finance by such firms.

To enable some control for the levels of finance to be carried out Kruskal-Wallis (K-W) one-way ANOVA tests were conducted to test for any differences between the replies from respondents in the four mutually exclusive groups dealing with only low-level finance (up to £1 million), only medium-level finance (£100,000–£50 million), only high-level finance (£10 million upwards) and other combinations of levels of finance. Similar tests were conducted for the three mutually exclusive groups comprising those providing only seed and/or start-up finance, those providing only management buy-in, buy-out and other major levels of finance and other combinations. There were only a few minor significant differences, which are not reported here. The effect of these was that the few of the companies studied which specialized in just

MBI/MBO and like stages of finance or only dealt with high-level finance (above £10 million) tended in some cases to take a less positive view of the role of IPRs and view IPRs as a less significant factor in investment decisions than other respondents. This might be expected, but if anything reinforces the conclusions reached and which are discussed later, since the other companies who were more concerned with earlier and smaller forms of finance tended to not just show higher ratings of the role of IPRs overall but also a higher difference between results where IPRs were thought to have the greatest influence and those where it was least, namely in the e-commerce and non-technical business sectors.

Industry sectors

Respondents were asked (Table 3.3) which industry sectors they would consider deals from and asked to indicate all that applied from among a range. These were predominantly technically based but included e-commerce and non-technical categories.

Most companies were involved in financing a wide range of businesses and only 21 per cent (24 companies) were involved in financing just one or two of the above sectors, whilst 57 per cent were involved in financing companies in four or more of the above sectors. As can be seen, the most popular sector was Electronics/Communications/IT but other interests were widely spread. The least popular was e-commerce, no doubt reflecting the dot.com fallout of recent years, but still 40 per cent of companies would consider funding such companies. The business angel-related companies tended to deal with a wide range of sectors and showed even less specialization than the venture capital companies.

Table 3.3 Industry sectors

Which industry sectors would you consider deals from? (Check all that apply with Y.)

	No.	(VC:BA)	%
Chemical/Pharmaceutical/Biotech	65	(51:14)	57.5
Electronics/Communications/IT	92	(74:18)	81.4
Other tangible technology	67	(50:17)	59.3
Software	83	(66:17)	73.5
E-commerce	45	(32:13)	39.8
Other non-technical	62	(47:15)	54.9
		(94:19)	

One criticism that might be levelled at the figures presented here is that, of the VCs responding, only 40 per cent would at present consider investments in e-commerce and only 55 per cent investments in other non-technical sectors. In seeking to study the effect of IPRs on investment in business methods one might think that the study should be confined to only those VCs prepared to invest in these two sectors at present. However, to do so would ignore the possibility that the others might not be investing in the sectors solely because of the post-dot.com boom conditions or lack of patent protection for business methods and should therefore have their views consulted as well because their views may well be relevant when conditions change. To investigate this a Mann-Whitney U test was conducted to see if answers to questions concerning patent protection (Tables 3.5–3.7) differed between respondents prepared to invest in the e-commerce and/or other non-technical sectors and those who were not prepared to at present. No significant differences were found. In any event it was noticeable that those answering parts of questions relating specifically to e-commerce and other non-technical sectors were primarily those prepared to invest in those sectors (which is suggested in the tables above by the numbers replying). Yet closer analysis showed that answers to questions relating specifically to business method patents (Tables 3.5–3.7) and regarding e-commerce from those prepared to invest in the e-commerce sector were generally slightly more positive about the role of IP in investment decisions (and occasionally statistically significantly so) relative to those not prepared to invest in the e-commerce sector at present. However, none of even these replies averaged more than 'very little' (2–3) in their responses. All this confirms, though, is that patents and IP mean a little more regarding e-commerce to those prepared to invest in e-commerce than those who will not at present but still very little and significantly less than the effect of patents in technical sectors and particularly the chemical, pharmaceutical and biotech sector. It does not, therefore, substantially affect the overall conclusions of this study.

Opinions regarding the role of IPRs in VC decisions

The remaining questions concerned the core issues with which this research is concerned, namely, the role that those who make VC investment decisions or advise those who do consider that IPRs play in those investment decisions. Intellectual property rights (IPRs) were defined in the questionnaire as comprising patents, trade marks, copyright, design rights and other rights protecting a company's intellectual property (IP). The replies for these questions are presented here along with the replies according to whether the respondent was associated with the business angel or the more general venture capital finance group of respondents. In each case two tailed p values for Mann-Whitney tests comparing average scores for each question are reported.

Whether IPRs are a significant factor in investment decisions

To begin to concentrate on the issue of how important IPRs are in VC investment decisions, respondents were asked how often IPRs are a significant factor in investment decisions in a variety of industry sectors. Again business angel-related respondents in general had a slightly lower opinion of the significance of IPRs with the exception of the two largely non-technical sectors of e-commerce and other non-technical companies.

However, none of these differences with the opinions of more conventional venture capital executives were significant. The overall differences between the various sectors were significant according to a Kendall's W test, despite only 35 cases involving all sectors. Overall, the importance of IPRs was seen as more significant in the more technical sectors and in particular in those associated with the Chemical/Pharmaceutical/Biotechnology sectors (see Table 3.4).

Table 3.4 Significance of IPRs in investment decisions by sector

Good people, good returns and a good business plan are generally seen as the most critical factors in an investment decision. Nonetheless, how often are intellectual property rights (IPR) a significant factor in whether or not to invest in a company in the following sectors? (Choose 1–5 on the following scale.)

Never = 1 Rarely = 2 Sometimes = 3 Frequently = 4 Always = 5

		Mean responses (N)			M-W (2-tail)
		Overall	**VC**	**BA**	**p value**
Chemical/Pharmaceutical/Biotech		3.85(72)	3.88(59)	3.69(13)	0.4475
Electronics/Communications/IT		3.65(91)	3.66(74)	3.59(17)	0.7473
Other tangible technology		3.53(75)	3.56(57)	3.44(18)	0.5295
Software		3.58(84)	3.65(67)	3.29(17)	0.1461
E-commerce		3.15(54)	3.13(39)	3.20(15)	0.7106
Other non-technical		2.80(66)	2.75(52)	3.00(14)	0.3834
Kendall's W test	Cases	W	Chi-Square	D.F.	Significance
	35	.3017	52.7899	5	.0000

The role of patent protection in investment decisions

The problem with the above question is that, whilst it reflects the current situation regarding the relative influence of IPRs in investment decisions,

Table 3.5 Significance of lack of patent protection in investment decisions by sector

To what extent would lack of patent protection prevent venture capital funding for a company in the following sectors? (Choose 1–5 on the following scale.)

Never = 1 Rarely = 2 Sometimes = 3 Frequently = 4 Always = 5

		Mean responses (N)			M-W (2-tail)
		Overall	VC	BA	p value
Chemical/Pharmaceutical/Biotech		3.85(73)	3.85(60)	3.85(13)	0.9390
Electronics/Communications/IT		3.30(93)	3.21(76)	3.71(17)	0.0061**
Other tangible technology		3.27(75)	3.18(57)	3.56(18)	0.0319**
Software		3.06(86)	3.00(69)	3.29(17)	0.2441
E-commerce		2.64(55)	2.56(41)	2.86(14)	0.2169
Other non-technical		2.55(69)	2.44(54)	2.93(15)	0.0610*
Kendall's W test	Cases	W	Chi-Square	D.F.	Significance
	36	.4132	74.3774	5	.0000

* Significant at a 10% probability threshold.

** At 5%.

it refers to IPRs in general. A more specific question was therefore asked which tried to ascertain whether lack of patent protection in particular would prevent venture capital funding for a company in various sectors (Table 3.5). Business angel-related respondents had an overall slightly higher and occasionally significantly higher opinion in some sectors (e.g., electronics and non-technical fields) that lack of patent protection might prevent venture capital funding. However, the main difference was between technical areas such as Chemical/Pharmaceutical/Biotechnology areas and non-technical areas, the former being an area where lack of patent protection was considered by all to be significantly more likely to prevent venture capital funding than in other sectors.

Effect of patent application ownership on investment attractiveness

Since most investment opportunities are trying to raise finance at a time when they have patent applications but no granted patents, respondents were asked the extent to which patent applications would increase investment opportunity attractiveness according to the sector involved (Table 3.6).

There were only slight differences between business angel- and venture capital company-based respondents and only two of those differences were significant. There was, however an overall significant difference between the various sectors with the effect of a patent application on attractiveness

Table 3.6 Significance of patent applications in investment decisions by sector

To what extent would ownership of patent applications by a business increase its attractiveness as an investment opportunity in the following sectors? (Choose 1–5 on the following scale.)

Never = 1 Rarely = 2 Sometimes = 3 Frequently = 4 Always = 5

	Mean responses (N)			**M-W (2-tail)**
	Overall	**VC**	**BA**	**p value**
Chemical/Pharmaceutical/Biotech	3.58(77)	3.53(62)	3.80(15)	0.2643
Electronics/Communications/IT	3.28(93)	3.21(75)	3.56(18)	0.0555*
Other tangible technology	3.29(76)	3.22(58)	3.50(18)	0.1507
Software	3.00(88)	2.97(70)	3.11(18)	0.3238
E-commerce	2.77(57)	2.69(42)	3.00(15)	0.1899
Other non-technical	2.69(70)	2.57(53)	3.06(17)	0.0155**

Kendall's W test	Cases	W	Chi-Square	D.F.	Significance
	40	.3237	64.7476	5	.0000

* Significant at a 10% probability threshold.

** At 5%.

being greatest in the Chemical/Pharmaceutical/Biotechnology sector and least in the e-commerce and non-technical sectors.

Thus far the data show quite clearly that, first, IPRs can increase the attractiveness of an investment opportunity in the eyes of venture capital executives and those advising business angels. Second, it is quite clear that that attractiveness-enhancing effect differs significantly by industry sector and not just as a result of the differing legal environment in each sector.

IPRs role in investment in business methods

In the questionnaire it was explained to respondents that one theoretical role of patents is to act as an incentive for investment and that this begs the question as to whether patents affect investment decisions in practice. Business method patents were highlighted as one area of particular interest. It was also explained that at present patents can be granted in the USA for all new and inventive business methods including non-technical ones (e.g., a method of running a mutual investment fund) whilst in the UK and Europe inventions must involve some form of technical effect to be patentable. Having then said that whether European countries, including the UK, should also grant patents for non-technical business methods was currently being debated respondents were asked the following series of questions concerning the

Table 3.7 Significance of BMPs in investment decisions by sector

If patents were available for non-technical business methods in the UK and Europe would this:
a) encourage investment that would not otherwise be made?
b) increase investment in developing such business methods?
c) make businesses which had applied for such patents more attractive investments than they are without them?
d) make businesses which had applied for such patents more attractive investments relative to other companies?
e) help those making investment decisions concerning such business methods?
f) benefit the VC industry through availability of patents for new and inventive venture capital-related business methods?
(Choose 1–5 on the following scale.)

Never = 1 Rarely = 2 Sometimes = 3 Frequently = 4 Always = 5

	Mean responses (N)			M-W (2-tail)
	Overall	VC	BA	p value
a	2.49(110)	2.45(91)	2.72(18)	0.1698
b	2.54(110)	2.49(92)	2.77(18)	0.0982*
c	2.65(110)	2.62(92)	2.83(18)	0.2097
d	2.70(107)	2.63(90)	3.06(18)	0.0242**
e	2.56(109)	2.47(91)	3.00(18)	0.0056**
f	2.47(109)	2.36(92)	3.06(17)	0.0005**

* Significant at a 10% probability threshold.

** At 5%.

possible impact of US-style business method patents for non-technical inventions becoming available in the UK and Europe. The overwhelming response to all these questions was that business method patents (BMPs) would have at most some but in the main very little effect on investment decisions (Table 3.7).

Taking the specific sub-questions in Table 3.7 in turn, the first (a) asked whether the availability of BMPs would encourage investment that would not otherwise be made. Obviously the effect of a BMP might be either to encourage more investment than might otherwise have occurred and/or it might cannibalize investment which would otherwise have gone to other relatively less attractive investment opportunities. BMPs on the whole were thought to be likely to encourage very little of the former (a). Viewed from the BMP perspective, the existence of BMPs might, of course, give rise to greater investment in developing business methods than would otherwise have occurred (b) but very little of this extra investment was thought likely either. The possibility that possession of BMPs would just have a relative effect of making those companies that possessed them more attractive investment opportunities received very little support either whether in absolute terms (c) or relative terms compared to other investment opportunities (d). In short, the effect of possession of business method patents, in contrast to patents and patent applications more generally and especially in technical sectors such as the Chemical/Pharmaceutical/Biotechnology sector, was seen by almost all respondents as having very little effect on investment decisions in businesses which possessed such patent applications.

One effect which has been commented on by some venture capital executives who were interviewed is the signalling effect of patent applications. In some cases it has been suggested that the possession of patent applications can be seen as an indicator of the competence of the management team for having taken the steps necessary to at least try to protect the company's IP, irrespective of the legal worth of the applications involved. In that respect, possession of patent applications by companies might be seen as contributing indirectly to the decision-making process. Answers to question (e), however, showed that BMP applications would have very little effect in helping make investment decisions.

At the same time, the more general role of patents and other IPRs in investment decisions also needs to be kept in perspective. One survey respondent commented:

> The patent process is too slow and lengthy to provide any information to early-stage investment decisions. Typically, a young business will have raised its first VC funding before it has a patent granted. Patent applications are virtually worthless as they have completely unknown value without spending an unreasonable amount of time/money on due diligence. In reality, 'tacit knowledge' is the most valuable form of intellectual property and this is judged subjectively during the investment process.

On the other hand, another survey respondent said:

> A patented technology is an interesting opportunity, but an unpatented product with good market opportunity and a skilled team of sales, marketing and support people is much more attractive a proposition. If the difference between two businesses is just IP rights, of course the business with the rights is more attractive, but more often than not, these rights only provide the holder with a competitive advantage, not necessarily market dominance.

Finally, the key area for the development of BMPs in the US was the financial services industry and it is therefore not impossible that one further effect on the venture capital industry of introducing BMPs would be to enable venture capital companies themselves to apply for business method patents. Respondents, however, saw this as likely to bring very little benefit to the venture capital industry (f).

Conclusions regarding patents and BMPs as incentives for R&D investment

The data presented show quite clearly that IPRs and patents and patent applications do have a positive, though not dominant, role to play in increasing the attractiveness of technical investments but that the effect of the introduction of BMPs would be certain not to have any great effect and would most likely have very little effect on investment decisions in the non-technical fields involved. One might add that the UK venture capital industry covered by this research, by giving greater weight to IPR in technical fields compared to those concerning BMPs, agrees with the European and UK patent offices in viewing a technical aspect to be necessary to make an effective patent application.

3.4 Discussion

An effective solution?

Most instances where governments use ends to justify means tend to be controversial. Patent systems are no exception. In using time-limited monopolies involving publication to encourage investment in and dissemination of inventions, governments use what might be thought of as an economic evil to achieve an economic good. This requires a balance to be kept, which is difficult because clear indicators to help decide where that balance should lie are hard to find and affected by many factors besides patents. Despite being a very specific case, the optimum balance for business method patents is unfortunately no clearer than for the patent system as a whole.

As a result of the uncertainty about its true effects, the patent system is not a precise policy measure. Edith Penrose (1951) said that 'a sweeping, non-discriminating, generously administered and unconditional patent grant is an expensive and blunt instrument'. It is arguably better than many other methods of encouraging innovation, such as prizes, in that, it does not reward inventors or, apart from system costs (and possibly hindering further different but related innovation), burden society when inventions fail. Yet whilst it can still give significant inventions great rewards, the question remains as to whether those inventions could have been obtained equally well without the patent system and even if not whether the blunt instrument could be sharpened and the patent system made more efficient.

What should an effective solution achieve?

There are arguably three main social benefits that a patent system seeks to obtain. The first and the one emphasized by the UK Patent Office consultation on business method patents,[5] is that of promoting investment in innovation that would not otherwise be made because of the risk of free-riding competition. There is also the aim of publication of inventions that would otherwise remain secret and the commoditization of inventions enabling their commercialization through sale or licensing, the latter being particularly important where overseas markets are critical, or where, more generally, resources for in-house exploitation are not available, thus limiting the benefits to inventors. These three roles of promoting investment, publication and commoditization in the cases where patents are most effective can all work together to produce an efficient system where the benefits outweigh the costs.

The costs of patent systems are well, if not precisely, known and inevitable. They include indirect but temporary costs of monopoly pricing, restriction of competition, potential hindrance of research and, where it exists, legal uncertainty, as well as the direct professional and administrative costs and official fees that any patent system involves. The essential question that needs asking in respect of any proposal to offer patents for new categories of inventions is thus whether the hoped for public benefits outlined above are truly present, outweigh these known costs and could not be obtained at lower or no cost in any other way.

In the case of business method patents in the USA, apparently no such analysis was carried out by the United States Court of Appeals for the Federal Circuit before deciding to 'lay to rest' the idea that they should not be patentable in the State Street Bank case judgment referred to earlier. Nor have economists since managed to produce a definitive answer as to whether BMPs would produce more benefits than costs. However, a brief consideration of the three potential benefits might guide us as to where the balance is likely to lie in this case.

What are the benefits of BMPs?

First is the scale of investment required in this field such that in the absence of the monopoly profits offered by patent protection, investment in development of business methods would be reduced or absent?

Second, in the absence of patent protection is it likely that the inventors of business methods would be able to protect them by means of secrecy and avoiding publication? Third, in the absence of patent protection would the lack of ability to commoditize new business methods so reduce the benefits that could be obtained from them that investment in their development would be reduced or absent?

In the case of the first question the current research suggests that the incentive effect of BMPs is minimal if it exists at all and is certainly lower than in the case of patents in other more technically based fields. The implication is that BMPs do *not* do a very good job of encouraging investment in new business methods. Furthermore, at least in the UK since the 1977 Patents Act came into force and expressly excluded BMPs, the absence of business method patents does not appear to have unduly hindered the development of new business methods in the UK. Finally, leaving aside their technical implementation, BMs would not appear to require any substantial investment in R&D compared to inventions in other more technical sectors.

The second question is as to whether inventors of new and inventive business methods might otherwise keep them secret in the absence of a system allowing for BMPs. However, in the first place this would not be possible with many business methods and, second, if it were, inventors might well keep them secret anyway even if BMPs were available. Publication benefits from BMPs are thus unlikely to be critical.

The last issue of commoditization, or the lack of it in the case where BMPs are not obtainable, is more interesting. First, franchising of businesses has been carried out for many years using existing IPRs without the use of BMPs. The question is thus whether there would be more innovation of business methods if BMPs were available to enable the resulting business methods to be more easily franchised or licensed.

This question resembles that encountered in the first question with the form of the carrot or benefit offered the innovator being different. In the case of a technically based innovation a key advantage of easy commoditization is that the consequent ease of licensing allows resource-poor businesses to get closer to being able to fully exploit their innovations than they would be able to using their own resources alone. For example, a start-up company with an invention that can be used throughout the world but without the resources to exploit the invention very widely initially, can approximate to that by licensing out the invention to others and thus reaping some at least of the benefits in the short term which would otherwise be difficult if not impossible to appropriate in the absence of the patent. However, in the case of the most common business method patents, which use e-commerce, the costs of exploiting such a business method globally are considerably reduced in any event by the global reach of the Internet, enabling small companies to scale up and expand their operations internationally at very low cost compared to conventional globalization strategies. As a result it seems likely that the commoditization benefits derived from BMPs in such cases may be low too.

Given the current research findings regarding investment incentives and the above considerations regarding the other potential benefits from BMPs it would seem that their costs are almost inevitably going to outweigh their benefits.

3.5 Conclusion

A UK Patent Office consultation exercise concluded in March 2001 with the view that:

> There is no sign, at least to date, of a want of innovation in computer-implemented business methods, and nor was there in the US before business methods became patentable in 1998. Intense innovation has characterized this field. The Government's conclusion is that those who favour some form of patentability for business methods have not provided the necessary evidence that it would be likely to increase innovation. Unless and until that evidence is available, ways of doing business should remain unpatentable.

The present investigation has encountered very little, if any evidence, that business method patents would increase innovation rather than just increase patent activity in the field of business methods. The specific evidence from consulting venture capitalists in the UK suggests that whilst patents, especially in the low patent density[6] technical fields of pharmaceuticals, chemicals and biotechnology, can play a substantial role in encouraging investment in innovation, making patent protection available for non-technical business methods would have very little effect on encouraging investment in such innovations that would not be made anyway. Though an identical survey was not carried out in the US, interviews carried out there as a separate exercise and not reported here support the suggestion that the situation there is not much different. Rather than encouraging innovation that would not otherwise occur, business method patents are viewed more as another means of appropriating intellectual assets that has to be used, more because they are there than because they are essential.

The research in the UK described here showed that if one assumed that all other factors were equal, a business method venture with a patent would be seen as slightly more attractive than one without but with very little effect on the absolute attractiveness. This minimal overall effect on investment in innovation would seem unlikely to outweigh the costs that the existence of such patent protection would bring in its wake.

Acknowledgements

The present research was carried out by the author as part of a larger project carried out together with Bob Hart and supported by the Intellectual Property Institute of London, which studied the issue of the introduction of business method patents in the US and legal and other factors affecting their potential introduction into the UK and Europe. The assistance of Simon Goeller of Said Business School with assembly of the mailing lists is also gratefully acknowledged.

Notes

1. Something illustrated, *inter alia*, by the relentless increase in the duration of copyright protection in recent years.
2. Article 52(2)(c) EPC; see also UK Patents Act 1977 S.1 (2)c.
3. 149 F.3d1368 (Fed.Cir.1998), rev'd 927 F.Supp. 502 (D. Mass. 1995), cert. denied,119 S.Ct.851 (1999).
4. Oxford Intellectual Property Research Centre: www.oiprc.ox.ac.uk
5. http://www.patent.gov.uk/about/consultations/conclusions.htm
6. High patent density refers to the number of patents per product – usually high in the case of markets such as automobiles and consumer products and low in the case of pharmaceuticals and chemical products.

References

Besen, S. M. and L. J. Raskind, 'An Introduction to the Law and Economics of Intellectual Property', *Journal of Economic Perspectives*, 5 (1) (1991), 3–27.

Branstetter, L. and M. Sakakibara, 'Do Stronger Patents induce more innovation? Evidence from the 1988 Japanese Patent Law Reforms', NBER Working Paper, 7066 (1999).

Jaffe, A. B., 'The US Patent System in Transition: Policy Innovation and the Innovation Process', *Research Policy*, 29 (2000), 531–57.

Kortum, S. and J. Lerner, 'What is Behind the Recent Surge in Patenting?', *Research Policy*, 28 (1) (1999), 1–22.

Kortum, S. and J. Lerner, 'Assessing the Contribution of Venture Capital to Innovation', *RAND Journal of Economics*, 31 (4) (2000), 674–92.

Lockett, A., G. Murray and M. Wright, 'Do UK Venture Capitalists still have a Bias against Investment in New Technology Firms', *Research Policy*, 31 (2002), 1009–30.

Machlup, F., 'An Economic Review of the Patent System: Study No.15 of the US Senate Subcommittee on Patents Trademarks and Copyrights', 85th Congress 2nd session (1958).

Machlup, F. and E. T. Penrose, 'The Patent Controversy in the Nineteenth Century', *Journal of Economic History*, 10 (1950), 1–29.

Murray, G. and J. Lott, 'Have UK Venture Capitalists a Bias against Investment in New Technology-Based Firms?' *Research Policy*, 24 (2) (1995), 283–99.

Penrose, E. T., *The Economics of the International Patent System* (Baltimore: Johns Hopkins Press, 1951).

Petersson, H., 'Venture Capital Firms and Intellectual Property', Department of Industrial Management and Economics, Chalmers University of Technology (2002).

Pitkethly, R. H., 'Patent Application Filing Incentives in Japan', Association of Japanese Business Studies, Ann Arbor, Michigan, AJBS (1995).

Pitkethly, R. H., 'Intellectual Property Strategy in Japanese and UK companies: Patent Licensing Decisions and Learning Opportunities', *Research Policy*, 30 (2001), 425–42.

Taylor, C. T. and Z. A. Silberston, *The Economic Impact of the Patent System*, (Cambridge: Cambridge University Press, 1973).

Part II

Knowledge Transfer and Intellectual Property Systems

4

Open Science and University Patenting: A Bibliometric Analysis of the Italian Case

Stefano Breschi, Francesco Lissoni and Fabio Montobbio

4.1 Introduction

This chapter addresses the issue of university patenting and its impact on the scientific activity of academic researchers. The issue is highly debated in Europe where legislators are trying to design policy instruments to support the technological transfer from university to industry and to create an optimal set of incentives to stimulate scientists' productivity. The relationship between patenting and publishing may be controversial because there are as many arguments claiming that the relationship is beneficial to both university and industry as reasons to fear that patenting may hinder the free diffusion of scientific knowledge or bias the scientists' choice of research topics.

We address the issue empirically with data at the individual level. We compare the number of scientific publications of a sample of 296 academic inventors and a sample of 296 matched controls, with patenting as a treatment variable. Section 4.2 qualitatively identifies the empirical model considering the different causal mechanisms that may explain a positive or a negative relationship between patenting and publishing. The empirical work exploits two datasets: one contains information on Italian 'academic inventors' (that is Italian academic researchers designated as inventors on patent documents); the other is based upon the *ad hoc* collection of publication data for both these 'academic inventors' and a sample of their 'non-inventor' colleagues, from the on-line version of ISI's *Science Citation Index*. Section 4.3 provides both a description of the data and the descriptive evidence. Section 4.4 presents the econometric exercise. Section 4.5 concludes.

4.2 The Relationship Between Patenting and Publishing at the Individual Level

The relationship between patenting and publishing may be negative at the individual level mainly for two reasons.[1] There may be a 'publication delay' effect and/or a 'basic-applied trade-off'. First, publication delays may be necessary to meet the novelty step requirement in all patent legislations throughout the world: only new ideas can be patented, and ideas that entered the common pool of knowledge (no matter how recently, and no matter by which means) through a published output are not new. Academic researchers that aim at taking a patent, either in their own name, or in the name of their universities or a business partner, should keep their inventions secret as long as the patent application has not been filed (Akers, 1999, p. 144).[2]

Second, the diversion of a researcher's attention from basic research to more applied targets may result in lower rates of publications in refereed journals, or in less ambitious publications with a lower impact on the scientific community. This can be expected to exert non-negligible effects only if patenting is non-occasional, especially if resulting from business-oriented research. Thus, we expect academic inventors with prolonged contacts with industry and more than one patent to be the most affected by the trade-off (for a discussion, see Breschi *et al.*, 2005a).[3]

There are at least three counter-arguments against the existence of a patenting–publishing trade-off at the individual level. First, there may be a 'resource effect'. This argument suggests that the individual researcher who chooses to address her/his research to IPR-relevant objectives does so in order to access additional resources. Scientists can access not just *financial* resources and expensive scientific instruments, but also 'focused' research questions (*cognitive* resources). Answers to research questions raised by technological puzzles may be at the same time economically valuable and scientifically relevant, up to the point of opening up new research avenues and disciplines (Mansfield, 1995, 1998; Rosenberg, 1990). We expect the resource effect to show up much more clearly for patents applied for by business companies, with the scientists appearing just as designated inventors, rather than by the scientists themselves or their universities (or public funding agencies). It may not be easy to tell the 'resource effect' apart from the 'publication delay' effect, despite their opposite impact on publication activity.

The two other counter-arguments against the publishing–patenting trade-off derive from long-debated questions in the sociology of science. We may label them the 'productivity fixed effect' and the 'augmented

Matthew effect'. Both of them suggest that academic inventors may be among the most productive scientists, namely those with the highest publication rates. The 'productivity fixed effect' argument simply suggests that both patents and publications are proxies of a scientist's productivity. The 'augmented Matthew effect' builds upon the classic remarks by Merton on the tendency of the priority reward system to benefit highly productive scientists, especially precocious ones, with a number of cumulative advantages, ranging from higher visibility and reputation, to ever-increasing ease of access to research opportunities and resources (Merton, 1988; for an empirical appraisal, Allison *et al.*, 1982).

4.3 Data and Descriptive Evidence

In this section we outline the main characteristics of the data. Data on patenting activity on academic professors come from the 'EP-INV-DOC' dataset, which lists 919 Italian academic inventors. The 'EP-INV-DOC' dataset originates from the complete list of professors and researchers who, in 2000, held a position in a scientific or technical discipline in an Italian university (including medical and engineering schools): names and surnames in that list were matched to names and surnames in the EP-INV database, which contains all patent applications to the European Patent Office which designate at least one inventor with an Italian address, from 1978 to early 2000. Overall, the EP-INV database contains information on 30,243 inventors and 38,868 patent applications (for a more comprehensive description, see Balconi *et al.*, 2004). For sake of simplicity, we will refer to patent applications simply as 'patents'.

The list of professors was provided by the Ministry of Education and Research (MIUR). It contains little more than 30,000 names, complete with age, affiliation, discipline and academic ranking (researcher, associate professor and full professor). Disciplines are defined according to a classification created for administrative purposes (to define candidates' profiles when new positions were offered); it is very detailed and allows some compression into broader categories, which we will refer to as 'fields'.[4] We focus on four disciplines with a very high share of academic inventors over the total number of professors in the discipline. These are: chemical engineering (this includes technology of materials, such as macromolecular compounds), biology, pharmacology and electronics and telecommunications, for a total of 301 academic inventors and 552 patents (see Table 4.1 and Table 4.A1).

We have selected for our exercise 296 academic inventors.[5] A control sample was then built, by matching each academic inventor to a professor

Table 4.1 University professors in Italy and academic inventors in the selected fields

Field	Professors, active in 2000	Academic inventors, number and (%)
Chemical engineering and materials technology	355	66 (18.5)
Pharmacology	613	84 (13.7)
Biology	1359	78 (5.7)
Electronics and telecommunications	630	73 (11.6)
Total	2957	301 (10.4)

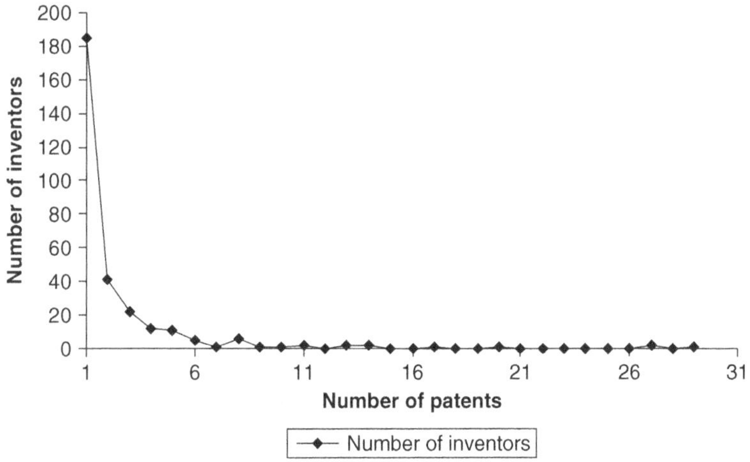

Figure 4.1 Distribution of the sample of academic inventors by number of patents
Source: EP-INV database.

in the same discipline, and possibly with the same academic position (full professor, associate professor or researcher), age and academic affiliation (in this order of importance).

Patent data

The distribution of patents across academic inventors is highly skewed; most professors have signed only one patent, and a very few more than five (Figure 4.1 and Table 4.2). This pattern is very similar to the well-established evidence on professors' publication records, which invariably shows the co-existence of a small number of hyper-productive

Table 4.2 Distribution (%) of academic inventors by number of patents and field

	Number of patents			
Fields	1	2–5	6+	
Chemical engineering and materials technology	60.9	32.8	6.3	*100*
Pharmacology	63.1	28.6	8.3	*100*
Biology	70.5	23.1	6.4	*100*
Electronics and telecommunications	56.2	31.5	12.3	*100*
Total	62.9	28.8	8.3	*100*

Source: EP-INV-DOC database.

'superstars', and a large number of professors with very few or no publications. The distribution would be even more skewed if we considered also the non-patenting professors (see again Table 4.1).

Most patents belong to business companies, as a result of contractual funding, with little meaningful differences across fields (Table 4.3). We cannot be sure that all academic inventors signed their patents when they were already working in a university. Some patents may be the outcome of former jobs as industrial researchers or employees of large public labs. However, we suspect these patents to be very few, since Italian professors usually start pursuing their academic career right after graduating (the definitive answer will, in any case, come from the ongoing interviews). As for IPRs over publicly funded research, in principle these belong to the sponsors (most often the MIUR ministry, the National Research Council and, in the past, ENEA, the National Agency for Alternative Energy). However, until recently, the decision to take the first step towards patenting was usually left to grant recipients, and if taken, the step may have met some bureaucratic resistance.

A similar explanation applies to the scarcity of patents owned by the universities: until recently, universities decided to take charge of the application procedure and expenses more to reward, often symbolically, some brilliant researcher, rather than as the outcome of a consistent exploitation strategy. As a result, few patent applications from publicly funded research are completed, and even less are extended outside the national level (so they do not appear in our dataset). It also happens that many professors take the shortcut of patenting in their own names: this explains the presence of a few inventors' own patents.

We also classify the inventors in two groups: 'occasional' and 'persistent'. The limited number of patents per inventor, and the limited

Table 4.3 Ownership of academic inventors' patents[1] by type of applicant and field: number of patents (and %)

	Business companies	'Open science' institutions[2]	Individuals[3]	Others	All applicant types
Chemical engineering and materials technology	125 *(78.1)*	18 *(11.3)*	15 *(9.4)*	2 *(1.3)*	160 *(100)*
Pharmacology	192 *(85.0)*	24 *(10.6)*	10 *(4.4)*	–	226 *(100)*
Biology	91 *(54.5)*	43 *(25.7)*	30 *(18.0)*	3 *(1.8)*	167 *(100)*
Electronics and telecommunications	199 *(81.9)*	28 *(11.5)*	13 *(5.3)*	3 *(1.2)*	243 *(100)*
All fields	607 *(76.3)*	109 *(14.2)*	68 *(8.5)*	8 *(1.0)*	796 *(100)*

[1] Patents owned by more than one applicant were counted more than once
[2] Universities, public labs and government agencies; both Italian and foreign
[3] Same applicants' and inventors' names

Source: EP-INV-DOC database.

commitment of universities in patenting their employees' findings, suggest that most academic inventors (as opposed to industrial researchers working for large R&D labs) are involved in the patenting process on a occasional basis. All inventors with just one patent belong to the 'occasional' category. As for the others, we distinguish between those whose patenting activity is concentrated in a few years (and whose patents are very likely to stem from just one research project) and those whose patents are separated by long time lags (who we suspect to have patented the results of more than one research project).

We distinguish also between those who patented for the first time before 1990 and those who patented for the first time between 1990 and 1995: for the former to be defined 'persistent', we require the lag between their last and first patent to be no less than half the time interval between their first patent and year 2000 (right censoring); for the latter we require the lag between their last and first patent to be no less than two thirds of the time interval between their first patent and year 2000. One additional category of inventors ('recent' inventors) gathers all inventors whose first patent is dated after 1995, and whose persistency we cannot judge (see Figure 4.2).

Figure 4.3 and Table 4.4 illustrate the distribution of the academic inventors in our sample according to the above-mentioned categorization, by field and number of 'patenting years' (years in which the inventor signed at least one patent). All inventors with more than five years of activity fall in the 'persistent' category. Thirty-five scientists (out of 91) with two to five years of activity also belong to the 'persistent' category.

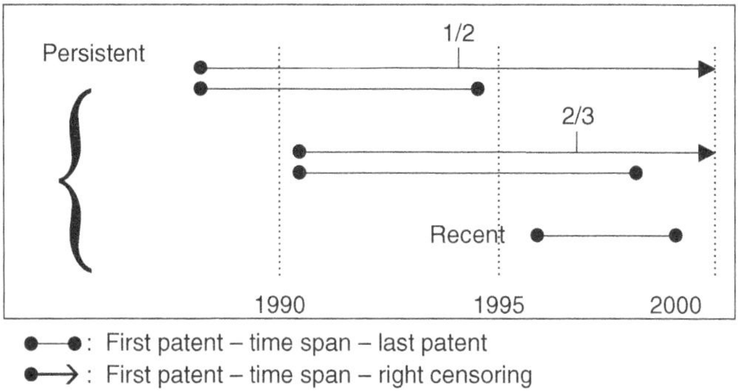

Figure 4.2 Persistent inventors: definition

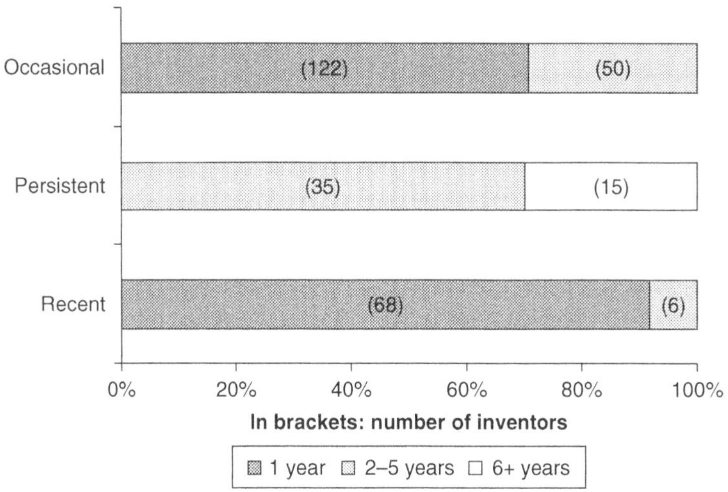

Figure 4.3 Academic inventors, by frequency of invention and number of patenting years

Note: 296 observations.

Source: EP-INV database.

In synthesis, inspection of data on academic inventors suggests that neither academic inventors in the chosen fields, nor their universities, seem to have pursued an active patenting policy. Patents signed by academic inventors are most often the result of contract research agreements between individual professors and a large number of business companies, which retain all the intellectual property rights over the

Table 4.4 Academic inventors, by frequency of invention and field (sample values)

	Occasional inventors, number and % (by field)	Persistent inventors, number and % (by field)	Recent inventors, number and % (by field)
Chemical engineering and materials technology	36 *(57.14)*	8 *(12.70)*	19 *(30.16)*
Pharmacology	50 *(60.24)*	17 *(20.48)*	16 *(19.28)*
Biology	50 *(64.10)*	10 *(12.82)*	18 *(23.08)*
Electronics and telecommunications	36 *(50.00)*	15 *(20.83)*	21 *(29.17)*
All field	172 *(58.11)*	50 *(16.89)*	74 *(25.00)*

research results. It follows that academic inventors' patents ought possibly to be seen as proxies of the involvement of professors in contract research projects: if continuative ('persistent' innovators), this involvement may indeed generate a positive 'resource' effect on the academic inventors' publication rate. At the same time, this suggests that business partners may have the final say over the academic inventors' publication tactics, and impose non-negligible publication delays.

Publication data

Publication data were collected from the 2003 on-line version of ISI's *Science Citation Index* for both 296 of the 301 of the academic inventors in the selected fields, and 296 'control' professors. The latter were chosen according to their academic position (which was required to match exactly that of the reference academic inventor) and age (control professor had to be preferably no more than five years younger/older than their counterparts). Controls were chosen from the same university of the academic inventors, or a near one. A detailed description of the matching procedure can be found in Breschi *et al.* (2005a). First, we calculated the average number of total publications of the inventors and their controls from 1975 to 2002. The average number of publications of the inventors is sensibly higher then their controls. Average figures are significantly higher in all fields (Table 4.5). Both the empirical literature on scientific productivity and the theoretical fundamentals of the sociology of science suggest that looking at mean comparisons may be misleading, since the distribution of professors by number of publications is usually found to be highly skewed to the right. Our data make no exception. Table 4.5 shows that all fields show a positive skewness index for both the inventors' and the controls' distribution. This table also

Table 4.5 Inventors versus control sample, publications (mean values and distribution skewness); by field and type of inventor, 1975–2003

	Controls			Inventors				
	Mean (1)	Median (2)	Skewness	Mean (3)	Median (4)	Skewness	(3) – (1)	(4) – (2)
Field								
Chemical engineering and materials technology	33.06	27	1.67	52.58	38	3.01	19.52	11
Pharmacology	44.56	41	1.09	57.37	50	1.14	12.81	9
Biology	48.12	36	1.95	68.62	52.5	2.74	20.5	16.5
Electronics and telecommunications	30.05	22.5	2.08	38.93	37.5	0.89	8.88	15
Inventor type								
Occasional	39	33	1.83	50.68	42	2.53	11.68	9
Persistent	44.1	35.5	1.27	76.78	59.5	2.95	32.68	24
Recent	37.5	30	2.08	49.6	40	1.93	12.1	10
All inventors	39.52	32	1.77	54.83	44	3.05	15.31	12

Source: Elaborations on EP-INV database and ISI *Science Citation Index*.

shows that the average number of publications of the inventors is always higher than the controls' mean value, and that the same holds for the median number of publications: together, these statistics suggest that the inventors' figures compare favourably against the controls' not because of some hyper-productive outlier, but as a result of a truly higher scientific productivity. We also notice that persistent inventors compare more favourably to their controls than occasional ones.

The superior productivity of inventors is confirmed when moving to yearly publication data. Figure 4.4 provides a snapshot of the mean number of publications for both the academic inventors and the control sample, for each year from 1975 to 2003. It suggests that the average scientific productivity of both inventors and controls has increased over time: whether this can be regarded as a hard fact or the mere result of the increasing propensity of Italian academics to publish on English-language SCI-monitored journals remains to be seen, but it is a not crucial concern of our research. More important, it is pointing at the clear superiority of academic inventors versus their controls, a superiority that roughly measures up to 1.5 papers per year.

Once again, persistency in invention looks like being associated to an even higher productivity: Figure 4.4 also reports the mean figures for the subgroups of persistent, recent and occasional inventors and it shows that the former are consistently more productive than all other inventors; the occasional ones are in the bottom position (among the inventors). As for comparing each type of inventor to its control group,

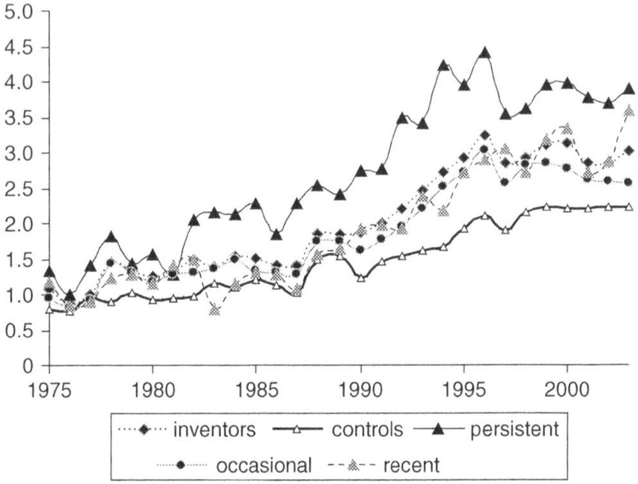

Figure 4.4 Average number of yearly publications; inventor versus control sample, 1975–2003

Source: Elaborations on EP-INV database and ISI *Science Citation Index*.

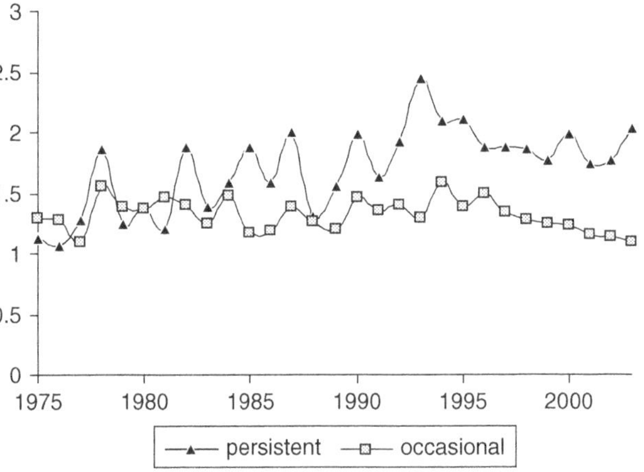

Figure 4.5 Average number of publications; inventor/control ratio, by inventor type, 1975–2003

Source: Elaborations on EP-INV database and ISI *Science Citation Index*.

Figure 4.5 reports the ratios between the average number of yearly publications of the persistent and occasional inventors' versus their controls' groups: persistent inventors compare more favourably to their controls than occasional ones do. Figure 4.5 also shows that controls apparently catch up with inventors in the late 1990s: one possible explanation for this trend could be the failure of many inventors to patent again during those years (notice that for recent inventors any catching-up is visible only in the last two years); alternatively, it may be some of our controls have turned into inventors, by signing patents in between 2000 and 2002 (the spell of time not covered by our data).

4.4 A Panel Data Analysis of Scientists' Publication Activity: The Effect of Patenting

In this section we use the longitudinal nature of our data to explore further the relationship between patenting and publishing. We perform a three-step exercise:

1. First we regress the yearly number of publications of each professor (inventors and controls alike) on his/her individual characteristics such as experience and disciplinary field, as well as on the characteristics of her/his academic institutions (size and prestige of her/his department).[6] In particular, we include each professor's status, whether she/he is an inventor or not. This tests directly whether inventors display, on average, higher scientific productivity than their controls. Regressions include also a full set of time dummies.
2. Second we use the patenting event as a treatment variable and we test whether *becoming* an inventor has a positive impact on the publication activity of a scientist. We build a variable ($postpat_{it}$) which is equal to one if $t \geq t_0$ and zero elsewhere. t_0 is the year of the first patent.
3. Finally, we test the impact of patenting on publication activity for the years immediately before and after the year in which the patent occurs. We use dummies to explore this dynamic behaviour and add seven time dummies, one for each year around the event, starting three years before the patent priority date (Dp_j, with $j = -3, \ldots, +3$; Dp_0 corresponds to the patent priority date). The coefficients can be interpreted as deviations of the number of yearly publications after controlling for time variant and individual (time invariant) heterogeneity: if there is a relationship between patenting and publishing, an unexplained pattern related to patenting activity should remain in the error terms and should be caught by the dummies' variables.

We estimate the following four specifications:

$$E(P_{it}|x) = \exp\left\{\beta inv_i + \sum_j \gamma_j ex_{ij} + \sum_j \delta_j sett_{ij} + \gamma Size\_dep_i + gender_i + \tau_t\right\} \quad (1)$$

$$E(P_{it}|x) = \exp\left\{\beta postpat_i + \sum_j \gamma_j ex_{ij} + \sum_j \delta_j sett_{ij} + \gamma Size\_dep_i + gender_i + c_i + \tau_t\right\} \quad (2)$$

$$E(P_{it}|x) = \exp\left\{\sum_{j=-3,+3} \beta_j Dp_{ij} + \sum_j \gamma_j ex_{ij} + \sum_j \delta_j sett_{ij} + \gamma Size\_dep_i + gender_i + c_i + \tau_t\right\} \quad (3)$$

$$E(P_{it}|x) = \exp\left\{\sum_{j=-3,+3} (\beta_j^{\star} I_{OCC})\, Dp_{ij} + \sum_{j=-3,+3} (\beta_j^{\star} I_{NO\_OCC})\, Dp_{ij} + \sum_j \gamma_j ex_{ij} + \sum_j \delta_j sett_{ij} + \gamma Size\_dep_i + gender_i + c_i + \tau_t\right\} \quad (4)$$

The explanatory variables we include in the regressions are:

- inv_i: a dummy variable equal to one for inventors.
- ex_{ji}: a set of binary variables for age categories; in particular we have four age categories (the base age is [25, 29]), ex_{1i} if age is in the interval [30, 39], ex_{2i} if age is [40, 49], ex_{3i} if age is [50, 59] and, finally, ex_{4i} if age [60, 70].
- c_i: unobserved individual time constant effect.
- $sett_{ji}$: a set of binary variables for the disciplinary fields of the professors. In particular $Dsett_1 = 1$ for Biology, zero elsewhere; finally, $Dsett_2 = 1$ for electronics and telecommunications, zero elsewhere. $Dsett_3 = 1$ for pharmacology, zero elsewhere; chemical engineering and materials technology is the base category.
- $gender_i$: this variable is one for women, zero elsewhere.
- $Size\_dep_{it}$: is the number of professors within the scientist's department divided by the total amount of professors in the scientific fields within the scientist's university. This controls for the size and importance of the department.
- Dp_j, with $j = -3, \ldots, +3$; dummies starting three years before the patent priority date. Dp_0 corresponds to the patent priority date.
- I_{OCC}: is a dummy variable equal to one if for occasional inventors and zero elsewhere.

- $I_{NO\_OCC} = 1 - I_{OCC}$: is a dummy variable equal to one for non-occasional inventors and zero elsewhere.
- All the regressions contain a full set of time dummies (τ_t) to control for time varying unobservables that are common across individuals.

Notwithstanding many qualitative limitations of our data, these variables are very much the same proved to be relevant by the sociological analysis of scientific productivity (Allison and Long, 1990; Long *et al.*, 1993; see also Turner and Mairesse, 2004).

Our panel is composed of 592 individuals for a maximum of 20 years. We selected the time period between 1980 and 1999 for which our patent data are more reliable. Moreover, we do not have the precise dates on which our professors started their academic careers. Therefore, we started including them in the sample when they are 25 years old. The panel therefore is unbalanced. Specifications (2), (3) and (4) are first estimated using fixed effects (LSDV) to control for unobserved individual heterogeneity. All time invariant variables in this case are dropped from the within estimation. In this case the dependent variable is re-calculated as $p_{it} = log(1 + P_{it})$ P_{it}: is the number of individual publications at time *t*. This is done because, for some individual observations, the number of publications is zero and the log of zero is not defined. Since publications are non-negative integers, any fixed effects model using least squares could create a bias in the estimated coefficients. We then use also a count data model. Since the distribution of individual publications is highly skewed, with significant overdispersion and a large number of zeros, specification (1) is also estimated using a negative binomial model, and specifications (2), (3) and (4) are also estimated using a fixed effects negative binomial model (Hausman *et al.*, 1984). In this case the dependent variable is P_{it}.

First step: inventors versus non-inventors

Table 4.6 (columns 1 and 2) reports the results from the regressions of the first specification. Our estimates confirm that inventors have a significantly higher propensity to publish. In particular, the coefficient of inv_i is equal to 0.32 in the negative binomial regression. This means that being an inventor increases the expected number of articles by 38 per cent, holding other variables constant. Conversely being a female scientist decreases it by 23 per cent, holding other variables constant.

In both regressions our time dummies (not reported) show that publications follow a non-linear quadratic trend over the 20-year period considered. Moreover, with respect to the base age, scientists display as expected significantly higher values of their publication levels, this

Table 4.6 Results of the estimation of specification (1) and (2), 1980–99

Dependent variable: Log (publications) in column (1) and (3); counts of publications in columns (2) and (4)

	OLS – pooled cross-section (1)	Negative binomial (2)	Within (3)	FE Negative binomial (4)
inv_i	0.17** *(0.12)*	0.32** *(0.62)*	–	–
$postpat_{it}$	–	–	0.15** *(0.02)*	0.15** *(0.03)*
$gender_i$	−0.14** *(0.02)*	−0.26** *(0.08)*	–	–
$Size\_dep_i$	0.02** *(0.00)*	0.04* *(0.02)*	–	–
ex_1 [30–39]	0.34** *(0.02)*	0.68** *(0.07)*	0.32** *(0.02)*	0.77** *(0.05)*
ex_2 [40–49]	0.33** *(0.02)*	0.67** *(0.08)*	0.29** *(0.04)*	0.77** *(0.07)*
ex_3 [50–59]	0.23** *(0.02)*	0.54** *(0.11)*	0.21** *(0.05)*	0.70** *(0.09)*
ex_4 [60+]	0.11** *(0.04)*	0.36* *(0.15)*	0.14* *(0.07)*	0.68** *(0.12)*
$Sett_1$ (Biology)	0.21** *(0.02)*	0.34** *(0.11)*	–	–
$Sett_2$ (Electronics and telecommunications)	−0.09** *(0.02)*	−0.21* *(0.10)*	–	–
$Sett_3$ (Pharmacology)	0.19** *(0.02)*	0.24** *(0.09)*	–	–
Cons	yes	yes	yes	yes
Time dummies	yes	yes	yes	yes
Individuals	592	592	592	590
Observations	10,696	10,696	10,696	10,673
R2 within	0.1463		0.1451	

** 99% sig. level; * 95%; standard errors in parentheses
ex(base) = 1 if $25 \leq age \leq 29$, zero elsewhere; $sett_{ji}$: the base is chemical engineering.

effect decreases with age. Finally, publications in pharmacology ($sett_3 = 1$) and biology ($sett_1 = 1$) are significantly higher than the base category and electronics and communications. Finally, $size\_dep_{it}$ is significantly positive. This indicates a positive department effect.

Second step: a treatment effect

Columns 3 and 4 of Table 4.6 show the results from specification 2. In this specification we use both linear and negative binomial fixed effect to control for individual heterogeneity. We find a positive impact of our treatment variable with both linear and count methods. The size of the coefficient is equal to 0.15. This means that becoming an inventor could improve the scientific productivity, holding other variable constant, of approximately 14 per cent. These results are similar to those found by Markiewicz and DiMinin (2004) and Azoulay *et al.* (2004) on US data. As we show in a companion paper (Breschi *et al.*, 2005b) these results may be affected by endogeneity because past publications might increase the probability of becoming an inventor. However, preliminary results using instrumental variables and the work of Azoulay *et al.* (2004) show that this result is robust to different specifications.

Third step: dynamic effects around the patent

Table 4.7 illustrates the results from specification 3 (columns 1 and 2) and 4 (columns 3a–3b and 4a–4b). In columns (1) and (2) we notice that the dummy variables are negative until two years before the patenting event (even if they cannot be considered significantly different from zero), and positive afterwards, with a peak on years −1, +1 and +3. This suggests that the regressions presented in the section 'First step: inventors versus non-inventors' (see p. 95), despite considering the impact on scientific productivity of being (at the present time or in the future) an academic inventor, tend to overestimate academic inventors' publication activity until two years before the patenting event, and underestimate it one year before, one year after and three years after the patent. These results suggest the existence of either a strong publication delay effect, and/or a resource effect.

In columns 3a, 4a, 3b and 4b estimations of specification 4 are presented. We examine more closely the dummies around the patenting year interacting them with a dummy for 'occasional' inventors (with only one patent), as opposed to 'non-occasional ones' (for these individuals we consider only the first patent). The differences are quite relevant and suggest that the nature of the relationship between patenting and publishing is different in the two cases. Occasional inventors have a peak in their publications one year before the patent. Patents probably are an occasional by-product of a successful research project. In the second case, when there is a more persistent patenting activity, inventors reach their peak in the publications later at year +1, +2 and at year +3. It looks as if the beneficial effect of patenting on publication rates lasted

Table 4.7 Results of the estimation of specification (3), 1980–99

Dependent variable: Log(publications) in column (1), 3a and 3b; publications counts in (2), (4a) and (4b)

	Occasional				Non-occasional	
	Within (1)	Fixed effects negative binomial (2)	Within (3a)	Fixed effects negative binomial (4a)	Within (3b)	Fixed effects negative binomial (4b)
Dp_{-3}	−0.04	−0.08	−0.00	−0.03	−0.11^{+}	−0.19^{+}
	(0.03)	(0.06)	(0.04)	(0.07)	(0.06)	(0.10)
Dp_{-2}	0.05†	0.05	0.10**	0.10^{+}	−0.06	−0.07
	(0.03)	(0.05)	(0.04)	(0.06)	(0.05)	(0.10)
Dp_{-1}	0.09**	0.11*	0.14**	0.16**	−0.00	−0.01
	(0.03)	(0.05)	(0.04)	(0.06)	(0.05)	(0.09)
Dp_{0}	0.07**	0.06†	0.08*	0.04	−0.02	−0.02
	(0.02)	(0.04)	(0.04)	(0.06)	(0.05)	(0.08)
Dp_{+1}	0.10**	0.09*	0.10**	0.10^{+}	0.11*	0.10
	(0.03)	(0.05)	(0.04)	(0.06)	(0.05)	(0.08)
Dp_{+2}	0.08*	0.06	0.05	0.02	0.14**	0.13^{+}
	(0.03)	(0.05)	(0.04)	(0.06)	(0.05)	(0.07)
Dp_{+3}	0.10**	0.09^{+}	0.05	0.00	0.17**	0.21**
	0.03	(0.05)	(0.04)	(0.07)	(0.05)	(0.07)
Individuals	592	590	592	590		
Observations	10,696	10,673	10,696	10,673		

All other estimated regressors omitted. Coefficients in (3a) and (3b) are obtained interacting Dp_{i} with a dummy for occasional and non-occasional inventors. The same occurs for columns 4a and 4b.
** 99% sig. level; * 95%; $^{+}$ 90%; † 85%; standard errors in brackets.

longer for persistent innovators, which is entirely consistent with the resource effect explanation and probably associated with a continuous patenting activity over time. Moreover, for non-occasional inventors coefficients are significantly negative three years before the patent. Again this is compatible with resource effects but cannot exclude, however, the possibility of a publication delay effect.

4.5 Conclusions

Our work shows that Italian academic inventors are highly productive scientists, indeed more productive than their non-inventor controls. The difference is particularly relevant for persistent inventors, namely those scientists who patent more than once over a long time period. The econometric exercise confirms the superiority of the scientific productivity of inventors relative to non-inventors. Moreover, we show that patents have a significantly positive impact in terms of increased number of publications within the scientist's academic career. Becoming an inventor could improve the scientific productivity, holding other variables constant, of approximately 14 per cent. Finally, the use of dummy variables in the dynamic analysis of the number of publications around the year of the patent shows that there is a pattern that is left unexplained by the individual heterogeneity, time dummies and by the treatment effect. This dynamic analysis shows that publishing activity tends to increase around the year of the patent. However, the nature of the relationship between publishing and patenting seems to be different for persistent and occasional inventors. For the latter the increase in the publishing activity starts two years before the patent and lasts only one year after. For the former there is a positive effect that extends also three years after the patent and there is no positive effect before the patent.

Taken together our evidence points at the existence of a 'productivity fixed effect' at the individual level and a 'resource effect', both of them creating a positive link between patenting and publishing activities. On the negative side, we cannot exclude the existence of some 'publication delay effect'. An important institutional specificity of the Italian case is that 75 per cent of the patents signed by at least one academic inventor belong to business companies. Those patents are often the result of research contracts, by which the business company retains all the intellectual property rights over the research results. It follows that our evidence suggests that contract research may generate a positive 'resource' effect on the academic inventors' publication rate, in particular when it expands over long time periods. Despite the institutional differences these results match closely those reached by Markiewicz and DiMinin (2004) and Azoulay *et al.* (2004) for the United States, the only other studies explicitly dedicated to the patenting–publishing trade-off outside Italy that we are aware of.[7] As for the superior productivity of academic inventors, this is confirmed by Stephan *et al.* (2004), who suggest the existence of a strong 'productivity fixed effect'.

It is impossible to derive any policy conclusion from our study. Of all the possible 'liaisons' between patenting and publishing we have studied the least dangerous, namely those occurring at the individual level. It remains possible that, by patenting their research results, academic inventors contribute to make them less accessible to other scientists, thus limiting the research effort at the systemic level.

We can say, however, that European legislators and university technology transfer offices should look closely at the specificity of the institutional environment before pushing academic scientists towards patenting their results (either in their own name or in the name of their universities). For the Italian case it may be that it is not patenting *per se* that boosts scientific productivity, but individual heterogeneity plus the advantage derived from solid links with industry, which in turn might require leaving IPR matters in the business partners' hands. If this conjecture turns out to be confirmed in our subsequent work, then legislators and technology transfer officers – wishing to strengthen those links – should avoid forcing university administrators and scientists to claim their own share of IPRs at all costs. The expected returns from any foreseeable licence are much less than the opportunity costs of putting the links with industry at risk.

Acknowledgements

A preliminary version of this paper benefited from comments received at a workshop on the empirical economic analysis of the academic sphere, BETA – Université Louis Pasteur, Strasbourg, 17 March 2004 and 10th International J. A. Schumpeter Society Conference, Milan, 9–12 June 2004. Further comments were provided by participants to the NBER (National Bureau of Economic Research) Productivity Seminars. Financial support from the Italian Ministry of Education and Research (PRIN 2003133821_003) and Università degli Studi dell'Insubria is gratefully acknowledged. Francesco Lissoni also received support from the Fulbright Commission, and hospitality from the MIT Sloan School of Management. Valerio Sterzi provided skilful research assistance.

Appendix

Table 4.A1 Disciplines (SSD) and fields: conversion table

Bio-chemistry (E05A)	Biology
Molecular biology (E05B)	Biology
Applied biology (E06X)	Biology
Human physiology (E04B)	Biology
Materials science and technology (I14A)	Chemical engineering and materials technology
Macromolecular compounds (I14B)	Chemical engineering and materials technology
Applied physics-chemistry (I15A)	Chemical engineering and materials technology
Chemical engineering (I15B)	Chemical engineering and materials technology
Industrial chemistry (I15E)	Chemical engineering and materials technology
Electronics (K01X)	Electronics and telecommunications
Electromagnetic fields (K02X)	Electronics and telecommunications
Telecommunications (K03X)	Electronics and telecommunications
Pharmaceutical chemistry (C07X)	Pharmacology
Applied pharmacology (C08X)	Pharmacology

Notes

1. In this section we briefly summarize the major causal links, focusing upon the individual level. However, there is a recent growth in the empirical literature addressing the impact on scientific activity of the increase in the patenting practice by universities, in particular after the Bayh-Dole Act. Henderson *et al.* (1998), Mowery and Ziedonis (2002), Agrawal and Henderson, 2002, Surlemont *et al.* (2003), Markiewicz and DiMinin (2004), Azoulay *et al.* (2004), Mowery and Sampat (2004) and Lerner (2004) discuss many aspects of the issues we touch upon in this section.
2. The publication delay may be mitigated by the so-called 'grace period' rule, which is in force in the US, Canada and Australia, and has been urged by many for European patents as well. The rule allows academic researchers to publish in advance their soon-to-be-patented inventions, as long as the publication does not occur too early (in the US, within 12 months of the patent application date).
3. Publication data may not be adequate to test the 'basic-applied trade-off' argument, as long as many journals are, in fact, dedicated to applied research. Some indicators of the orientation of the journal towards basic versus applied research (such as classifications by experts, or cruder measures such as ISI's impact factor or cited half life) ought to be employed to weigh each published article. An even better weight is provided by the number of citations received by each article, which are also made available by ISI: next drafts of this paper will indeed make use of them (see Breschi *et al.*, 2005a).
4. The major limitation of the MIUR list and, as a consequence, of the EP-INV-DOC database, is that it includes only those professors and researchers who had passed a competitive examination for a tenured position (from now on, we will refer to them simply as 'professors'). Thus our data miss the large number of fixed-term appointees who, at the time, had been working in one or more universities for one or more years, as well as all the PhD students, post-doc fellows, and technicians. In the current Italian system, assistant professor (called 'researcher') and associate professor positions, despite being only the first two steps of the academic career, are not offered as fixed-term appointments, but as tenured ones. The main differences with the position of full professor lie in wage and administrative power.
5. For a more detailed description of the sample and matching methodology we refer to Breschi *et al.* (2005a) where we provide data cross-tabulations by field, age and number of patents. Most of the selected inventors are full professors, aged between 40 and 60. The mean age of both the inventors and their patents increases slightly in the chemical engineering field, while the opposite holds for inventors in electronics and telecommunications.
6. In principle, the characteristics of institutions may vary, either because the institutions themselves gets smaller or bigger, and gain or lose prestige, or because professors move from one university to another. However, we have data on universities only for 2000, and no data on the professors' career before then. So, also the characteristics of institutions appear as fixed effects in our regression.
7. On Italy, see Calderini and Franzoni (2004). Data on academic inventors, but not yet on their publications, can also be found in Meyer *et al.* (2003) for the case of Finland.

References

Agrawal, A. and R. Henderson, 'Putting Patents in Context: Exploring Knowledge Transfer from MIT', *Management Science*, 48 (2002), 44–60.

Akers, N. J., 'The European Patent System: An Introduction for Patent Searchers', *World Patent Information*, 21 (1999), 135–63.

Allison, P. D. and J. S. Long, 'Departmental Effects on Scientific Productivity', *American Sociological Review*, 55 (1990), 469–78.

Allison, P. D., J. S. Long and T. D. Krauze, 'Cumulative Advantage and Inequality in Science', *American Sociological Review*, 47 (1982), 615–25.

Azoulay, P., W. Ding and T. Stuart, 'The Effect of Academic Patenting on (Public) Research Output', paper presented at the NBER Summer Institute: Academic Science and Entrepreneurship: Dual Engines of Growth?, Cambridge, MA, 23 July (2004).

Balconi, M., S. Breschi and F. Lissoni, 'Networks of Inventors and The Role of Academia: An Exploration of Italian Patent Data', *Research Policy*, 33 (2004), 127–45.

Breschi, S., F. Lissoni and F. Montobbio, 'The Scientific Productivity of Academic Inventors: New Evidence from Italian Data', *WP Cespri*, 168 (2005a): http:\\www.cespri.unibocconi.it

Breschi, S., F. Lissoni and F. Montobbio, 'From Publishing to Patenting: How to Become an Academic Inventor?', *WP Cespri* (2005b) forthcoming.

Calderini, M. and C. Franzoni, 'Is Academic Patenting Detrimental to High Quality research? An Empirical Analysis of the Relationship between Scientific Careers and Patent Application', *WP Cespri*, 162 (2004).

Hausman, J. A., B. Hall and Z. Griliches, 'Econometric Models for Count Data and an Application to the Patents–R&D Relationship', *Econometrica*, 52 (1984), 909–38.

Henderson, R., A. B. Jaffe and M. Trajtenberg, 'Universities as a Source of Commercial Technology: A Detailed Analysis of University Patenting 1965–1988', *Review of Economics and Statistics* (1998), 119–27.

Lerner, J., 'The University and the Start-Up: Lessons from the Past Two Decades', *The Journal of Technology Transfer*, 30 (1–2) (2004), 49–56.

Long, J. S., P. D. Allison and R. McGinnis, 'Rank Advancement in Academic Careers: Sex Differences and the Effects of Productivity', *American Sociological Review*, 58 (1993), 703–22.

Mansfield, E., 'Academic Research Underlying Industrial Innovations: Sources, Characteristics, and Financing', *Review of Economics and Statistics*, 77 (1995), 55–65.

Mansfield, E., 'Academic Research and Industrial Innovation: An Update of Empirical Findings', *Research Policy*, 26 (1998), 773–6.

Markiewicz, K. R. and A. DiMinin, 'Commercializing the Laboratory: The Relationship Between Faculty Patenting and Publishing', Econ 222/PHDBA 297-T: Seminar On Innovation, Haas School of Business (2004).

Merton, R. K., 'The Matthew Effect in Science, II. Cumulative Advantage and the Symbolism of Intellectual Property', *ISIS*, 79 (1988), 606–23.

Meyer, M., T. Siniläinen, J. T. Utecht, 'Towards Hybrid Triple Helix Indicators: A Study of University-Related Patents and a Survey of Academic Inventors', *Scientometrics*, 58 (2003), 321–50.

Mowery, D. C. and B. Sampat, 'The Bayh-Dole Act of 1980 and University–Industry Technology Transfer: A Model for Other OECD Governments?', *Journal of Technology Transfer*, 30 (1–2) (2004), 115–27.

Mowery, D. C. and A. A. Ziedonis, 'Academic Patent Quality before and after the Bayh–Dole Act in the United States', *Research Policy*, 31 (3) Issue 3 (2002), 399–418.

Rosenberg, N., 'Why do firms do basic research (with their own money)?', *Research Policy*, 19 (1990), 165–74.

Stephan, P. A., S. Gurmu, A. J. Sumell and G. Black, 'Who's Patenting in the University? Evidence from the Survey of Doctorare Recipients', paper presented at the workshop on The Empirical Economic Analysis of the Academic Sphere, BETA – Université Louis Pasteur, Strasbourg, 17 March (2004).

Surlemont, F., B. Surlemont and F. Nlemvo, 'Toward a Typology of University Spin-offs', *Small Business Economics*, 21 (2003), 355–69.

Turner, L. and J. Mairesse, 'Individual Productivity Differences in Scientific Research: An Econometric Study of the Publications of French Physicists', paper presented at the workshop on The Empirical Economic Analysis of the Academic Sphere, BETA – Université Louis Pasteur, Strasbourg, 17 March (2004).

5
Brain Drain and R&D Activities of Multinationals

Michele Cincera

5.1 Introduction

Over the recent years, European policy-makers have been more and more concerned about emigration flows for qualified scientists beyond Europe's borders. This so-called scientific 'brain drain' is on the rise and could represent a threat to Europe's knowledge-based economy. A recent report of the European Commission (2003) gives evidence that the brain drain of people born in the EU is increasing. For instance, about 75 per cent of EU-born US doctorate recipients who graduated between 1991 and 2000 had no specific plans to return to the EU, and more and more are choosing to stay in the US. The most important reasons which keep EU-born scientists and engineers abroad relate to the quality of work. Better prospects and projects, and easier access to leading technologies are most often cited as reasons for plans to work abroad. Another aspect to explaining emigration flows of highly skilled workers is that the production factors used in the production process, including alongside traditional inputs, human and knowledge capital, are increasingly mobile across national borders. These factors play an important role in economic growth and international competition for these inputs have increased their cross-border mobility. It is, therefore, important to have a better understanding of the main determinants that affect the direction and the magnitude of these flows of inputs as well as their economic impact for both the origin and destination countries. In the economic literature on multinational enterprises (MNEs), forces such as scale economies, trade and transaction costs, as well as the abundance factor are often mentioned to explain the location and investment decisions of workers, firms and in particular MNEs.

The purpose of this chapter is to shed some light on one aspect of this international mobility of factors by examining the interactions between the emigration of highly skilled workers and the presence of subsidiaries of foreign MNEs in a small open economy, like Belgium. Most empirical evidence indicates that inward foreign direct investment (FDI) in R&D has a positive impact on the demand of highly skilled workers in the host country. As a result, high levels of inward FDI can be expected to diminish the importance of brain drain, that is the net emigration rate of highly educated people. In that case, we can talk about a reduced brain drain. Furthermore, MNEs' investment decisions bring to the host economy new qualified personnel from the headquarters. In that case we can talk about a 'brain gain'. Finally, 'brain exchange' between MNEs' affiliates and local firms can arise through a variety of direct and indirect channels such as, for example, knowledge spillovers, patent licensing, formal R&D collaborative agreements or informal contacts between scientists and engineers and training of the R&D personnel hired in the host country.

A second objective of this chapter is to assess the main determinants, that is market-driven and technology-push factors, that affect the delocalization of MNEs' R&D activities in a host economy. On the one hand, the core activity of MNEs' foreign subsidiaries may consist of adapting products and processes developed in the first place at the headquarters to the need of local markets. On the other hand, a well-trained and educated workforce may not only retain domestic firms but also attract foreign MNEs, which in turn invest in physical capital, R&D and training activities. These questions are investigated by means of descriptive statistics and indicators based on patent statistics from the two main patent offices in the world, the European Patent Office (EPO) and its US homologue (USPTO).

The plan of the chapter is as follows. Section 5.2 reviews the main impacts of MNEs' R&D activities in host countries as well as the main determinants that affect their investment and location decisions. Section 5.3 presents the dataset and derives the main hypothesis of the study. The main empirical findings are reported in section 5.4. Some concluding remarks and policy implications are set out in the last section.

5.2 R&D Activities of MNEs

FDI in the area of R&D is an increasing phenomenon that has already been subjected to various research. MNEs largely dominate the Belgian innovation system and a first question that is worth examining concerns the impacts of this high degree of internationalization of science and technology activities for the local economy.

Impacts of MNEs' R&D activities

In a survey, Blomström and Kokko (1998) examine the effects of knowledge spillovers generated by the R&D activities of MNEs' subsidiaries. From the host country's perspective, these externalities not only influence the R&D of domestic firms operating in the same MNE's industry but also of firms located in other industry sectors. According to the studies surveyed, these effects have in general a positive impact on domestic R&D. However, they systematically vary across countries and industries and increase with the local capability and the level of competition. On the other hand the effects of MNEs' R&D activities on the home country are more difficult to identify.

As far as the Belgian economy is concerned, there have been only a few studies examining the impact of international spillovers in the local economy. Veugelers and Vanden Houte (1990), in an analysis based on Belgian R&D firms, find that the higher the presence of multinationals in an industry, the weaker is the innovative effort of domestic firms in the same industry. Cincera (2005) reports a similar result, though the key variable is not the level of R&D effort but the output of this activity as measured by the number of patent applications. Fecher (1990) estimates a positive impact of domestic R&D spillovers on Belgian firms' productivity performance, while no effect of international spillovers is found. More recently, Veugelers and Cassiman (1999) find that MNEs are more likely to transfer technology to the Belgian economy. However, the main conclusion of the study is that it is not so much the international character of the firm, but rather its access to the international technology market that is important for generating external knowledge transfers to the local economy.

MNEs' activities can also affect the labour market in host countries, in particular the demand for and the supply of highly skilled workers (Slaughter, 2002). According to the author, on the demand side, inward FDI stimulates the demand for more skilled workers in host countries through several channels. Demand for highly skilled workers may increase when (direct) technology transfer from the MNE to subsidiaries take place. But even more indirect mechanisms such as knowledge spillovers, market-driven technology flows or investment in capital related to technology innovations may increase the demand for highly skilled workers. On the supply side, MNEs can facilitate investments in human capital via short-term firm-level activities such as training or via long-term country level activities that collectively contribute to the overall macro environment in which fiscal policy can support education policy.

Determinants of MNEs' R&D activities

When considering the degree of internationalization of R&D, it should be noted that technology production has usually been centralized in the host country of MNEs. The reduction of the costs related to communications and control, economies of scale in R&D and a better coordination between central and peripheral research labs are often mentioned in the literature to explain this situation (Terpstra, 1985).[1] However, during the past decade, the involvement of MNEs in overseas R&D has increased significantly. Companies all over the world are investing more and more in overseas R&D as a tool to increase their competitive advantages and to exploit their resources in order to create higher quality products.[2] MNEs have accelerated the pace of their direct investments in overseas R&D, and have established or acquired multiple R&D laboratories abroad and are increasingly integrating these laboratories into global R&D networks.[3]

According to Granstrand *et al.* (1992), the reasons for the ongoing process of increased decentralization and internationalization of R&D activities can be explained by three main categories of factors: demand-side, supply-side and environmental- or institutional-related factors. The demand-side factors include a greater adaptation of products and technologies to the needs of local markets, a higher proximity to customers, an increase of competitiveness through the transfer of technology and the pressures of subsidiaries to enhance their status within a corporation. Among the main supply-side factors, the monitoring of technology developed abroad and the hiring of a foreign and barely mobile highly skilled labour can be mentioned. Finally, the environmental factors include the legislation on intellectual property, the provision of R&D incentives by the domestic government, such as tax advantages and R&D subsidies, and governmental pressures to improve the subsidiary's capabilities beyond the simple assembly of proven products to innovative activities.

Belderbos (2001) identifies two different motives for overseas R&D activities. The first motive, which consists in the exploitation of the firm's technology abroad, means that companies adapt their products and processes to suit the local market and manufacturing processes and to fulfil local standards or manufacturing conditions. The second motive is the sourcing of foreign technology, which explains the founding of basic R&D for the world market. In this case, firms attempt to gain access to specific expertise in the local science base and hire foreign skilled engineers and researchers. The notions of home base augmenting (HBA) and home base exploiting (HBE) are often used to characterize these motives. For Kuemmerle (1999), HBA sites are more likely to be located near universities or public research and technology organizations. HBA units have increasingly been used as part of the MNE's strategy to build up and exploit science and technology (S&T) know-how located beyond the boundaries of the group, while the activities of HBE sites are more aimed at transferring the knowledge developed within the group. Newly established subsidiaries generally focus on the design and the development of products to meet local markets' needs in exploiting the mother company's existing technologies, while R&D activities of acquired subsidiaries are more concerned with applied research and scanning of local technologies.

5.3 Data and Hypotheses

Among the main indicators of science and technology activities available to economists, patent statistics have probably been the most extensively used.[4] However, like other technological indicators, patent statistics have their own weaknesses. The same weight given to patents by simply counting them is an important drawback of this indicator. In reality, the pure technical content as well as the intrinsic economic value of a patent may vary widely among patents. Moreover, not all inventions are patented, nor all are patentable, and other existing methods in appropriating the outcomes of R&D activities may be preferred.[5] The propensity to patent may change substantially over time, across countries and among technological sectors. For example, it is generally recognized that the propensity to patent is important in sectors such as machinery or chemicals but very weak in aerospace and in software since, in the latter industries, inventions can be more easily imitated.

Data

The European Patent Office (EPO) and its US homologue (USPTO) are the main sources of information in this study. All patents with at least one Belgian inventor have been extracted from the ESPACE-BULLETIN database for European patents and from the dataset released by Hall *et al.* (2001) on the NBER (National Bureau for Economic Research) website for US patents.[6] Table 5.1 lists the main variables available for each patent document, which are subsequently used in the descriptive analysis.

A main difference between these two databases is that European patents refer to patent applications, while for the US, the patents are the ones that are granted.[7] Another difference is that information on patent citations is only used for US patents. The year in which the patent has

Table 5.1 List of variables for patent data

Variables	EPO	USPTO
Application year	x	x
Name of the applicant	x	x
Country of residence of the applicant	x	x
Applicant is part of a foreign group		x
Name of the inventor(s)	x	x
Country of residence of the inventor(s)	x	x
Technological sector	**IPC**	**USPC**
Number of claims		x
Number of citations received		x
Share of self-citations made with respect to total number of citations		x

Notes: IPC = International Patents Classification; USPC = US Patent Classification.

been applied rather than granted is considered for both data sources. According to Jaffe (1986) and Tong and Frame (1994), patents classified by date of application are preferable because they reflect the moment when a firm realizes an innovation and because of the existence of long lags between the filing of a patent application and a patent grant.[8]

Three categories of patent applicants can be distinguished according to the criterion of whether the patent owner is a Belgian firm, a Belgian subsidiary of a foreign MNE or a foreign company.[9] The latter category represents patents involving at least one inventor residing in Belgium but which were applied for by non-Belgian firms. This can happen when the output of the R&D performed by the subsidiary is directly patented by the multinational in its home country. Several factors can explain this strategy. First, the IP department of a large firm with important patenting activities is generally located at the headquarters of the MNE and not in its foreign subsidiaries. Second, contrary to other countries like the US or the UK (Bertin and Wyatt, 1988), the Belgian patent law does not request a first filing in Belgium if an invention has been generated on the domestic territory. Third, the geographic distance between the MNE's home base and the host country can be another reason explaining a lower patenting propensity. Maskus (1998), for instance, finds that the number of patents filed by US subsidiaries in host countries positively depends on the strength of intellectual property rights protection of the latter, as well as on the geographic distance to the US.

Table 5.2 Hypotheses

Hypothesis 1	Home base augmenting (HBA) R&D activities are more important in technological sectors in which Belgium holds scientific comparative advantages
Hypothesis 2	Patents resulting from HBA activities have a higher technological and economic value
Hypothesis 3	Patents resulting from home base exploiting (HBE) R&D activities have a lower technological and economic value
Hypothesis 4	Brain drain is negatively correlated with the importance of MNEs' R&D activities in the local innovation system
Hypothesis 5	MNEs' R&D delocalization increases the demand for local researchers brain gain)
Hypothesis 6	MNEs' R&D delocalization stimulates the exchange of ideas and knowledge between local and foreign researchers and inventors (brain exchange)

Hypothesis

The objectives of this chapter are twofold. First, it aims to investigate the main determinants of the delocalization of MNEs' R&D investments. Second, it seeks to assess the impact of MNEs' foreign subsidiaries' R&D activities on the local labour market for highly skilled workers. To that end, six hypotheses have been formulated (see Table 5.2).

Hypotheses 1–3 are concerned with the first objective, hypotheses 4–6 with the second. As regards Hypothesis 1, if the main reasons for MNEs to delocalize abroad are the access to the local science base, and to benefit from the availability of a highly educated labour force in order to augment its own knowledge base, then we can expect a positive correlation between the scientific fields where the host economy holds scientific relative advantages and R&D (and as result patents) activities carried out by the MNEs subsidiaries in the host country. In order to test this hypothesis, the scientific revealed comparative advantage (SRCA) index has been constructed on the basis of the number of scientific publications contained in the ISI-web of science database. A second indicator based on citations has been considered as well. The number of citations per scientific publication can be used as a proxy for its quality and importance. Therefore, if scientific publications in a given scientific field are more cited on average in a country or a region as compared to a reference group, the relative strength of the region's scientific base can be expected to be higher.

As previously discussed, on the one hand MNEs will invest in HBA R&D activities in order to increase the group's knowledge base as a result of potential spillovers arising from local productive R&D organizations such as universities, publicly funded research institutes and innovative competitors, or to make effective use of the general strong local technological and research infrastructures. On the other hand, MNEs will engage in HBE R&D activities abroad to further exploit their own research capabilities in a foreign environment. These activities typically concern the development and adaptation of existing technologies to the local market conditions such as consumer tastes, environmental legislation or standards. Given the different nature of these two types of research activities, the technological and economic value of HBA R&D output as measured by patenting can be expected to be higher when compared to HBE ones (Hypotheses 2 and 3). Therefore the value of patents related to HBA R&D should be higher when compared to the one generated by HBE R&D. Several indicators have been suggested in the literature to assess the value of a patent.[10] For instance, the claims provide a definition of what the patent protects. The scope of protection will be higher, the higher the number of claims and several studies have found a significant correlation between the number of claims and the patent value (Lanjouw and Schankerman, 1999). As for scientific publications, the number of citations by subsequent patents is another well known indicator for assessing the value of patent (Hall *et al.*, 2000).[11] Citations that come from patents assigned to a same firm or MNE refer to previous patented inventions of that firm. These so-called self-citations are therefore more likely to be linked with home-based exploiting R&D activities aimed at improving and adapting existing protected inventions.

As far as the impact of MNEs' R&D activities on the labour market in the host country is concerned, three effects are investigated. The first effect refers to the idea that the higher the presence of foreign R&D MNEs in a host country the less important is the brain drain or the emigration of highly skilled workers from that country. In order to test this assumption (Hypothesis 4), the degree of internationalization of R&D activities, as measured by the share of patents with at least one Belgian inventor and applied for by Belgian subsidiaries of foreign MNEs and foreign firms in the host country's total count of patents, is compared to the rate of emigration of highly educated persons. Hypothesis 5 examines whether FDI in R&D are associated with a 'brain gain', that is, an increase in the demand for local researchers by the foreign MNEs. This hypothesis can be tested by comparing the number of new inventors in patent documents applied for by foreign subsidiaries and domestic firms. Finally, Hypothesis 6 tests whether the MNE's R&D delocalization stimulates the exchange of ideas and knowledge between local and foreign researchers and inventors. This 'brain exchange' can be assessed by identifying the inventors' country of residence documented in co-invented patents.

5.4 Empirical Findings

The high internationalization of the Belgian technological base

The share of foreign companies and subsidiaries of foreign MNEs in national innovative activities as measured by patents with at least one Belgian inventor represents more than 80 per cent of the total number of patents at the end of the 1990. This share is by far the largest among the industrialized countries (Patel and Pavitt, 1991) and, as can been seen in Table 5.3, it has steadily increased over the past two decades. In the 1980, the share was about 60 per cent, which suggests that there have been strong linkages between MNEs and the Belgian science and

Table 5.3 Patents with Belgian inventors, share of foreign applicants, 1983–99

	EPO-FOR	USPTO-FOR	USPTO-FOR + SUBS
1983	32.7	40.3	58.5
1984	31.2	37.3	58.2
1985	34.5	39.0	54.7
1986	33.8	42.2	55.9
1987	30.3	39.2	53.3
1988	36.5	41.2	57.0
1989	37.7	44.0	58.6
1990	41.3	40.8	63.1
1991	40.5	43.5	66.6
1992	42.5	43.3	66.4
1993	40.6	45.7	73.1
1994	43.8	45.1	75.0
1995	42.6	41.1	70.5
1996	46.4	42.8	75.0
1997	44.8	46.1	76.8
1998	39.4	56.2	84.1
1999	35.4	57.1	85.7

Notes: EPO-FOR and USPTO-FOR refer to foreign applicants and USPTO-FOR + SUBS includes Belgian subsidiaries of foreign MNEs in addition to foreign applicants.

Source: EPO and Hall *et al.* (2001) databases.

technology base for a long time.[12] Another feature that emerges from Table 5.3 is the higher importance of foreign companies as compared to Belgian subsidiaries of foreign MNEs in terms of patent applications. The share of the former represents about 70 per cent of the total number of patents applied for by these two categories of applicants. This indicates that patents are mostly applied for by the headquarters of the local subsidiaries' mother companies.

Table 5.4 shows the geographic origin of foreign companies and subsidiaries of foreign MNEs that applied for patents involving at least one Belgian inventor over the period 1983–99. As a whole, for both European and American patents, two countries namely Germany and the US, largely dominate the picture. Belgium's main trade partners and neighbours, France, the Netherlands and the United Kingdom, also appear to be important. All in all, these five countries represent 87.0 per cent of European patents and 92.8 per cent of US patents of the total number of patents with Belgian inventors applied for by foreign applicants (Belgian subsidiaries of foreign MNEs and foreign firms).

On the basis of the technological class of each patent, it is possible to examine the main technological fields in which foreign applicants are most present, as well as their relative importance as compared to the Belgian applicants.[13] The main technological fields in which foreign applicants are the most active are reported in Tables 5.5, 5.6 and 5.7.[14] In terms of European patents (Table 5.3), chemistry (42.8 per cent) is by far the most important technological class in terms of patents applied for by foreign companies. Electrical materials and equipment and technologies related to material processing in textiles and paper (6.4 per cent each) are

Table 5.4 Patents with Belgian inventors: origin of foreign applicants (in %), 1983–99

	USPTO-FOR	USPTO-SUBS	EPO-FOR
DE	14	64	15
US	52	33	39
FR	8	2	12
NL	12		14
GB	6		7
Other	7	1	13

Notes: EPO-FOR and USPTO-FOR refer to foreign applicants and USPTO-SUBS to Belgian subsidiaries of foreign MNEs.

Source: EPO and Hall *et al*. (2001) databases.

Table 5.5 Patents with Belgian inventors by technology class, EPO applications by foreign companies, 1983–99

Technology sector	% tot col	% tot row
Chemical and petrol industry, basic materials chemistry	14.9	74.0
Macromolecular chemistry, polymers	13.3	62.2
Organic fine chemistry	6.7	45.0
Electrical machinery and apparatus, electrical energy	6.4	55.4
Materials processing, textiles, paper	6.4	34.3
Handling, printing	5.8	33.5
Telecommunications	5.5	56.9
Biotechnology	4.3	43.5
Pharmaceuticals, cosmetics	3.6	44.7
Materials, metallurgy	3.5	36.8
Total	100.0	40.0

Notes: % tot col = % of patents by technological class with respect to total number of patents; % tot row = % of patents applied for by foreign firms in a given technological class with respect to total number of patents (with at least one Belgian inventor) applied in that class.

Source: EPO database.

Table 5.6 Patents with Belgian inventors by technology class, USPTO applications by Belgian subsidiaries of foreign MNEs, 1983–99

Technology sector	% tot col	% tot row
Miscellaneous chemical	40.0	36.0
Drugs	14.2	42.6
Miscellaneous others	8.6	24.2
Organic compounds	6.2	24.5
Optics	4.9	60.3
Nuclear and X-rays	3.7	49.7
Materials processing and handling	3.1	11.6
Resins	3.0	7.0
Communications	2.3	15.5
Computer peripherals	2.2	79.2
Total	100.0	21.2

Notes: % tot col = % of patents by technological class with respect to total number of patents; % tot row = % of patents applied for by MNEs' subsidiaries in a given technological class with respect to total number of patents applied in that class.

Source: Hall *et al.* (2001) database.

Table 5.7 Patents with Belgian inventors by technology class, USPTO applications by foreign companies, 1983–99

Technology sector	% tot col	% tot row
Miscellaneous chemical	21.1	40.8
Resins	12.5	62.3
Materials processing and handling	5.5	44.7
Miscellaneous others	5.4	32.4
Communications	5.1	72.8
Drugs	4.9	31.8
Organic compounds	4.1	34.4
Electrical devices	3.4	75.0
Biotechnology	3.3	54.2
Agriculture, husbandry, food	3.2	68.0
Total	100.0	45.5

Notes: % tot col = % of patents by technological class with respect to total number of patents; % tot row = % of patents applied for by foreign firms in a given technological class with respect to total number of patents applied in that class.

Source: Hall *et al.* (2001) database.

the other major technological fields. In terms of US patents, subsidiaries of foreign companies (Table 5.4) and foreign companies (Table 5.5) appear to be again specialized in the chemical and pharmaceutical sectors (54.2 per cent).

Market driven versus technology-push factors

The high dependence of the Belgian innovation system with respect to foreign MNEs could be an important reason for its lower propensity to patent.[15] Subsidiaries can be specialized in the adaptation to the Belgian market of products and services developed and patented in the first place in the research labs of the multinational. These subsidiaries could also be involved in HBA research activities, the local availability of a highly qualified workforce and an appealing knowledge base being the main reasons for their presence in the foreign country. In the first case, one can expect a lower propensity to patent for a given amount of R&D given that the original invention is already protected. In both cases the output of R&D performed by the subsidiary can be directly patented by the multinational in its home country and not in Belgium. Finally, the geographic distance between the MNE's home base and the host country can be another reason for explaining a lower patenting propensity.

Table 5.8 analyses the scientific revealed comparative advantages index of Belgium as regards scientific publications across scientific fields:

$$\mathrm{SRCA}_{ij} = \frac{\left(n_{ij} \Big/ \sum_{i} n_{ij}\right)}{\left(\sum_{j} n_{ij} \Big/ \sum_{i,j} n_{ij}\right)}$$

where n_{ij} is the number of publications of the jth country in the ith scientific field.

Three reference groups are considered: the world, the OECD and the EU-15. Table 5.8 also reports for each scientific field the difference of the average number of citations to scientific papers between Belgium and the three reference groups. With respect to the OECD reference group, Belgium appears to hold strong comparative advantages in scientific fields closely related to agriculture (agricultural sciences, plant and animal science), biochemistry (immunology, microbiology, pharmacology and toxicology) and clinical medicine. Even though there is no direct correspondence between the technological classification of patents and the one for scientific publications, the scientific areas where Belgium appears to be better positioned could explain the relatively high importance of (both EPO an USPTO) patents applied for by foreign subsidiaries and foreign firms in related technological areas such as drugs, organic fine chemistry or biotechnology.[16] The main reasons for the delocalization of R&D activities in that case may be the benefits associated in accessing the local scientific base and know-how available in these technological fields. However, this hypothesis does not appear to hold for the patents applied in electrical devices, material processing and handling, communications and computers, as Belgium's scientific position in material and computer sciences, mathematics and engineering appears to be relatively less favourable. However, for the last three scientific fields, the average number of citations per publication is significantly higher in Belgium as compared to the OECD reference group.

An alternative way to examine this question is to look at the relative value of patents applied for by foreign subsidiaries and foreign firms as compared to domestic ones. Patents associated with research activities aimed at increasing the knowledge base of the foreign group can be expected to be of higher value, at least from a technological point of view, as compared to the ones related to the development and adaptation

Table 5.8 Scientific Revealed Comparative Advantages based on scientific publications and citations per paper (1993–2003)[a]

	SRCA			Citations per paper		
	World[b]	OECD[c]	UE15	World[b]	OECD[c]	UE15
Agricultural sciences	1.02	1.10	1.03	64	8	9
Biology and biochemistry	1.08	1.01	1.07	76	5	14
Chemistry	0.93	1.08	0.96	58	−4	1
Clinical medicine	1.24	1.12	1.08	50	15	16
Computer science	0.98	0.97	0.97	43	13	20
Economics and business	1.07	0.95	1.22	41	20	31
Engineering	0.89	0.97	1.03	74	23	25
Environment/Ecology	0.99	0.97	1.01	22	−6	−4
Geosciences	0.62	0.63	0.62	19	−2	1
Immunology	1.22	1.07	1.09	53	21	30
Materials science	0.77	0.92	0.88	36	−6	0
Mathematics	0.95	1.03	0.96	63	28	31
Microbiology	1.41	1.35	1.24	69	27	30
Molecular biology and genetics	1.02	0.91	0.99	18	−8	−3
Multidisciplinary	0.43	0.64	0.78	−27	−14	−3
Neuroscience and behaviour	0.83	0.74	0.79	33	−1	3
Pharmacology and toxicology	1.25	1.22	1.20	39	−2	3
Physics	0.92	1.05	0.93	−4	−9	−6
Plant and animal science	1.24	1.27	1.29	43	−2	−1
Psychiatry/Psychology	0.70	0.60	0.83	29	3	2
Social sciences, general	0.44	0.39	0.64	−2	−5	−3
Space science	0.76	0.74	0.64	7	−22	−17

Notes:
[a] Difference of average number of citations to scientific papers between Belgium and the three reference groups.
[b] 152 countries.
[c] Australia, Austria, Belgium, Canada, Denmark, Finland, France, Germany, Greece, Ireland, Israel, Italy, Japan, Luxembourg, Netherlands, Norway, Portugal, Spain, Sweden, Switzerland, United Kingdom, USA.

Source: ISI web of science.

of existing technologies to the needs of the local economy. As previously discussed, patents characterized by an above average number of claims, a high frequency of citations received and a low frequency of self-citations, can be expected to be of higher value. Therefore, these patents should reflect more research activities aimed at increasing the knowledge base of the mother company. Table 5.9 summarizes these three indicators for the US patents with at least one Belgian inventor applied for by Belgian firms, foreign subsidiaries and foreign firms. With regards to the average number of self-citations, we observe that the patents of foreign firms and subsidiaries have systematically more self-citations. This can be explained by the fact that the average size of the patent's portfolio of the foreign companies is much more important as compared to the domestic firms.[17] As a result, the probability of being self-cited is much higher. With respect to the domestic firms, this indicator has, however, a much higher value for the foreign patents assigned to organic compounds, drugs and biotechnology. Conversely, the value of this indicator is relatively lower for patents in electrical devices and material processing and handling. According to the average number of claims and the average number of citations received, foreign firms and subsidiaries appear to perform better in four technological sectors, namely chemicals, communications, electrical devices and optics. Except for chemicals, the number of self-citations is also relatively lower. Consequently, the patents assigned to these technological classes can be

Table 5.9 Patents with Belgian inventors: average number of claims, average number of citations received and number of self-citations

	CLAIMS			CITREC			SELFCIT		
	1	2	Δ	1	2	Δ	1	2	Δ
Organic compounds	9.7	8.1	−1.6	2.1	2.7	0.5	0.08	0.26	0.17
Resins	13.4	13.6	0.2	4.4	3.5	−0.9	0.09	0.18	0.09
Miscellaneous chemical	11.3	12.8	1.5	3.5	5.7	2.2	0.13	0.24	0.11
Communications	12.4	13.6	1.2	2.7	5.0	2.4	0.01	0.09	0.08
Computer peripherals	11.2	11.3	0.1	3.2	5.8	2.5	0.06	0.14	0.08
Drugs	11.3	12.5	1.2	3.9	3.5	−0.4	0.10	0.40	0.30
Biotechnology	19.7	13.4	−6.3	1.7	1.8	0.2	0.02	0.28	0.26
Electrical devices	10.8	11.6	0.8	1.7	3.2	1.5	0.05	0.08	0.03
Nuclear and X-rays	12.7	11.9	−0.8	2.3	4.4	2.1	0.06	0.11	0.06
Materials processing and handling	12.3	12.0	−0.3	4.1	4.3	0.2	0.06	0.09	0.03
Optics	13.3	15.3	2.0	2.4	4.7	2.3	0.06	0.13	0.07
Agriculture, husbandry, food	13.4	12.7	−0.7	3.5	3.4	−0.1	0.05	0.12	0.07
Miscellaneous others	13.5	12.5	−1.0	3.0	4.6	1.6	0.08	0.14	0.06
Total	11.9	12.6	0.7	3.5	4.3	0.8	0.08	0.18	0.10

Notes: CLAIMS = average number of claims; CITREC = average number of citations received; SELFCIT = average number of citations made; 1 = domestic applicants; 2 = patent applied for by foreign subsidiaries and firms; Δ = difference between 1 and 2.

Source: Hall *et al.* (2001) database.

expected to be of higher economic value and as such may reflect the outcomes of R&D activities of the HBA type. Patents assigned to organic compounds and biotechnology, however, have on average a lower number of claims and are more self-cited. Therefore, these patents can be expected to have a lower value and may be more related to R&D activities aimed at adapting or improving existing inventions carried out in the mother company's research labs. For the other technology classes, it is more difficult to identify the type of R&D carried out by the foreign firms and subsidiaries as no clear-cut patterns emerge from the values taken by the three indicators.

On the whole, the indicators reported in Table 5.9 give a somewhat different picture than the conclusions based on the scientific comparative advantages of Belgium. Patents related to biotechnology, organic compounds and fine chemistry have a relatively lower technical and economic value but correspond to scientific fields in which Belgium is comparatively better positioned, that is, the importance of scientific activities in terms of publications is relatively more important as compared to the OECD average. Foreign firms could therefore be interested in investing in HBE R&D activities to benefit from the availability of a highly qualified local workforce. Conversely, patents classified in electrical devices, communications and computers appear to have a relatively higher economic value. Whilst Belgium does not hold particular scientific comparative advantages in the corresponding scientific fields, their performance in terms of citations is well above the average score observed at the OECD level. Therefore, the local expertise and scientific excellence in these sectors could be one of the main driving forces explaining the MNEs' decision to invest in R&D in the foreign economy.

MNEs' R&D activities and brain drain

Another main objective of this chapter is to shed some light on the importance of MNEs' R&D activities and the emigration of highly qualified workers. As previously discussed, the higher the presence of foreign R&D subsidiaries in a host country, the higher the demand for domestic researchers and therefore the lower the importance of emigration or brain drain. The dataset constructed by Docquier and Marfouk (2004) gathers information regarding immigration and emigration rates of highly educated workers for about 150 countries.[18] This harmonized dataset is based on country population censuses for two periods: 1990 and 2000. Table 5.10 indicates that Belgium is one of the most internationalized countries in the world in terms of patents with domestic

Table 5.10 Emigration rate of population with tertiary education (1990 and 2000) and EPO patents (1987–9/1997–9) with domestic inventors applied for by foreign applicants; EU-15 = 100

	Emigration rate – tertiary education		Share of foreign applicants	
	1990	2000	1987–9	1997–9
Austria	159.5	125.6	215.4	191.4
Belgium	59.1	67.4	351.9	280.7
Denmark	65.3	77.3	185.8	124.0
Finland	61.2	89.6	81.8	52.9
France	45.5	45.0	86.7	96.4
Germany	143.7	110.5	60.1	62.3
Greece	159.2	167.7	316.5	165.3
Ireland	320.8	404.7	280.2	219.6
Italy	88.8	87.1	75.1	90.3
Luxembourg	99.2	94.7	448.1	393.2
Netherlands	87.0	94.2	120.9	104.3
Portugal	148.3	181.9	472.8	316.9
Spain	31.2	30.2	179.2	168.2
Sweden	44.6	50.4	111.9	93.4
United Kingdom	142.8	173.5	166.3	194.6
EU-15	100.0	100.0	100.0	100.0

Source: Docquier and Marfouk (2004) and EPO databases.

inventors applied for by foreign companies. Only two countries, Luxembourg and Portugal, exhibit higher scores. However, the market shares of these countries in terms of patenting activities are marginal. Then, the emigration rate in Belgium, for both periods, is about half the performance obtained at the EU level (59.1 and 67.4 in 1990 and 2000 respectively), while the degree of internationalization as measured by the presence of foreign firms in patenting activities is about three times larger in Belgium as compared to the EU (351.9 and 280.7 for the periods 1987–9 and 1997–9 respectively).

Table 5.11 reports the results of a fixed effects panel data regression based on the relationship between emigration rates and the importance of foreign companies in national R&D activities as measured by EPO patent applications. The Hausman test statistic leads one to reject the random-effect model and the negative coefficient associated with the importance of foreign R&D activities in the host country is statistically significant at the 10 per cent level. This finding suggests that higher degrees of R&D internationalization are associated with lower rates of

Table 5.11 Relationship between emigration rate of people with tertiary education and internationalization of R&D activities (share of foreign applicants in patents with at least one domestic inventor)

	Estimated coefficient	**Standard error**
Constant	150.21*	20.41
% of foreign firms in domestic patents	−0.1840**	0.1057
Number of observations	30	
F-test	33.67	[0.0000]
Hausman test	4.89	[0.0271]
R_a^2	0.0723	

Notes: Standard error in brackets; *(**) statistically significant at the 1% (resp. 10%) level; p-value in square brackets; F-test for fixed effects (H0: $\alpha 1 = \ldots = \alpha 15 = 0$); Hausman test (H0: βrandom effects − βfixed effects ~ 0).

emigration of highly educated workers and as a result the importance of brain drain is smaller.

As discussed in section 5.2, the presence of foreign MNEs in the host country positively affects the labour market by increasing the demand for local researchers. Table 5.12 shows the number of 'new' Belgian inventors in all domestic and foreign patents for the period 1983–99.[19] It follows that for the foreign subsidiaries and firms, this number is of the same order of magnitude as for Belgian companies. In other words, if the foreign firms would not have invested in Belgium, the number of new inventors would have been half of the current number. It can be noted that the share of new inventors based in Belgium in foreign applications has grown more rapidly compared to the share in domestic ones. It should thus be noted that the term 'Belgian inventor' refers to the country of residence of the inventor and not to his or her citizenship. It is unfortunately not possible to identify the nationality of these Belgian inventors, but it can be assumed that a non-negligible share of them are researchers of the MNEs' mother company that moved to Belgium when the subsidiary was established. Therefore, this additional availability of 'imported' human capital produces a 'brain gain' for the host country.

The residence country of inventors of 'co-invented' patents provides another indicator not only of the level of R&D internationalization but also of the importance of ideas exchanges and knowledge spillovers among inventors involved in a joint research project. Table 5.13 shows that the share of foreign co-inventors in patent applications with at least

Table 5.12 Number of 'new' inventors in US patents applied for by Belgian and foreign firms (1983–99)

	DOM	FOR
1983	82	82
1984	99	74
1985	110	102
1986	138	115
1987	123	123
1988	102	122
1989	147	140
1990	133	132
1991	117	144
1992	126	147
1993	119	173
1994	185	226
1995	220	273
1996	188	219
1997	112	214
1998	31	65
1999	1	2

Notes: DOM = Domestic applications; FOR = foreign applications.

Source: Hall *et al*. (2001) database.

Table 5.13 Share of co-inventors by country of residence and by type of applicants (Belgian firm, foreign subsidiary and foreign firm), USPTO, 1983–99

	Belgian firms	Belgian subsidiaries of foreign firms	Foreign firms
Belgium	94.0	91.5	62.1
USA	0.8	1.9	13.7
Germany	1.9	0.6	8.3
France	1.2	2.1	3.8
Netherlands	0.7	0.3	4.2
United Kingdom	0.2	1.0	2.6

Source: Hall *et al*. (2001) database.

one Belgian inventor is higher for patents applied for by foreign subsidiaries (8.5 per cent) and in particular by foreign firms (37.9 per cent). Regarding foreign applicants, US and German co-inventors are particularly important. The growing internationalization of R&D activities creates more and more interactions, or 'brain exchange', between Belgian and foreign inventors, which in turn produce positive knowledge externalities in the local economy.

5.5 Conclusion

Based on European and US patent statistics, this chapter attempts to identify the main determinants explaining the decision of MNEs to delocalize their R&D to a small open economy. The impact of these activities on the local labour market for highly skilled workers is examined as well. Regarding the first question, the scientific fields where Belgium holds comparative advantages with respect to the OECD, that is, agriculture, biochemistry and clinical medicine, appear to be positively correlated with the technological classes in which the number of patents applied for by foreign subsidiaries and firms are relatively the most important. It could therefore be concluded that the main motive for R&D MNEs to invest in Belgium is to gain access to specific knowledge resources, which are abundant in the local economy. The indicators based on the patent scope, the number of received citations and the number of self-citations reveal a relatively low value of the patents applied for by the foreign subsidiaries and assigned to these technological classes, which suggests that the main objective of the MNEs' R&D units operating in these sectors may be the transfer and adaptation of existing knowledge to the host country. At the other end, the sourcing of foreign technologies and competencies within the local S&T base appear to be the main driving force of foreign firms and subsidiaries' R&D activities (as measured by patents) in electrical devices, communications and computers sectors. In terms of comparative advantages, Belgium is not particularly well positioned in the scientific fields corresponding to these technological sectors. Yet, the importance and quality of the output of these scientific fields as measured by citations is relatively higher as compared to the OECD reference group. Furthermore, the patents assigned to these technological classes and applied for by the foreign firms and MNEs' subsidiaries appear to have a relative higher economic value. As regards the effects of MNEs on the demand for local R&D personnel, the results suggest a reduced brain drain (negative correlation between the rate of emigration of highly educated people and the level of internationalization of R&D activities), a positive 'brain gain' (higher number of new inventors in patents applied for by foreign subsidiaries and MNEs as compared to domestic firms) and an important 'brain exchange' (higher number of foreign inventors in co-invented patents applied for by foreign subsidiaries and firms) in the host country.

The results of this study lead to several important policy implications, although one has to be cautious in drawing any firm conclusions at this stage of the research.

First, MNEs' R&D activities abroad indisputably generate positive spillovers in the host country through a positive demand for highly qualified people in the host country. As a result, a strengthening of policies designed to attract FDI in research and innovation activities is highly desirable. Among these policies, we can mention financial incentives such as R&D tax concession and subsidies, the improvement of the local infrastructure and quality of the workforce or measures directed at decreasing the importance of administrative burdens and easing the starting of new businesses.

Second, S&T collaborations are another important source of spillovers brought by foreign R&D subsidiaries in the local economy. Such formal and informal agreements between scientists from different companies and research organizations represent an efficient means by which partners can exchange ideas, acquire new technological capabilities and improve their innovative performances. Technology policies aimed at promoting collaborative agreements should therefore be encouraged and further strengthened.

Third, the development by multinationals of external networks of relationships with local counterparts can also be a source of knowledge spillovers from the subsidiary to the parent company, foreign affiliates gaining access to external knowledge sources and application abilities in the host country. This 'repatriation' of local research results and the exploitation of their commercial outcomes in the MNE's home country may represent a serious loss of income from the point of view of the host country. It is therefore important to correctly assess the trade-off between the gains of FDI-induced knowledge spillovers and the benefits of research activities that spill out outside the domestic borders. With that respect, policies aimed at better internalizing the fruits of foreign affiliates' R&D and at anchoring their economic exploitation in the domestic economy deserve particular attention.

Given these preliminary results, further analysis and data collections would be helpful in order better to identify and support the policy implications implied by the high degree of internationalization of R&D

investment in Belgium. The following are among the main questions to be addressed in future research. What forces determine the location decisions of MNEs' R&D activities? What are the benefits of MNEs' R&D activities in the host/home countries? What are the reasons for R&D clusters in economic hubs (role of public research organizations and universities as key drivers)? What kind of cost-effective policy instruments can be implemented to attract foreign and to retain domestic MNEs' R&D activities (R&D direct and indirect support, education policies)? What policies are likely to attract and retain highly skilled workers (language training, citizenship policies)?

As far as the last question is concerned, two recent initiatives at the EU level are worth mentioning (European Commission, 2003): the launch of the development of the 'European Researcher's Charter' and the outline of a 'Code of Conduct for the Recruitment of Researchers'. The first initiative consists of a framework for the career management of human R&D resources, based on voluntary regulation and the second is based on best practices to improve recruitment methods.

Acknowledgements

The author is grateful to the Belgian Federal Ministry of Science Policy for supporting this research as well as to Michel Beine, Frédéric Docquier and Lydia Greunz for comments and helpful discussions on earlier drafts and suggestions received from seminar participants at INNO-tec, University of Munich and the AEA Conference on 'Innovation and Intellectual Property: Economic and Managerial Perspectives', Singapore, 15–16 July 2004. The usual disclaimer applies.

Notes

1. As pointed out by Cantwell and Santangelo (1999), non-codified technological activities that necessitate highly tacit capabilities will in general require a higher proximity.
2. Angel and Savage (1996) and Belderbos (2001), among others, analyse the determinants of the localization of Japanese R&D labs abroad; Cantwell and Harding (1998) measure the R&D internationalization of German firms; Dunning and Narula (1995) and Florida (1997) examine the R&D activities of foreign firms in the US, and Pearce and Papanstassiou (1999) in the UK.
3. Research joint ventures, firm's acquisitions and the establishment of greenfield units are the three main ways to access a foreign market.
4. For the relevance of patent statistics as an indicator of science and technology activities, see for instance Bound *et al.* (1984), Basberg (1987), Glisman and Horn (1988), Griliches (1990) or Archibugi and Pianta (1992).
5. Industrial secrecy or lead time are two well-known examples.
6. www.nber.org/patents.

See also http://www.bl.uk/services/information/patents/spec.html#des for more information on the contents of a patent specification.

7. The share of patents granted as a percentage of filed applications was 67 per cent for European patents and 68 per cent for US ones over the period 1995–9 (Quillen and Webster, 2001).
8. On average, according to the EPO, it takes just over three years between the filing of the patent application and the patent grant.
9. Information gathered by the Belgian central balance sheet office contains the composition of the shareholders. When more than 50 per cent of shareholders are from abroad, the firm is considered to be a subsidiary of a foreign group.
10. See Harhoff *et al.* (2003) for a recent review of studies on various indicators used to estimate the economic value of patents.
11. The authors find a positive correlation between the firm market value and the stock of citation-weighted patents.
12. The indicator of the internationalization of technology based on more recent patent data proposed by Cincera (2005) confirms these results.
13. Unfortunately, technological classes according to which European and US patents are classified are not directly comparable. European patents are classified according to the International Patent Classification. US patents are classified according to IPC and according to the US patent classification (USPC). Only the latter is available in the database of Hall *et al.* (2001).
14. European patents are classified according to the classification system jointly developed by the German Fraunhofer Institute of Systems and Innovation Research (ISI), the French Patent Office (INPI) and the 'Observatoire des Sciences et des Techniques' (OST). This so called 'OST/INPI/ISI' classification is based on the International Patent Classification and distinguishes between 30 different technological fields. US patents are classified according to the classification proposed by Hall *et al.* (2001) which consists of 36 technological classes based on the USPTO classification system.
15. As shown in Capron and Cincera (2000), the R&D productivity index as measured by the ratio of patents on R&D expenditures was 95 for Belgium in 1995 against 100 for the EU average.
16. See, however, Verbeek *et al.* (2002), who developed a linkage scheme based on patent citation data to link the science and technology systems.
17. The average total number of patents (irrespective of the country of residence of the inventor) applied for (at the USPTO) by Belgian firms is 14.6 against 1459.1 for foreign companies and subsidiaries (with at least one patent involving at least one Belgian inventor).
18. The emigration rates is defined as the emigration stock by educational attainment as a proportion of the labour force born in the sending country.
19. By 'new' inventors, we mean inventors that appear for the first time in the patent document. They are identified on the basis of their last and first names and city of residence.

References

Angel, D. P. and L. A. Savage, 'Global localization? Japanese research and development laboratories in the USA', *Environment and Planning A*, 28(5) (1996), 819–33.

Archibugi, D. and M. Pianta, 'Specialization and size technological activities in industrial countries: The analysis of patent data', *Research Policy*, 21(1) (1992), 79–93.

Arrow, K., 'Economic Welfare and the Allocation of Resources for Invention', in R. Nelson (ed.), *The Rate and Direction of Inventive Activity* (Princeton: Princeton University Press, 1962), 609–26.

Basberg, B. L., 'Patents and the measurement of technological change: a survey of the literature', *Research Policy*, 16 (1987), 131–41.

Belderbos, R., 'Overseas innovations by Japanese firms: An analysis of patent and subsidiary data', *Research Policy*, 30(2) (2001), 313–32.

Bertin, G. and S. Wyatt, *Multinationals and Industrial Property: The Control of the World's Technology* (Hemel Hempstead, UK: Harvester Wheatsheaf, 1988).

Blomström, M. and A. Kokko, 'Multinational corporations and spillovers', *Journal of Economic Surveys*, 12(2) (1998), 247–77.

Bound, J., C. Cummins, Z. Griliches, B. H. Hall and A. B. Jaffe, 'Who Does R&D and Who Patents?', in Z. Griliches (ed.), *R&D, Patents and Productivity* (Chicago: University of Chicago, 1984), 21–54.

Cantwell, J. and R. Harding, 'The internationalisation of German companies' R&D', *National Institute Economic Review*, 163 (1998), 99–125.

Cantwell, J. and G. D. Santangelo, 'The frontier of international technology networks: Sourcing abroad the most highly tacit capabilities', *Information Economics and Policy*, 11(1) (1999), 101–23.

Capron, H. and M. Cincera, 'Technological Performance', in H. Capron and W. Meersen (eds), *The National Innovation System of Belgium* (Heidelberg: Physica-verlag, 175–97).

Cincera, M., 'The link between firms' R&D by type of activity and source of funding and the decision to patent', working paper DULBEA, no. 10-05.RS (April 2005).

Cohen, W. M., 'Empirical studies of innovative activities', in P. Stoneman (ed.), *Handbook of the Economics of Innovation and Technological Change* (Oxford, UK: Blackwell, 1995), 182–264.

Docquier F. and A. Marfouk, 'Measuring the international mobility of skilled workers (1990–2000) – Release 1.0', Worldbank Policy Research 3381 (2004).

Dunning, J. H. and R. Narula, 'The R&D activities of foreign firms in the United States', *International Studies of Management and Organisation*, 25 (1995), 39–73.

European Commission, 'The brain drain – emigration flows for qualified scientists' (2003).

Fecher, F., 'Effets directs et indirects de la R&D sur la productivité: une analyse de l'industrie manufacturière belge', *Cahiers Economiques de Bruxelles*, 128 (1990), 459–82.

Florida, R., 'The globalization of R&D: Results of a survey of foreign-affiliated R&D laboratories in the USA', *Research Policy*, 26(1) (1997), 85–103.

Geroski, P., 'Markets for Technology: Knowledge, Innovation and Appropriability', in P. Stoneman (ed.), *Handbook of the Economics of Innovation and Technological Change* (Oxford: Blackwell, 1995).

Glisman, H. H. and E. I. Horn, 'Comparative invention performance of major industrial countries: patterns and explanations', *Management Sciences*, 34(10), (1988), 1169–87.

Granstrand, O., *The Economics and Management of Intellectual Property, Towards Intellectual Capitalism* (London: Edward Edgar, 1999).

Granstrand, O., L. Hakanson and S. Sjolander, *Technology Management and International Business* (Chichester: Wiley, 1992).

Griliches, Z., 'Patent Statistics as Economic Indicators: A Survey', *Journal of Economic Literature*, 28(4), (1990), 1661–1707).

Hall, B. H., A. B. Jaffe and M. Trajtenberg, 'Market Value and Patent Citations: A First Look', NBER Working Paper 7741 (2000).

Hall, B. H., A. Jaffe and M. Trajtenberg, 'The NBER Patent Citations Data File: Lessons, Insights and Methodological Tools', NBER Working Paper 8498 (2001).

Harhoff, D., M. Scherer and K. Vopel, 'Citations, family size, opposition and the value of patent rights', *Research Policy*, 32(8) (2003), 1343–63.

Jaffe, A., 'Technological opportunity and spillovers of R&D', *American Economic Review*, 76 (1986), 984–1001.

Kuemmerle, W., 'Foreign direct investment in industrial research in the pharmaceutical and electronics industries – Results from a survey of multinational firms', *Research Policy*, 28(2–3) (1999), 179–93.

Lanjouw, J. and M. Schankerman, 'The quality of ideas: measuring innovation with multiple indicators', NBER Working Paper 7345 (1999).

Maskus, K., 'The international regulation of intellectual property', *Weltwirtschaftliches Archiv*, 123(2) (1998), 186–208.

Patel, P. and K. Pavitt, 'Large firms in the production of the world's technology: An important case of non-globalization', *Journal of International Business Studies*, 22 (1991), 1–20.

Pearce, R. and M. Papanastassiou, 'Overseas R&D and the strategic evolution of MNEs: evidence from laboratories in the UK', *Research Policy*, 28(1) (1999), 23–41.

Quillen, C. and O. Webster, 'Continuing patent applications and performance of the US patent office', *Federal Circuit Bar Journal*, 1 (2001), 1–21.

Slaughter, M., 'Does inward foreign direct investment contribute to skill upgrading in developing countries?' CEPA Working Paper 2002–08 (2002).

Terpstra, V., 'International product policy: the role of foreign R&D', in H. V. Wortzel and L. V. Wortzel (eds), *Strategic Management of Multinational Corporations: The Essentials* (New York: Wiley, 1985).

Tong, X. and J. D. Frame, 'Measuring national technological performance with patent claims data, '*Research Policy*', 23(2) (1994), 133–41.

Verbeek, A., K. Debackere, M. Luwel, P. Andries, E. Zimmermann and F. Deleus, 'Linking science to technology: Using bibliographic references in patents to build linkage schemes', *Scientometrics*, 54(3) (2002), 399–420.

Veugelers, R. and B. Cassiman, 'Importance of international linkages for local know-how flows: Some econometric evidence from Belgium', CEPR Discussion Paper DP2337 (1999).

Veugelers, R. and P. Vanden Houte, 'Domestic R&D in the presence of multinational enterprises', *International Journal of Industrial Organization*, 8 (1990), 1–15.

6
Do Stronger Intellectual Property Rights Induce More Patents?

Sung Jin Kang and Hwan Joo Seo

6.1 Introduction

The patent system has long been recognized as an important policy instrument for the promotion of innovation and technology transfers. This trend is evidenced by the agreement on trade-related aspects of intellectual property rights (TRIPs) under the GATT-WTO of 1994. The main reason to protect patents is due to two main characteristics of innovation: non-rival and partially non-excludable (Romer, 1990). Non-rival means that the use of a particular innovation by a producer does not preclude other entrepreneurs from using it, whereas partially non-excludable implies that the innovator is often unable completely to prevent others from using the innovation without authorization.

However, there has been an ongoing debate on whether stronger IPRs encourage or retard innovative activities (see Maskus (2000) and Gallini (2002) for an extensive survey). Nordhaus (1969), who initiated an economic analysis of the patent system, shows that by granting innovators temporary monopoly power the protection of intellectual property enhances the incentives to allocate more efforts to R&D and innovative activities, and further encourages technology transfers through a reduction in transaction costs related to intellectual property. However, recent empirical and theoretical studies have not yielded a clear conclusion on whether the strengthening of IPRs leads to more or less innovation.

Theoretical studies by Scotchmer (1991), Helpman (1993), Heller and Eisenberg (1996), Bessen and Maskin (2000) and Shapiro (2000) were pessimistic on the impacts of IPRs on innovative activity. For example, Helpman finds that stronger IPRs would diminish both the northern rate of innovation and southern welfare when imitation is the only channel of technology transfer. Strengthened IPRs would raise imitation costs, restrict technology diffusion, and thus reduce long-run incentives to innovate. This is possible because if innovative firms expect slower loss of their technological advantages they could earn higher profits per innovation, thereby reducing the need to engage in R&D.

Lai (1998) and Yang and Maskus (2001), however, suggest an opposite effect: tighter IPRs would increase innovation and technology transfers. Lai found that tighter IPRs would promote product innovation and technology diffusion if production were transferred through foreign direct investment rather than through imitation. By assuming licensing as a transfer mechanism, Yang and Maskus indicate that, by reducing licensing costs, stronger IPRs would lead to higher economic returns to the licensor and would liberate resources for innovation, thereby leading to both greater innovation and licensing.

While the studies discussed above have focused on the effects of IPRs alone, recent studies have turned to the observation that the effects of IPRs could be strengthened and maximized under appropriate institutional and economic contexts (Coriat and Orsi, 2002; Hall, 2002; Lall, 2003). For example, Coriat and Orsi suggest that the increasing trend of patents of US companies in the 1980s might have stemmed from the combined effects of the strengthening of IPRs (the introduction of the Bayh-Dole Act and the creation of the Court of Appeals for the Federal Circuit (CAFC)) and institutional change in the financial sector between the late 1970s and early 1980s. Alongside the changes in IPRs, a series of new regulations such as new Employee Retirement Income Securities Act (ERISA) pension fund regulations and NASDAQ's transformation were introduced. These regulatory changes aimed to encourage the entry of venture capital into the small and new hi-tech firms coming out of the research sector. Therefore, it was possible to finance new and risky companies that otherwise would never have obtained sufficient funding for the commercialization of their innovations. Supporting the hypothesis of Coriat and Orsi, Kortum and Lerner (2000) show that the productivity of R&D in a better financial environment (for example, financing by venture capital) was about three times higher than that only with an internal financial source. In addition, they show that even though the share of venture capital of total R&D investment is only less than 3 per cent, the contribution to patents was about 8 per cent between 1983 and 1992 and increased to 14 per cent in 1998.

In addition to financial support, Mansfield (1986) posed a hypothesis on other determinants: economic impacts of IPRs will be maximized with better capability of technology adoption and highly developed structure of industries. Lall (2003) suggested a similar hypothesis in which the impacts of the strengthening of IPRs might be varied according to the level of economic development and local technological capability.

This paper tests the hypotheses suggested by traditional and recent research. Subsequently, it investigates the impacts of the strengthening of IPRs alone by testing the robustness of the results through introducing complementary factors such as industrial structure, social capability and trade regime. In addition, we hypothesize that the effectiveness of IPRs might not be identical across countries but may vary according to their economic and institutional contexts. By using a long-run, cross-country, panel data analysis, this paper shows that the strengthening of IPRs alone does not strongly affect the innovation process. Considering the joint effects of other complementary environments with IPRs, however, it is shown that the strengthening of IPRs promotes innovative activity. A more important finding is that all countries are not positively affected.

The paper is organized as follows. Section 6.2 reviews recent empirical evidence for the theoretical hypotheses discussed above. After estimation model specification and the data are discussed in sections 6.3, 6.4 discusses the estimation results. Finally, section 6.5 concludes.

6.2 Empirical Evidence

Recent research has called into question the effectiveness of patents as a tool to provide incentives for the innovations. Most of the empirical studies have focused on the impacts of IPRs alone without consideration of institutional complementarity and show that strengthened IPRs have not led to an increase of innovative effort or output (see Jaffe, 2000; Kortum and Lerner, 2000; Hall and Ziedonis, 2001; Sakakibara and Branstetter, 2001; Lerner, 2002). As an exception, Kanwar and Evenson (2003) indicate the significance of IPRs as an incentive to encourage innovations.

Kortum and Lerner (1999) investigate diverse hypotheses to explain the recent overall surge in US patenting. They fail to find empirical support for the close connection between the overall rise in patents and the strengthening of IPRs (in particular the creation of CAFC) in the US They attribute the overall increase in patenting activity to a change in the management of R&D, reoriented towards more applied research, with an increase in research productivity caused by the introduction of information and communication technology (ICT) and the investment of venture capital, rather than to a series of patent reforms. Moreover, the survey evidence by Cohen *et al.* (2000) also supports the ineffectiveness of patents for the protection of inventions. They find that enterprises consider patents as less effective instruments for the protection of their intellectual properties relative to alternative mechanisms such as secrecy and lead-time.

In the analyses of the relationship between the Bayh-Dole Act and innovation, Henderson *et al.* (1998), Mowery and Sampat (2001), Mowery *et al.* (2001) and Mowery and Ziedonis (2002) examine whether the Bayh-Dole Act of 1980 has stimulated the quantitative and qualitative development of patents of US universities. They found the number of patents registered by US colleges has increased since the early 1970s, which implies that the number of patents might have increased independently of the Bayh-Dole Act. Furthermore, the quality of patents measured by the frequency of citation decreased after the introduction of the Act.

Thus, studies on the source of the increased number of US patents since the 1980s have shown that there is no compelling evidence that the policies to strengthen IPRs such as the Bayh-Dole Act and the establishment of the CAFC have contributed to the promotion of patents. Furthermore Sakakibara and Branstetter (2001) examine the case of Japanese patent reform of 1988, which allowed transformation from a single claim system to a multiclaim system. They also show that there is no significant evidence that the strengthening of IPRs in 1988, through the expansion of patent scope and the increase of patent length, contributed to innovative activity in Japan.

In contrast, cross-country studies seem to show relatively positive effects of IPR policies (Gould and Gruben, 1996; Lerner, 2002; Kanwar and Evenson, 2003). Studying 177 patent-related policy shifts in 60 countries over 150 years, Lerner found that the strengthening of IPRs shows an inverted-U relation with innovations. Utilizing cross-country data, Kanwar and Evenson show that intellectual property protection (defined as an index of patent rights) has a strong positive effect on technological change (defined by R&D investment expenditure). The same finding results even after several pertinent control variables are allowed for.

The empirical studies discussed above have suggested mixed evidence. In general, the studies on individual countries (US and Japan) do not support the positive effect of IPRs, whereas the cross-country studies do.

6.3 Model Specification and Descriptive Statistics

To estimate the determinants of innovative activity, the definition of innovative activity should be clarified. Kanwar and Evenson (2003) define it as the R&D expenditure ratio to gross national product rather than patent applications. This paper, however, interprets R&D expenditure as an input to produce patents.[1] This hypothesis is consistent with the idea of innovation function suggested by the endogenous growth theories initiated by Romer (1990) and Grossman and Helpman (1991). They assume that technology change is a function of R&D input approximated by the number of labourers employed by the R&D sector or R&D expenditure. Thus, we assume that patents are an indirect measure of inventive activity by using R&D expenditure as an input.

For the estimation, we assume that patent production uses R&D expenditure as a ratio of GDP (RD) as an input in addition to other supporting factors. Thus, the following log-linear equations are used:

$$P_{it} = c + \alpha_1 RD_{it} + \alpha_2 IPR_{it} + \sum_{j=1}^{J} \beta_j X_{ijt} + u_i + \varepsilon_{it} \quad (1)$$

$$P_{it} = c + \alpha_1 RD_{it} + \alpha_2 IPR_{it} + \sum_{j=1}^{J} \gamma_j X_{ijt} IPR_{it} + u_i + \varepsilon_{it} \quad (2)$$

Here, P_{it} is defined as the natural log of the number of patents per 1,000 people in country i at time t. It is the annual number of utility patents applications filed in the United States by country of origin. These data were originally compiled by the United States Patent and Trademark Office (USPTO) and reported to the World Intellectual Property Organization (WIPO) each year.[2] The country of origin of an application is based on the residence of the first-named inventor. And u is a country-specific residual and ε is a well-defined stochastic error term.

As the main independent variables, RD and IPR reflect the ratio of R&D expenditure to GDP and the index of intellectual property rights (IPRs) respectively. The first set of data is from the statistical yearbook on-line database of UNESCO and the second is from Ginarte and Park (1997) for 1960–90 and Park and Wagh in the *Economic Freedom of the World: 2002 Annual Report* (2002) for 1995 and 2000. The index was constructed for each of the 110 countries between 1960 and 1990 and the 64 countries in 1995 and 2000 every five years. The index incorporates five aspects of patent laws: the extent of coverage, membership in international patent agreements, duration of protection, provisions for loss of protection, and enforcement mechanisms. The index was scored in the range from 0 to 5, with higher values indicating stronger patent protection.

Other variables indicated by a matrix, X, test the joint effect with the strengthening of IPRs over periods. They are the natural log of real GDP per capita (*gdp*), the institutional environment (*IE*), the ratio of high-technology exports to manufactured exports (*HT*), the ratio of ICT expenditure to GDP (*ICT*) and trade shares (*Openness*).

The difference between equations (1) and (2) is in the fourth term which implies a set of independent variables with or without an interaction term of IPR. Thus, equation (1) is intended to test the effect of IPR alone, while equation (2) is intended to test the effect of IPR interacted with other independent variables. We designated the first specification as the 'baseline model' and the second as the 'extended model'.

These variables are derived from the literature on economic development and technological change. Lall (2003) and the World Bank (2001) propose that the potential significance of IPRs varies according to the countries' levels of economic development. Therefore, *gdp* is introduced to control the level of economic development and the pro-cyclical movement of patent applications. The data are sourced from the Penn World Table 6.1. Geroski and Walters (1995) found that the level of patent activity of UK firms generally rose over the years and varied pro-cyclically.

Mansfield (1986) found large differences by industries in the innovation-promoting role of patents. His survey revealed that 65 per cent of inventions in pharmaceutics, 30 per cent in chemicals, 18 per cent in

Table 6.1 Summary statistics

	1981–5	1986–90	1991–5	1996–2000	1981–2000
P	0.03	0.03	0.03	0.04	0.03
	(0.05)	(0.06)	(0.06)	(0.08)	(0.06)
gdp	8.24	8.32	8.37	8.46	8.35
	(1.01)	(1.07)	(1.09)	(1.10)	(1.07)
RD	1.17	1.34	1.21	1.12	1.20
	(1.09)	(0.97)	(0.85)	(1.06)	(1.10)
IPR	2.43	2.46	2.71	3.07	2.68
	(0.91)	(0.94)	(1.11)	(0.99)	(1.02)
IE	4.50	4.49	4.87	5.35	4.86
	(1.96)	(2.25)	(2.45)	(2.36)	(2.36)
HT	n.a.	0.10	0.09	0.11	0.10
		(0.11)	(0.11)	(0.14)	(0.13)
ICT	n.a.	n.a.	0.05	0.06	0.05
			(0.02)	(0.02)	(0.02)
Openness	0.73	0.71	0.80	0.85	0.78
	(0.43)	(0.43)	(0.47)	(0.46)	(0.45)

Notes
(1) n.a. means the data are not available.
(2) Standard deviation is in the parentheses.

petroleum, 15 per cent in machinery, 12 per cent in metal products, 8 per cent in primary metals and 4 per cent in electrical machinery would have been deterred without patent protection. Thus, the importance of IPRs to promote innovation may vary across industries and correspondingly the economic impacts of IPRs must be dependent on the industrial structure or the trade structure in each country. We, therefore, use HT to reflect the sophistication of industrial structure in each country.

It is well known that openness to trade contributes to economic growth (Gould and Gruben, 1996; Aghion and Howitt, 1998). These effects appear to be slightly stronger in relatively open trade regimes as the competitive pressure in these regimes stimulates innovative activity in domestic industries. We present results based on trade regimes as defined by trade shares (i.e., exports plus imports as a share of GDP). However, unlike Gould and Gruben, we are trying to find a direct relationship between openness and innovative activity. This is because an insignificant relationship between openness and economic growth does not necessarily mean that openness does not promote innovation. It may simply result from the contribution of an innovation to economic growth not being strong enough. Thus, we test the direct effect of openness to an innovative activity.

Arora and Gambardella (1994) and Kortum and Lerner (1999) argue that application of ICT to the discovery process may have substantially promoted the productivity of R&D and expanded the knowledge base through the expansion and sharing of knowledge in the US. To capture the impacts of ICT diffusion on innovative activities, we propose to use the ratio of ICT investment to GDP.

Finally, *IE* is assumed to affect innovation as well. The summary index constructed by the Fraser Institute is based on 23 components designed to identify the consistency of institutional arrangements and policies with economic freedom in seven major areas. The data are indexed on a 1–10 scale at five-year intervals from 1970 to 1995 and every year afterwards. The missing data of other years are generated by a linearly interpolate method. Since it may be assumed that the institutional environment changes smoothly, this assumption might not affect the estimation results. The higher value of the index indicates a better institution or social infrastructure. The core ingredients are personal choice, legal protection of property rights, freedom of exchange, reliance on markets, use of money and market allocation of capital. Individuals have economic freedom when: (a) their property, acquired without the use of force, fraud, or theft, is protected from physical invasions by others and (b) they are not forced to use, exchange, or give their property to another as long as their actions do not violate the identical rights of others.

Figure 6.1 shows the trends of the number of patents per 1,000 persons and the IPR index between 1981 and 2000. As Figure 6.1 shows, there is a monotonic increase in the number of patents and a higher increase especially after the mid-1990s, indicating an increasing trend in the growth rate of the number of patents. In addition, it is shown that the trend of the IPR index in the 1980s was quite stable at 2.4, while it has increased to about 3.0 since 1990.[3]

Table 6.1 shows summary statistics of the variables used in the estimation of the next section. Except for the R&D expenditure ratio, all values show an increasing trend over the period. The trend of the R&D expenditure ratio is clarified in Figure 6.2 by isolating the data for OECD member countries as well, thereby indicating an increasing trend since 1980 for OECD countries, while non-OECD countries had a decreasing trend between 1990 and 1995 and then an increasing trend after 1995. However, the value was still lower in 1995 than that before 1990. From Figure 6.2, we can infer that this decreasing trend may have resulted from non-OECD member countries.

Since the variables used in the estimation might be highly correlated, Table 6.2 reports their correlation coefficients. In general, the *IPR* index and *IE* are highly correlated with *gdp*. Thus, to test the effect of these correlations on the estimation results, we estimate the equation both with and without combining these variables.

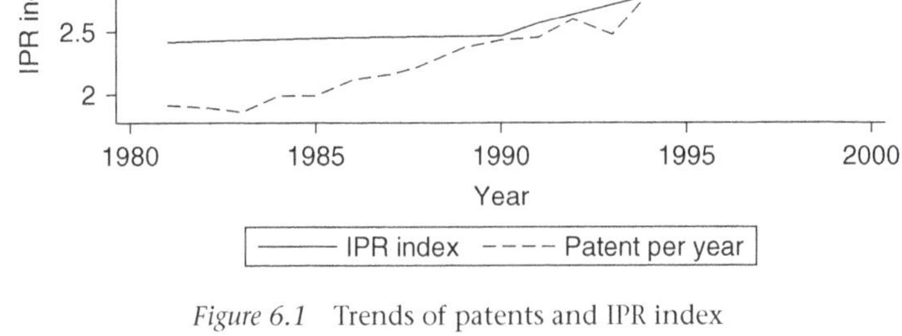

Figure 6.1 Trends of patents and IPR index

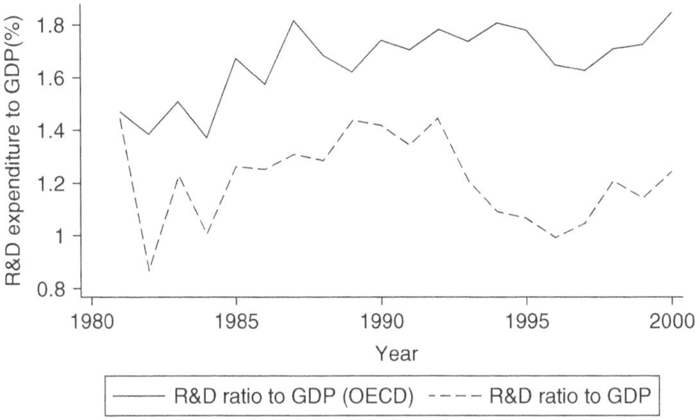

Figure 6.2 Trends of R&D expenditure ratio to GDP

Table 6.2 Correlation coefficients

	P	gdp	RD	IPR	IE	HT	ICT	Openness
P	1.00							
gdp	0.66	1.00						
RD	0.79	0.67	1.00					
IPR	0.62	0.82	0.69	1.00				
IE	0.45	0.79	0.39	0.57	1.00			
HT	0.52	0.49	0.45	0.37	0.50	1.00		
ICT	0.53	0.68	0.52	0.62	0.63	0.36	1.00	
Openness	−0.12	0.19	−0.08	−0.05	0.23	0.34	0.18	1.00

6.4 Estimation Results of the Baseline Model

In order to determine the separate impact of IPRs, Table 6.3 reports the estimation results of IPRs with other conditioning variables but without interaction with IPRs (called the 'baseline model'). Two different models indicate that IPRs without interactions with other conditioning variables are not statistically significant.[4] In order to examine the difference of the estimation results between fixed- and random-effect model specifications, two results are reported.

To avoid possible bias due to highly correlated control variables, each model is estimated with different combinations of control variables, in addition to the three main variables, *gdp*, *RD* and *IPR*. As other model specifications show similar results, only two results are reported.

Table 6.3 Panel estimation results of baseline models

	Model 1		Model 2		Model 2A	
	Fixed	Random	Fixed	Random	Fixed	Random
RD	0.019	0.02	0.019	0.019	0.025	0.023
	(4.98)**	(5.42)**	(4.96)**	(4.94)**	(4.07)**	(5.16)**
gdp	0.103	0.05	0.105	0.053	0.129	0.053
	(4.76)**	(3.43)**	(4.41)**	(3.53)**	(4.07)**	(2.97)**
IPR	0.007	0.013	0.01	0.013	0.008	0.015
	(0.78)	(1.58)	(1.13)	(1.6)	(0.74)	(1.62)
IE	0.001	−0.0003	−0.00002	−0.001	−0.001	−0.001
	(0.2)	(−0.08)	(−0.01)	(−0.22)	(−0.14)	(−0.26)
HT	0.059	0.101	0.077	0.166	0.045	0.156
	1.02	(2.11)*	(1.21)	(3.02)**	(0.60)	(2.49)*
ICT	0.383	0.375	0.332	0.333	0.497	0.460
	(2.60)**	(2.58)**	(2.18)*	(2.24)*	(3.00)**	(2.90)**
Openness			−0.003	−0.016	0.003	−0.006
			(−0.12)	(−1.11)	(0.14)	(−0.39)
Constant	−0.996	−0.505	−1.019	−0.521	−1.252	−0.554
	(−5.26)**	(−4.40)**	(−4.95)**	(−4.50)**	(−4.59)**	(−3.96)**
Observations	250	250	245	245	218	218
Number of countries	41	41	40	40	39	39
sigma_u	0.07	0.05	0.07	0.05	0.085	0.054
sigma_e	0.02	0.02	0.02	0.02	0.016	0.016
Rho	0.96	0.91	0.96	0.91	0.967	0.923
P(u_i = 0)	0.00		0.00		0.00	
overall R^2	0.53	0.58	0.56	0.63	0.55	0.63

Notes
(1) Robust t statistics in parentheses.
(2) * significant at 5%; ** significant at 1%.
(3) rho indicates the fraction of variance due to u_i and P(u_i = 0) represents p-values for F-test in which all $u_i = 0$.

First of all, *gdp* and *RD* are positively and significantly correlated with the number of patents. As in the findings of Geroski and Walters (1995) for the UK firms, the positive and significant coefficient for income per capita (*gdp*) implies that this is clear evidence of a secular relation between the level of innovative activities and the level of economic activity, even for cross-country analysis.

ICT, which reflects the social infrastructure, is positively related with the number of patents, while *HT*, the degree of sophistication of industrial structure in exports, plays a positive role. The variable, which reflects trade regime, *Openness*, is not significant. This implies that the competitive pressure under an open economy might not stimulate innovative activity. This is in contrast with the results of Kanwar and Evenson (2003), who show that openness played a significant role in promoting R&D expenditure. As an alternative, we used a black market premium index but with the same outcome.

The most important variable, *IPR*, is not significant for either estimation, fixed- or random-effect panel estimation, even though the coefficients for random-effect panel estimation become relatively higher. In general, it can be interpreted that *IPR* alone, without the joint support of other supporting variables, cannot directly affect innovative activity.

Two independent variables, *gdp* and *IPR*, might be endogenous. Grossman and Lai (2004) and Lai and Yang (2004) show that differences in market size and differences in R&D capacity generate national differences in optimal patent policies. Moreover, Gould and Gruben (1996) found no strong direct effects of patents on economic growth, but there was a significantly positive effect when patents interacted with a measure of openness to trade. Even though this study uses the level of real GDP per capita rather than economic growth rate as an independent variable, we test their possible endogeneity. We estimate instrumental variables and two-stage least squares for panel-data models (see Baltagi (2001) for a discussion on estimation process). Due to difficulties in choosing instrumental variables, we selected lagged values of *gdp* and/or *IPR* in addition to all other independent variables as instrumental variables. Estimation results are quite consistent with those of estimation without considering endogenous problem.

As an example, Model 2A in Table 6.3 reports the instrumental variable estimation results by assuming both *gdp* and *IPR* are endogenous. The results are quite consistent with the estimation results of Models 1 and 2. *RD*, *gdp* and *ICT* are significant, while *IPR* alone does not play a significant role.

Tables 6.4 and 6.5 report the panel estimation results of the extended model by considering the joint effects of IPR and other independent variables. Model 2 in Table 6.3 is used as a benchmark. *RD* plays a positive and significant role throughout all five models in Tables 6.4 and 6.5.

Model 3 in Table 6.4 includes an interaction term of *IPR* with *gdp* to the second model in Table 6.3. As in Table 6.3, *HT* and *ICT* are significant. Unlike the results of Table 6.3, however, *IPR* itself and an interaction term are significant.

In Model 4, even though IE is not significant without consideration of the joint effect with IPRs (Table 6.3), the coefficient for *IE* becomes significant for the random-effect estimation (i.e., the *t*-value rises for the fixed-effect model as well). In addition, *HT* and *ICT* are positive and significant as before.

In Model 5, HT itself and an interaction term are significant and the coefficients for other independent variables, gdp and *ICT*, are positive and significant. Furthermore, the interaction term between *IPR* and *ICT*

Table 6.4 Panel estimation results of extended models

	Model 3		Model 4	
	Fixed	Random	Fixed	Random
RD	0.015	0.017	0.019	0.018
	(4.37)**	(5.16)**	(4.82)**	(4.93)**
gdp	−0.214	−0.136	0.092	0.045
	(−4.86)**	(−5.61)**	(3.56)**	(3.12)**
IPR	−0.707	−0.555	−0.03	−0.082
	(−8.06)**	(−9.08)**	(−0.92)	(−2.96)**
IE	0.003	0.001	−0.018	−0.042
	(0.89)	(0.16)	(−1.25)	(−3.49)**
HT	0.087	0.096	0.078	0.146
	(1.58)	(2.00)*	(1.23)	(2.70)**
ICT	0.422	0.381	0.355	0.385
	(3.19)**	(3.02)**	(2.32)*	(2.64)**
Openness	−0.019	−0.022	−0.005	−0.018
	(−1.06)	(−1.72)	(−0.24)	(−1.24)
*gdp**IPR*	0.077	0.061		
	(8.21)**	(9.37)**		
*IE**IPR*			0.006	0.013
			(1.3)	(3.60)**
Constant	1.923	1.208	−0.774	−0.171
	(4.81)**	(5.66)**	(−2.78)**	(−1.17)
Observations	245	245	245	245
Number of countries	40	40	40	40
sigma_u	0.06	0.05	0.07	0.05
sigma_e	0.01	0.01	0.02	0.02
Rho	0.95	0.92	0.95	0.90
P(u_i = 0)	0.00		0.00	
overall R^2	0.67	0.71	0.59	0.68

Notes
(1) Robust t statistics in parentheses.
(2) * significant at 5%; ** significant at 1%.
(3) rho indicates the fraction of variance due to u_i and P(u_i = 0) represents p-values for F-test that all u_i = 0.

in Model 6 is significant, thereby maintaining the same results for other independent variables like other models.

What is interesting is the estimation result for *Openness* in Model 7. As mentioned above, Openness was not significant in Table 6.3. When an interaction term is considered, however, it becomes marginally significant. This implies that open economies experience greater competition and need to acquire advanced technologies in order to promote product

Table 6.5 Panel estimation results of extended models

	Model 5		Model 6		Model 7	
	Fixed	Random	Fixed	Random	Fixed	Random
RD	0.017	0.017	0.015	0.015	0.018	0.018
	(4.71)**	(5.11)**	(4.31)**	(4.71)**	(4.56)**	(4.73)**
gdp	0.048	0.034	0.059	0.049	0.094	0.051
	(1.99)*	(2.48)*	(2.66)**	(3.72)**	(3.85)**	(3.55)**
IPR	−0.005	−0.013	−0.034	−0.038	−0.005	−0.003
	(−0.58)	(−1.54)	(−3.32)**	(−4.15)**	(−0.39)	(−0.25)
IE	0.001	0.002	0.001	0.0002	0.0004	−0.0001
	(0.23)	(0.54)	(0.27)	(0.08)	(0.1)	(−0.03)
HT	−0.841	−0.858	0.061	0.107	0.072	0.164
	(−5.04)**	(−6.01)**	(1.09)	(2.22)*	(1.13)	(3.01)**
ICT	0.396	0.418	−3.576	−3.926	0.344	0.35
	(2.80)**	(3.11)**	(−6.56)**	(−7.92)**	(2.27)*	(2.34)*
Openness	−0.02	−0.024	−0.011	−0.022	−0.097	−0.103
	(−1.02)	(−1.81)	(−0.61)	(−1.69)	(−1.74)	(−2.25)*
*HT*IPR*	0.262	0.283				
	(5.88)**	(7.65)**				
*ICT*IPR*			1.138	1.237		
			(7.40)**	(8.89)**		
Openness**IPR*					0.027	0.025
					(1.83)	(1.92)
Constant	−0.422	−0.274	−0.429	−0.314	−0.862	−0.459
	(−1.96)	(−2.54)*	(−2.16)*	(−2.99)**	(−3.89)**	(−4.10)**
Observations	245	245	245	245	245	245
Number of countries	40	40	40	40	40	40
sigma_u	0.05	0.04	0.05	0.04	0.07	0.04
sigma_e	0.01	0.01	0.01	0.01	0.02	0.02
Rho	0.93	0.90	0.93	0.91	0.95	0.89
P(u_i = 0)	0.00		0.00			
Overall R^2	0.69	0.72	0.68	0.71	0.55	0.61

Notes:
(1) Robust t statistics in parentheses.
(2) * significant at 5%; ** significant at 1%.
(3) rho indicates the fraction of variance due to u_i and P(u_i = 0) represents p-values for F-test that all $u_i = 0$.

quality. Moreover, firms in an open economy are more likely to undertake effective technology transfers and adaptation to local circumstances. However, the different estimation results in Models 2 and 7 suggest that innovation will be more evident in economies with protection for intellectual property.[5]

6.5 Estimation Results of the Extended Model

As we see from the theoretical and empirical literature review in sections 6.1 and 6.2, the effects of IPR on innovative activities are quite mixed.

This can be interpreted to indicate that countries might be either positively or negatively affected. By using the estimation results of equation (2), the direction/sign of the effect for an individual country can be easily identified.

From the coefficient for the interaction terms through Models 3 to 7 in Tables 6.4 and 6.5, the IPR effect is easily calculated. For the interaction term with IPR, x, the marginal IPR effect from equation (2) is calculated as:

$$\frac{\partial P_{it}}{\partial IPR_{it}} = \alpha_2 + \gamma_j X_{jt} \tag{3}$$

The *IPR* effect on innovative activity depends on α_2 (the coefficient on *IPR*) and γ_j(the coefficient on an interaction term of IPR and X_j). To calculate the effect of IPRs, we use the mean value of an independent variable over a specific period. Thus, the sign of the IPR effect depends on the values of the two coefficients and the mean value of each independent variable. If the effect in equation (3) is positive, it implies that IPR improves the innovative activity for a specific level of IE, *X*. If it shows negative, however, for a specific institutional level, IPRs can deter innovative activities of that country.

In addition, the countries which were positively or negatively affected are identified. First, the threshold value of each independent variable which makes equation (3) equal zero can be calculated. Then, through comparison between the mean value and threshold value of each independent variable, we can easily identify the countries with positive or negative effect.

Table 6.6 reports these two results from the estimation results in Tables 6.4 and 6.5. First, with Model 3 in Table 6.6 and using the mean value of *gdp* over 20 years, 9.50, in the fixed-effect model, the IPR effect is positive and significant. For the fixed-effect estimation result, the IPR effect is $-0.707 + 0.077gdp$. By using the mean value of *gdp* across countries between 1981 and 2000, 9.50 ('mean' in the table), the *IPR* effect is 0.025 ('effect' in the table). This result supports the argument that IPR with an interaction of *gdp* plays a positive role, while IPR alone plays an insignificant role in Table 6.3.

In a similar vein, Models 4 through 7 use interaction terms of other independent variables with *IPR*. The effects of *IPR* with *HT* (Model 5) and *ICT* (Model 6) are similar at about 0.030, while the effects with *IE* (Model 4) and *Openness* (Model 7) are both about 0.014. Thus, the large effect of IPRs when they are jointly considered with *HT* or *ICT* implies

Table 6.6 Effects of IPR and thresholds of institutional environments

		Model 3 (gdp)		Model 4 (IE)		Model 5 (HT)		Model 6 (ICT)		Model 7 (ICT)	
		Fixed	Random	Fixed	Random	Fixed	Random	Fixed	Random	Fixed	Random
IPR effect											
	mean	9.50	9.50	7.44	7.44	0.14	0.14	0.06	0.06	0.64	0.64
	effect	0.025	0.025	0.015	0.015	0.031	0.026	0.034	0.036	0.012	0.013
Threshold		9.18	9.10	5.00	6.31	0.02	0.05	0.03	0.03	0.19	0.12
Number of countries											
	positively	21	24	33	22	37	31	32	32	37	40
	negatively	19	16	7	18	3	9	8	8	3	0

that the sophistication of industrial structure and ICT diffusion play a significant role in promoting innovative activities. These findings are in agreement with those by Mansfield (1986), Arora and Gambardella (1994) and Kortum and Lerner (1999).

Second, equation (3) supports the argument that all countries are not equally affected. For Model 3 by fixed-effect estimation, the threshold value of *gdp* that makes the *IPR* effect equal 0 is 9.18 ('threshold' in the table), which equates to an actual GDP per capita of US$ 9,701 at the 1995 international price. Using this threshold value, we identified that 21 out of 40 countries were positively affected, while the remaining 19 were negatively affected. For the random-effect model, the threshold value of *gdp* becomes slightly lower (9.10) so that 24 countries were positively affected and 16 negatively. Thus, the countries with negative effect might support the arguments by Helpman (1993), who assumes the imitation channel in developing countries. When the global IPRs system is strengthened by the adoption of a minimum standard, imitation becomes harder, which decreases its rate of occurrence and thereby slows down the rate of innovation. The list of countries used in the estimation is in Table 6.A1 of the Appendix and the identified countries which were positively or negatively affected are listed in Table 6.A2 of the Appendix.

For Models 4 to 7, the threshold values for each IE are calculated and the countries with positive or negative effects are identified. For fixed-effect estimation, 33 and 32 countries had larger mean values than the threshold values of IE and ICT, respectively, indicating that they were positively affected. In the same way, 37 countries were positively affected under consideration of threshold values of *HT* and trade shares (*Openness*).

6.6 Conclusion

In this study, we have investigated the impact of the strengthening of IPRs on innovative activity, using cross-country data over the past two decades. The following is a summary of our results.

First, there is no evidence that stronger IPRs alone boost innovation measured by the number of patent applications, even when several pertinent control variables are considered. Second, there is strong evidence that IPRs are positively and significantly related with innovations once other complementary aspects of the environment for innovation, such as the stage of economic development, industrial structure, trade regime and IE are jointly instigated. Third, even following consideration of the complementary condition, some countries were positively affected while others were negatively affected. This result implies that the effectiveness of IPRs might not be identical across countries but may vary according to the economic and institutional contexts of each country. For example, only countries with per capita GDP above about US$ 9,000 gain positive benefit from the strengthening of IPRs.

The recent introduction of global minimum standards for IPRs through TRIPs in the WTO raises a considerable debate about whether the strengthening of IPRs increases or decreases innovation. Results from our analysis show that innovation is not automatically improved by the strengthening of IPRs. A policy change to strengthen the protection of IPRs can improve economic performance only when the supplementary institutional changes in other economic areas take place concurrently. The building of a more competitive domestic market structure through openness to trade, incessant upgrading of industry structure, the enhancement of economic efficiency through the construction of a market-friendly environment, and the presence of adequate infrastructures such as ICT are crucial if IPRs are to become an effective policy instrument.

Appendices

Table 6.A1 List of countries for fixed-effect panel estimation

Variable	Positive	Negative
gdp	2, 3, 6, 7, 11, 12, 14, 15, 16, 17, 18, 19, 23, 24, 25, 26, 29, 30, 31, 35, 38	1, 4, 5, 8, 9, 10, 13, 20, 21, 22, 27, 28, 32, 33, 34, 36, 37, 39, 40
IE	1, 2, 3, 6, 7, 8, 10, 11, 12, 13, 14, 15, 16, 17, 18, 19, 20, 21, 23, 24, 25, 26, 27, 28, 29, 30, 31, 35, 36, 37, 38, 39, 40	4, 5, 9, 22, 32, 33, 34
HT	1, 2, 3, 4, 5, 6, 7, 9, 10, 11, 12, 14, 15, 16, 17, 18, 19, 20, 21, 22, 23, 24, 25, 26, 27, 28, 29, 30, 31, 32, 33, 34, 35, 36, 37, 38, 40	8, 13, 39
ICT	1, 2, 3, 5, 6, 7, 8, 9, 10, 11, 12, 14, 15, 16, 17, 18, 19, 20, 23, 24, 25, 26, 27, 28, 29, 30, 31, 32, 35, 38, 40	4, 13, 21, 22, 33, 34, 36, 37
Openness	2, 3, 4, 6, 7, 8, 9, 10, 11, 12, 13, 14, 15, 16, 17, 18, 19, 20, 21, 23, 24, 25, 26, 27, 28, 29, 30, 31, 32, 33, 34, 35, 36, 37, 38, 40	1, 5, 22

Table 6.A2 List of countries

1	Argentina	11	Czech Republic	21	Indonesia	31	New Zealand
2	Australia	12	Denmark	22	India	32	Poland
3	Austria	13	Egypt	23	Ireland	33	Romania
4	Bulgaria	14	Spain	24	Israel	34	Russia
5	Brazil	15	France	25	Italy	35	Sweden
6	Canada	16	United Kingdom	26	Japan	36	Thailand
7	Switzerland	17	Germany	27	Republic of Korea	37	Turkey
8	Chile	18	Greece	28	Mexico	38	USA
9	China	19	Hong Kong	29	Netherlands	39	Venezuela
10	Colombia	20	Hungary	30	Norway	40	South Africa

Notes

1. See Griliches (1990), Trajtenberg (1990), Kortum (1997) and Kanwar and Evenson (2003) for further discussion.
2. The patent data might underestimate the number of patents of each country because they did not include the patents registered in the original country. However, as the data which considered domestically registered patents might reflect different criteria for patent registration, they might be subject to bias as well. Thus, this paper uses the patents registered in the USA only to reflect the same criteria for patent registration.
3. The difference does not reflect a sample selection issue. The number of countries with an IPR index in 1980, 1985 and 1990 was 110, but in 1995 and 2000 it was only 64. However, the average value of the IPR index was not so different. For example, the average index value in 1980 was 2.41 and 2.42 for 219 and 64 countries, respectively, even though the value for the latter sample was slightly higher. The values for other years are slightly higher (0.01 in 1985 and 0.02 in 2000) but not significantly. Thus, the sample selection does not affect the trends of the IPR index in the 1980s.
4. Year or five-year period dummies are not significant through all estimation specifications and they do not affect the estimation results significantly, so they are not included in the estimation throughout the paper.
5. Gould and Gruben (1996) show that while patent alone does not play a significant role in promoting economic growth, patents interacting with openness does. Their result might be consistent with our estimation results on the IPR effect on innovative activities (patents). In other words, our estimation results can be interpreted to indicate that intellectual property interacting with openness promotes innovative activities, which will lead in turn to higher economic growth.

References

Aghion, P. and P. Howitt, *Endogenous Growth Theory* (Cambridge: MIT Press, 1998).

Arora, A. and A. Gambardella, 1994, 'The Changing Technology of Technological Change: General and Abstract Knowledge and the Division of Innovative Labor', *Research Policy*, 23 (1994), 523–32.

Baltagi, B. H., *Econometric Analysis of Panel Data*, 2nd edn (New York: John Wiley & Sons, 2001).

Bessen, J. and E. Maskin, 'Sequential Innovation, Patents and Imitation', MIT Working Paper, No. 00–0,1(2000).

Cohen, W. M., R. R. Nelson and J. P. Walsh, 'Protecting Their Intellectual Assets: Appropriability Conditions and Why US Manufacturing Firms Patent (or Not)', NBER Working Paper 7552 (2000).

Coriat, B. and F. Orsi, 'Establishing a New Intellectual Property Rights Regime in the United States: Origins, Content and Problem', *Research Policy*, 31 (2002), 1491–507.

Gallini, N. T., 'The Economics of Patents: Lessons from Recent US Patent Reform', *Journal of Economic Perspectives*, 16 (2002), 131–54.

Geroski, P. A. and C. F. Walters, 'Innovative Activity over Business Cycle', *Economic Journal*, 105 (1995), 916–28.

Ginarte, J. C. and W. G. Park, 1997, 'Determinants of Patent Rights: A Cross National Study', *Research Policy*, 26 (1997), 283–301.

Gould, D. M. and W. C. Gruben, 'The Role of Intellectual Property Rights in Economic Growth', *Journal of Development Economics*, 48 (1996), 323–50.

Griliches, Z., 'Patent Statistics as Economic Indicators: a Survey', *Journal of Economic Literature*, 28 (1990), 1661–707.

Grossman, G. M. and E. Helpman, *Innovation and Growth in the Global Economy* (Cambridge: MIT Press, 1991).

Grossman, G. M. and E. L.-C. Lai, 'International Protection of Intellectual Property', *American Economic Review*, 94 (2004), 1635–54.

Hall, B. H., 'The Financing of Research and Development', NBER Working Paper 8773, (2002).

Hall, B. H. and R. H. Ziedonis, 'The Patent Paradox Revisited: An Empirical Study of Patenting in the US Semiconductor Industry, 1975–1995', *RAND Journal of Economics*, 32 (2001), 101–28.

Heller, M. A. and R. Eisenberg 'Can Patents Deter Innovation? The Anti-Commons in Biomedical Research', *Science*, 280 (1996), 698–701.

Helpman, E., 'Innovation, Imitation, and Intellectual Property Rights', *Econometrica*, 61 (1993), 1247–80.

Henderson, R., A. B. Jaffe and M. Trajtenberg, 'Universities as a Source of Commercial Technology: a Detailed Analysis of University Patenting, 1965–1988', *Review of Economics and Statistics*, 80 (1998), 127–99.

Jaffe, A. B., 'The US Patent System in Transition: Policy Innovation and the Innovation Process', *Research Policy*, 29 (2000), 531–57.

Kanwar, S. and R. Evenson, 'Does Intellectual Property Protection Spur Technological Change?', *Oxford Economic Papers*, 55 (2003), 235–64.

Kortum, S., 'Research, Patenting and Technological Change', *Econometrica*, 65 (1997), 1389–419.

Kortum, S. and J. Lerner, 'What is Behind the Recent Surge in Patenting?', *Research Policy*, 28 (1999), 1–22.

Kortum, S. and J. Lerner, 'Assessing the Contribution of Venture Capital to Innovation', *RAND Journal of Economics*, 31 (2000), 674–92.

Lai, E. L.-C., 'Intellectual Property Rights Protection and the Rate of Product Innovation', *Journal of Development Economics*, 55 (1998), 115–30.

Lai, E. L.-C. and I. K. Yang, 'International Protection of Intellectual Property: An Empirical Investigation', paper presented at the International Conference

'Recent Advances in International Economics III: Intellectual Property Protection and International Trade', Hong Kong, 24–25 May (2004).
Lall, S., 'Indicators of the Relative Importance of IPRs in Developing Countries', *Research Policy*, 32 (2003), 1657–80.
Lerner, J. 'Patent Protection and Innovation Over 150 Years', NBER Working Paper 8977 (2002).
Mansfield, E. 'Patents and Innovation: an Empirical Study', *Management Science*, 32 (1986), 173–81.
Maskus, K., *Intellectual Property Rights in the Global Economy* (Washington, DC: Institute for International Economics, 2000).
Mowery, D. and B. Sampat, 'Patenting and Licensing University Inventions: Lessons from the History of the Research Corporations', Industrial and Corporate Change, 10(2) (2001), 317–55.
Mowery, D. C. and N. S. Bhaven, 'University Patents and Patent Policy Debates in the USA, 1925–1980', *Industrial and Corporate Change*, 10 (2001), 781–814.
Mowery, D. C. and A. Ziedonis, 'Academic Patent Quality and Quantity before and after the Bayh-Dole Act in the United States', *Research Policy*, 31 (2002), 399–418.
Mowery, D. C., B. Sampat and A. Ziedonis, 'The Growth of Patenting and Licensing by US Universities: an Assessment of the Effects of the Bayh-Dole Act of 1980', *Research Policy*, 30 (2001), 99–119.
Nordhaus, W. D., *Invention, Growth, and Welfare: A Theoretical Treatment of Technological Change* (Cambridge: MIT Press, 1969).
Park, W. G. and A. Wagh, 'Index of Patent Rights', in *Economic Freedom of the World: 2002 Annual Report* (Vancouver: Fraser Institute, 2002).
Romer, P., 'Endogenous Technological Change', *Journal of Political Economy*, 98 (1990), S71–102.
Sakakibara, M. and L. Branstetter, 'Do Stronger Patents Induce More Innovation? Evidence from the 1988 Japanese Patent Law Reforms', *RAND Journal of Economics*, 32 (2001), 77–100.
Scotchmer, S., 'Standing on the Shoulders of Giants: Cumulative Research and the Patent Law', *Journal of Economic Perspectives*, 5 (1991), 29–42.
Shapiro, C., 'Navigating the Patent Thicket: Cross Licenses, Patent Pools, and Standard Setting', *Innovation Policy & the Economy*, 1 (2000), 119–50.
Trajtenberg, M., 'A Penny for Your Quotes: Patent Citations and the Value of Innovation', *RAND Journal of Economics*, 21 (1990), 172–87.
World Bank, 'Intellectual Property: Balancing Incentives with Competitive Access', in *Global Economic Prospects* (Washington, DC: World Bank, 2001).
Yang, G. and K. Maskus, 'Intellectual Property Rights, Licensing, and Innovation in an Endogenous Product Cycle Model', *Journal of International Economics*, 53 (2001), 169–87.

Part III

Innovation Management and Intellectual Property Rights

7
What Is Different About Innovation in Asia?

Arnoud De Meyer and Sam Garg

7.1 Introduction[1]

East Asia, a group of countries including the ASEAN group as well as Taiwan, South Korea and China[2] have witnessed a high economic growth during the 1980s and the first half of the 1990s. It has been convincingly argued that this economic growth was fuelled by adding foreign direct investment to a large pool of local, often highly skilled labour. But it has become clear that this formula has reached its limits (Lingle, 1997; Krugman, 1994), particularly after the financial crisis of 1997–9. Moreover, the emergence of China as a manufacturing base for the world and the recent developments in India in particular in the service industries have rendered it improbable for most companies operating from East and South East Asia to pursue a competitive strategy exclusively based on low prices and thus low production factor costs. One can expect that China, and in a later stage India, will be the major sources of low-cost production for the rest of the world (Clarke, 1999). Even if the labour costs rise in the coastal provinces of China or the main cities of India, there will always be a pool of cheap labour a little bit further into the inner provinces and the countryside. China and India will remain exporters of price deflation for many years to come. Most economic commentators argue thus that a macroeconomic strategy based on capital injection to leverage the available workforce will not be sufficient any more and that East and South East Asian countries and their companies will have to invest in the development of new products, services and processes (APO, 2003; Wolff and Yoshida, 2001).

Being successful with innovations requires more than originality and good luck. Since the early 1970s in the USA and Europe, and since the mid-1980s in Japan, scholars and practitioners have developed empirically supported lessons about how to manage innovation (Shavinina, 2003). On many of the occasions that one of the authors was involved in executive programme or lecture series for Asian audiences to discuss these lessons, we often heard Asian managers argue that the application of these lessons in Asia may well be different. The argument was not that the lessons did not apply, but rather that the specific circumstances in East Asia were such that the implementation would be radically different. Some scholars have put forward similar arguments. Couchman *et al.* (1999) argue that there is diversity in the way concepts like concurrent engineering are implemented, and illustrate this with data from Australia and Indonesia. Tang and Yeo (2003) and Hsu and Chen (2003) describe some of the specifics of the innovation systems in, respectively, Singapore and Taiwan. Zain *et al.* (2002) compare innovation management between the German and Malaysian subsidiaries of a European multinational and find that both subsidiaries follow similar innovation processes, but that different types of problems and critical success factors were applicable to both subsidiaries. The Malaysian subsidiary faced more behavioural problems, while the German subsidiary encountered more technical problems.

In this chapter we want to report on a study of how the implementation of innovation management concepts is indeed different in Asia.

7.2 The Research Project

How did we proceed? In a first phase of the research we went out to gather information about innovation management in Asia through interviews with privileged observers, such as scholars, leaders of innovative firms and policy-makers. The information gathered through these interviews was complemented with extensive desk research. We collected files on about 30 innovative firms or innovative clusters and for each of these cases we explored what could be the differences in implementation of innovation management lessons between Asia and the industrialized world. The preliminary results of this study were reported in De Meyer and Garg (2004a) and are extensively described and commented on in De Meyer and Garg (2005). They provided a large number of hypotheses about innovation management in Asia that could be classified in five different categories. In a second step, we developed on the basis of this exploratory study a questionnaire, which was sent to a wide group of senior managers in East and South Asia. In particular we translated the hypotheses developed during the first phase into 34 statements about innovation in Asia. These statements were then submitted to a panel of senior managers operating in Asia in order to get their opinion on how they influenced, positively or negatively, the practice of innovation management in Asia. The detailed analysis and results are reported elsewhere (De Meyer and Garg, 2004b). Here we limit it to a summary.

7.3 What Did We Learn from the Case Files?

Before we address some of the preliminary results of the exploratory study we need to state an important caveat. We did not study, either through the case studies or through the desk research, breakthrough innovations. In most of the cases we observed opportunistic adaptations of products or services to the local markets, or exploitation of local market advantages. For example, we studied the case of Banyan Tree Hotels and Resorts, a Singapore-based chain. It would be difficult to argue that such a chain of luxurious and well-located holiday resorts is a breakthrough innovation. But what this company has done is to redefine completely what the customer will experience during a long weekend in one of its resorts. This redefinition puts the emphasis on the individual experience under the aptly chosen slogan 'a sanctuary for the senses' and takes advantage of the quite exquisite physical environment of some Asian islands, as well as the image of personalized service that is often identified with Asia. In this way the company offers a new value proposition in the way our colleagues Kim and Mauborgne (1997) define value innovation.

It very quickly became obvious to us that many of the lessons we have learned over the last 30 years about innovation management do apply in Asia. For example, the case of 'MyWeb.com' (De Meyer and Chua, 2000), a small producer of electronic set-top boxes which enabled access to Internet via TV monitors, is an almost classic story of an entrepreneurial venture; the company's demise was largely due to the same reasons why start-ups go under anywhere in the world. Likewise, the efforts that Banyan Tree Hotels and Resorts put into brand building are largely similar to those one would find elsewhere in the world for a small organization.

But that is not the point of this chapter. Here we will look at what the additional hurdles can be for an innovator operating in Asia. As we said, we could classify our empirical findings based on the case files in five broad categories. In the following paragraphs we will detail these.

Table 7.1 Number of engineers and scientists in R&D per million persons in some selected countries

Country	Engineers per million
China	459
Japan	4960
Korea	2138
Singapore	3282
Hong Kong	93
Thailand	102
India	158
USA	4103

Source: World Bank, 2002.

Inadequate resources

Contrary to what one may perceive when one is confronted with the absolute numbers of populations or engineers and scientists in China, India or South East Asia, there is quite a dearth of capable technologists in many of these countries when it comes to innovation. In Table 7.1 we have listed the number of engineers and scientists active in R&D per million people and this based on data provided by the World Bank for 2002. It is noticeable that the number of engineers employed in R&D, while large in absolute terms, is still low in proportion to the total population in countries like China, Thailand, Indonesia or India in comparison with Japan or the United States. Even in Korea we still have a significantly lower number of engineers compared to these two countries. And what is equally important is that while we do not have hard data on the qualifications of the technical staff, we got the impression through the interviews that companies in Asia are confronted, on top of the shortage, with a lack of quality of training.

Engineering capability is one aspect of resources. Finance is another. Several times it was explained to us that the Asian financial markets simply miss the sophistication and the willingness to invest in innovation. Risk management is not one of the strengths of Asian financial institutions and the consequence of this is a lower propensity to invest in innovative projects. While this difference may seem small, it can have a significant effect on international competition.

A third area where they may be a lack of resources is in the field of design. Chinese clothes producers lack the basic skills to come up with attractive designs, even for the taste of the local population. As a consequence, they still use, to a large extent, expensive Western designers (Plafker, 2004).

Beyond the human and financial resources we discovered two resources related to what one might call an inadequate mindset. You may correctly argue that a mindset is not a resource in the traditional sense of the word, but we think that the right mindset is a condition for successful innovation and can thus be considered to be a sort of resource.

First, many of the managers in Asia, in particular the ones that have been successful in the past, have a clear mindset that drives them in the direction of cost reduction, as opposed to new value creation. They simply have been very successful with it in the past, and often perceive low labour cost and access to cheap natural resources as the cornerstone of their competitive advantage. Making the mental switch from being a receiver of technology and a producer for a principal in the industrialized world towards assuming the role of a proactive innovator for local and international markets is not an obvious move for them.

Second, many Asian managers still think too often in terms of product and natural resources as opposed to process capabilities maps (De Meyer *et al.*, 2005). Asian firms are used to getting blueprints of products that they need to build for a principal somewhere else in the world. Their business model is based on recombining and producing existing products and components. Innovators often have to recombine their process capabilities in order to design and develop new solutions for new needs.

The difference between the early chip factories in Singapore and Taiwan can illustrate this. In Singapore the chip-making industry bought turnkey factories but there was little local knowledge about the intricacies of wafer production. In Taiwan the wafer production was often developed by engineers who had spend the better part of their professional life in the United States working for US companies and who had developed an intimate knowledge about the production processes. The first group thought in terms of products and off-the-shelf technology. The second group had a clear map of the process capabilities needed to have a continuous evolution of wafer production. It is the second group that has been more successful in the short and medium term in rolling out innovations.

Ineffective market input

We found that for Asian companies the application of good marketing concepts becomes a challenge because of the geographical distance from sophisticated and trend-setting markets, as well as the lack of reliable market data. More specifically we found the following:

- The average Asian company has a limited understanding of, or experience with, marketing. Many of the companies in our sample, whether it is the automotive producer Aapico, Shin satellite in Thailand or Biocon (De Meyer and Bhardwaj, 2003b) in India, had excellent technological capabilities but little knowledge about brand building, developing sophisticated distribution channels or even advertising.
- A substantial disadvantage for innovation by Asian companies is that they are quite far removed from the sophisticated consumer markets in industrialized countries. Japan, which has been the trend-setting market for Asia, the United States or some of the leading markets in Europe are all geographically very far away; also in a cultural sense they are very distant. Asian companies need to have an extremely long marketing arm to be able to tap into the intimate market knowledge that is needed to develop new products or services.
- Let us not underestimate the fact that there are sophisticated local markets in development. Singapore, Hong Kong or Taipei offer lots of opportunities for fashion designers. Manila is by far the most sophisticated market in the world for Short Message Service (SMS) as we described in the case 'Pinoy2Pinoy' (De Meyer and Bhardwaj, 2003a). But these markets are often still embryonic and not mature enough to be a source for products that can be rolled out worldwide.
- Many of the Asian markets are still quite closed, if not parochial. There are historical reasons for that. Quite a few Asian nations have had a less than happy relationship with each other in the past or are culturally quite far apart from each other. The differences between Buddhist Thailand and Muslim Malaysia are quite substantial. And the historic differences between China and Japan still influence the buying patterns in both countries (Klein and Ettenson, 2000). This renders it perhaps more difficult to develop Asian products for Asian wide markets.
- Finally, there is an absolute lack of reliable market data. In many cases it just isn't there. In other cases it may be available, but no one trusts its. The lack of accuracy on market data and the simplistic way of collecting it in China has been well documented. We found that most of the time companies had no good market data available.

The strong historic role of the government hinders true innovation

Virtually all Asian governments have played and play a strong role in the development of the local economy. Governments have chosen, in the past, sectors in which they wanted their national champions to be present. More often than not they have an important stake in the leading companies, either through direct participation in the equity or by having a strong voice in their management. This may have been an appropriate policy for economies that needed to catch up or for companies that were acting as a sub-contractor for principals in other parts of the world. But when it comes to driving innovation this is definitely less indicated. Nowhere in the world do governments have a particularly good track record in choosing winners in terms of innovation. And if the innovative companies are independent from the government they are confronted with the following additional hurdles:

- The regulatory environment favourable to innovators and entrepreneurship is often lacking: innovators need good IPR protection and, in particular, the enforcement of these rights; they need also legislation that enables the fast creation of companies, but if the innovation is not successful they equally need legislation that allows them to stop the business in an efficient and clean way.
- The public sector is, in many Asian countries, still one of the most important purchasers. Local governments tend to be conservative in their procurement and do not favour local innovators over well-established international brands.
- Pro-business policies and regulations have often favoured local entrepreneurs that took advantage of information asymmetry through their good contacts with the government: they did not need to innovate, simply to set up shop and create jobs. Favouring insiders with trade protection and insider information does not favour necessarily innovative developments.

Perception of a certain 'Asianness'

Some aspects that are associated with Asia or Asian cultures impede innovation or make it more difficult to penetrate new markets with Asian innovations. First, there is the structure of local companies. We do not want to make sweeping generalizations, but we have observed that in many cases firms in Asia are either family owned or have a strong family culture. This leads to a certain level of authoritarianism, and organizations with quite subservient and sometimes disengaged employees. Authority is often delegated to a limited extent and the top, wanting to keep control over the firm, becomes a bottleneck in decision-making and the stimulation of creativity.

Second, Asian goods were often perceived in industrialized countries to be cheap goods. Asian factories were often seen as suitable for low-cost but also low-value work. This perception is still prevalent and in the interviews we were offered several anecdotes regarding how senior managers in European headquarters would confound the manufacturing capabilities of a Thai or Malaysian company with the stereotyped perceptions these managers had about holiday experiences they had enjoyed in those countries.

This perceived low quality in export markets is sometimes reinforced by a low self-perception by Asian companies. It may be a somewhat irrelevant example but we are still struck by the observation that in many Asian capitals the mannequins used in fashion houses have Caucasian traits (barring those countries where this is explicitly forbidden). This is an example to us of how Asian companies still don't see their own markets as mature and leading.

Finally, there is often a misunderstanding of what entrepreneurship really is. We were often told how great and strong the entrepreneurship is in the Chinese business world. But a careful examination of many success stories about Chinese entrepreneurship reveals that, in fact, these are often success stories about trading, exploiting information asymmetry (which is sometimes a nice expression for unhealthy collusion between government and business) and real estate deals. There is definitely nothing wrong with many of these activities, but they are not about value creation through innovative products and processes.

Lack of appreciation for intangibles

Finally, we observed in our discussions and case studies a very strong lack of appreciation for the intangible side of innovation: brand building is often neglected, or simply reduced to a name tag; lip service is paid to the protection of intellectual property rights, but nobody seems to care a lot about copying of software or other intangible content. While there are good Asian brands outside Japan, with the exception of Samsung none has made it to the top 100 brands in the world.

Only hard tangible products seem to have real value in many eyes. Perhaps it has something to do with the fact that till now Asian companies had a very strong negative trade balance concerning intellectual property rights. They had to pay the royalties and for the licences and they did not receive a lot. Appreciation for the intangibles may rise the moment these companies can get some benefit from it. In fact, that is what you see happening today in China or Thailand. This lack of a good IPR system is now felt throughout the region and countries like

Singapore have made it a policy to implement a tough IPR regime. Even China is moving towards better protection of IPR and is cracking down on fakes, from computer chips to life-saving medicines. The situation has become so bad for the Chinese government and its citizens (in particular in terms of health and safety) that the issue of IPR has been raised at the highest levels of government (Balfour, 2005).

A second aspect of this lack of appreciation for intangibles is the absence of good design capabilities. Asian companies invest in development, carry out marketing, apply the latest techniques of finance, but often do not have the design capabilities that help to set a product apart. Japan is currently developing as a design powerhouse in Asia and is determining the fashion and the trends. But in the rest of Asia, be it Seoul, Singapore, Hong Kong or Shanghai, there is no critical mass of good designers, be it within the companies or on a freelance basis (Plafker, 2004).

7.4 Confirming These Hypotheses Through Large-Scale Survey

The results of the case studies led to many hypotheses about what really hinders innovation management in Asia. But handling so many qualitative observations leads to incomprehensible results. It does not allow us to say which one is the most important, or whether some hurdles were more important for some groups and less for others. Therefore we decided to test some of these through a large-scale survey.

The results of the interviews were translated in 32 statements about the key success factors that would affect innovation management in a positive or negative way (see Table 7.2 for the full list). This was combined with a few questions about the company and the respondent, as well as a set of questions about the change in the competitive environment and the evolution of the need to innovate. The respondents were also given an opportunity to choose the top three challenges amongst those highlighted in 34 statements and highlight any other challenges not covered in 34 statements. Through a questionnaire we collected the opinion of 336 senior managers operating in Asia on the importance of each of the statements for innovation in Asia. The composition of the sample is described in Table 7.3.

We want to highlight two shortcomings of the sample. While it is reasonably diverse in terms of geography, there is perhaps an overrepresentation of respondents located in Singapore. But one should take into account that, in many cases, Singapore acts as a hub for the region.

Table 7.2 List of statements used in the survey

1. Disengaged and subservient employees
2. Over-reliance on creative improvisations
3. Insufficient project management capabilities
4. Greater emphasis on market share than on profitability
5. Quality of competitive intelligence
6. Stigma associated with failure
7. Quality of
   a. Engineers
   b. Designers
   c. Managers
8. Inadequate risk capital
9. Few role models of successful innovative companies in the country or the region
10. Quick imitation of innovative business models/products/services by competitors
11. Inapplicability of innovative management lessons from the West
12. Strong cost reduction attitude
13. Lack of pressure from financial markets
14. Unsophisticated existing customer base
15. Asian markets are either too small or too heterogeneous for profitable innovation
16. Lack of reliable marketing data
17. Inadequate access to significant number of 'early adopter' type of customers
18. Asian customers perceive the Western goods to be better than the Asian ones
19. Prospects of good growth for the company even without innovation
20. Inability to recombine/reconfigure existing capabilities into new products/services
21. Western markets look down on Asian products and services
22. Lack of involvement of Asian companies in setting up global standards
23. Lack of self-confidence of Asian employees in international business
24. Geographical distance with the Western markets makes it difficult to understand their needs
25. Mainstream international business media reporting in English tend to focus on negative Asian business news
26. Government intervention in business in the home country of your company
27. Strong and conservative public sector leaves few opportunities for private sector
28. Inadequate protection of intellectual property rights
29. Lack of strong brand
30. Conservative business partners
31. Lack of diversity in the workforce
32. Insufficient attention to details

Table 7.3 Sample composition

Descriptor	Percentage
Company headquarters (n = 336)	
Asian	57.4
Non-Asian	42.5
Title of respondent (n = 336)	
President, CEO, managing director	35.2
General management	29.2
Functional management	11.9
No answer	23.5
Industry composition (n = 335)	
Industry	48.8
Services	52.1
Geographical composition (n = 336) (of the location of the respondent)	
Singapore	34.2
Mainland China	10.4
Hong Kong	8.9
Malaysia	7.1
India	6.5
Korea	4.5
Thailand	3.0
Taiwan	2.7
Philippines	2.1
Sri Lanka	0.9
Pakistan	0.9
Others	2.7
Undetermined	16.1

Many regional headquarters are located in the city state. When a researcher wants senior managers to respond, one automatically ends up with many responses from a Singapore location.

Second, any questionnaire suffers from self-selection by the respondents. Most, if not all, of the respondents are of the opinion that innovation is becoming significantly more important in the competition than it used to be five years ago. We probably received proportionally more responses from managers interested in innovation than from those for whom innovation is still irrelevant. For our study this was an advantage rather than a disadvantage: we may assume that our respondents are more acutely aware of the hurdles and advantages for innovation in South East Asia.

Table 7.4 Perceived changes in the environment compared to five years ago

Score	Intensity of the competition	Current importance of innovation	Score	Frequency of innovation in the industry
Significantly higher	73%	56%	Very frequent	18%
Higher	22	35	Frequent	42
No difference	4	9		34
Lower	2	1		6
Significantly lower	0	0	Almost never	0
Mean	1.35	1.54		2.29

1: significantly higher/very frequent; 5: significantly lower/almost never.

How did we analyse the survey data?

For each of the 32 items and for the questions regarding the intensity of competition and the importance of innovation, we had asked the respondents to score on a scale from 1 (very negative effect on the innovation in your company) to 5 (very positive effect on the innovation in your company). We also asked the respondents to indicate their top three challenges. In Tables 7.5a and 7.5b one will find the top and bottom items for the two analyses.

In order to get a better grip on the data we applied two straightforward multivariate techniques. We reduced the number of 32 key influencing factors to a set of ten factors through a factor analysis with varimax rotation. The ten factors explain 58 per cent of the variance. The first five factors account for 40 per cent of the variance.

These factors can be interpreted as ten dimensions along which the senior managers that participated in the survey differed. Once we had these ten dimensions, we applied a cluster analysis to find four clusters of respondents that have common characteristics. We determined to cluster in four groups after inspection of the dendrogram. These four clusters can be seen as four groups of managers that have a common view on the problems they face with respect to innovation.

Results from the survey

Importance of innovation to the respondents

As an introduction to the questionnaire we asked a few questions about the current importance of innovation compared to the past and the changing competitive environment (Table 7.4). Our respondents argue that innovation is frequent in their industry, and that the intensity of the competition is significantly rising and innovation is currently significantly higher than it used to be five years ago. It was interesting to see that the three indicators are actually significantly correlated with each other. In other words, a higher intensity of competition leads to a stronger need to innovate and is actually also translated in a higher frequency of innovation. But it could also be seen from the attached importance that the frequency of innovation lags behind the intensity and importance of innovation, perhaps indicating the challenges of innovation.

Hurdles and success factors for innovation in Asia

In Tables 7.5a and 7.5b you will see the statements that describe the most positive and most negative influences on the management of innovation in Asia. In the first table you will find the ranking based on the individual scores for each of the statements. In the second table you will find the ranking on the basis of the answer to the question: which of these factors do you see as the most challenging?

As one would expect the two tables have some statements in common and some differences. Which factors have a negative impact on the ability to innovate? Insufficient project management capabilities, the inability to reconfigure existing capabilities of the company into new products or services and inadequate IPR protection stand out in both types of analysis. They are complemented with the negative impact of quick imitation of innovative products by competitors, weaknesses in

Table 7.5a Most positive and negative factors based on the individual scores of each item (on a scale from 1 to 5)

Most positive factors (or not hindering innovation)	**Most negative factors (or perceived to be a hurdle)**
Quality of managers	Quick imitation of innovative products by competitors
Quality of engineers	Inadequate protection of IPR
Quality of designers	Insufficient project management capabilities
Quality of competitive intelligence	Inability to reconfigure existing capabilities into new products
Asian customers perceive Western goods to be better than Asian ones	Unsophisticated existing customer base
Strong cost reduction attitude	Lack of reliable marketing data

Table 7.5b Most- and least-often cited factors as top three challenges for innovation (n = 290)*

Least-often cited top challenges	Most-often cited top challenges
Mainstream international business media focus on negative news from Asia	Disengaged employees Strong cost reduction attitude
Geographical distance with the Western markets	Insufficient project management capabilities
Asian consumers perceive Western goods to be better than the Asian ones	Inability to reconfigure existing capabilities into new products
Lack of pressure from financial markets	Inadequate IPR protection
Western markets look down on Asian goods	Inadequate risk capital

* The number of respondents is slightly lower than for the other questions. Not all respondents filled in the question about these three challenges.

marketing, lack of employee engagement for innovation, and insufficient risk capital.

And what is not a problem? The respondents seem to have fewer problems with the intrinsic quality of the people (and score themselves as managers as a strong positive factor) and don't seem to think that some of the statements that reflect an underdog mentality (e.g., negative reports by the business press, negative perceptions of Asian versus Western goods or distance from the markets) have a negative impact on the innovation process.

Something that seems difficult to explain is the ambiguous impact of a strong cost reduction attitude, which does not appear to be a negative factor when one looks at the individual scores of the 32 statements, but is cited among the top three hurdles to overcome. The reason is simple: the score on this item is strongly bi-modal, that is, some respondents consider it to be negligible while others see this as a very important hurdle for innovation. The same respondents who score it as an important hurdle mention it also consistently as one of the most important challenges.

We originally thought that the positive or negative impact of key factors for innovation would be perceived differently by managers depending on whether their companies have headquarters inside or outside Asia (described as Asian and non Asian companies). But we were wrong. There are not that many statements for which we find significant differences. We find only five items on which managers of Asian companies are significantly more positive than their counterparts from non-Asian companies:

- the negative impact of insufficient project management capabilities
- the degree to which Western management methods can be applied in Asia
- the negative influence of a cost reduction attitude
- the lack of reliable market data
- and the negative impact of inadequate IPR protection.

It does appear that the managers of non-Asian companies are a bit more negative about the management capabilities of their staff or of Asian management in general. But, all in all, the number of significant differences is really not high.

Understanding how the senior managers really differ in their opinion

Interpreting a list of 32 statements remains a laborious exercise and therefore we reduced them through an appropriate statistical technique to the underlying factors that really describe how the respondents have a different view on the difficulties of implementing innovation in Asia. We found ten underlying factors that explain the differences in opinion in our sample of 336 senior managers. In the order of decreasing importance, they are as follows:

1. The most important factor that explains the differences in how senior managers feel about the hurdles for innovation reflects the *absence of an environment in Asia in which it is easy to operate as an innovator.* It is a factor that combines the lack of market data or of trend-setting customers combined with the stigma associated with failure. These factors don't make it easy for some innovators to pursue their projects, while others don't seem to be bothered by it.
2. The second differentiating factor groups a few items that reflect the *underdog mentality* of the Asian company. To what extent are Asian companies involved in setting international standards? Do they lack confidence? Have they good market perception? Do they see the international business press as constantly negative about Asia? Again some managers see this as a real hurdle, while others don't seem to be affected.
3. The third differentiating factor is the one that groups *the lack of some knowledge resources,* for example, the lack of quality of knowledge workers or the lack of reliable competitive intelligence.

4. The fourth factor points at the *inertia that is created by the forces of tradition in Asian business.*
5. The next factor groups some items that have to do with the *lack of basic management models and lessons specifically applicable to innovation management in Asia.*
6. Two statements that reflect the *negative impact of government* compose the sixth factor.
7. A seventh factor reflects the fact that for some companies there is *no perceived need to innovate.*
8. The two statements composing the eighth factor reflect the *lack of external pressure and business rewards for innovation.*
9. Factor nine is related to *the lack of good market understanding.*
10. The last and tenth factor represents the negative impact on innovation of *the traditional cost reduction attitude.*

Once again, we wanted to know whether the significant differences that we observed in the original 32 items between respondents from Asian and non-Asian companies were confirmed in the ten factors. There is only one factor where there is a real difference: managers of non-Asian firms felt that the perceived need to innovate was lower than managers of Asian firms did. The important observation seems to us, however, that on the factors that explain the highest variance there is no difference between Asian and non-Asian managers.

Classifying the sample into groups

Having ten factors that explain the differences between the respondents, we can now explore to what extent the group of 336 respondents could be placed into groups with common characteristics. We found four distinct groups with strong common characteristics (Table 7.6).

Managers in the first group consider the lack of the existence of appropriate management methods and the lack of a perceived need to innovate to be important hurdles. But they think, on the other hand, that the underdog mentality, the inertia due to the traditional Asian approach to management and the lack of external rewards for innovation do not hinder them too much. This may suggest that this is a cluster of managers that see the major challenge for Asian innovation as the need to get incentives to innovate. They also require the development of appropriate innovation management methods. They can perhaps be seen as people who want to innovate but don't know-how and seem to be still at the beginning of the innovation journey. We will call them *innovation starters.*

Table 7.6 Innovation types

Type	Are having trouble with	But do have fewer problems with
Innovation starters	• appropriate management methods for innovation • lack of a perceived need to innovate	• underdog mentality • inertia due to traditional Asian management style • lack of external rewards for innovation
Tradition fighters	• underdog mentality • inertia due to traditional Asian management style	• availability of knowledge resources • lack of a perceived need to innovate
Poor in knowledge resources	• availability of knowledge resources	• appropriate management methods for innovation
Stuck in the muck	• external rewards for innovation • influence of the government • underdog mentality	• availability of knowledge resources • appropriate management methods for innovation • cost reduction attitude

The respondents in the second cluster feel positive concerning the support that the economic environment can provide for innovation. They have no problems with the availability of knowledge resources and don't feel so much constrained by a perceived non existing need to innovate. On the other hand, they feel somewhat negative about the underdog mentality and negative about the inertia created by the traditional Asian approach to management and a typical cost reduction attitude. They seem to believe one can easily innovate in Asia if one can overcome some of the traditional behavioural hurdles for innovation in Asia. They may well be those managers who are already innovating but feel they are constrained by some administrative heritage from the past both in their firm and in the environment. We will call this group the *tradition fighters*.

The third cluster scores average on most factors, except for two of them. They have no problems with the lack of appropriate management models, but they strongly feel that they do not have the right resources available in the firm. This group perceives themselves to be poor in knowledge competencies needed for innovation. We will call the respondents in this group the *poor in knowledge resources*.

The fourth and last cluster seems to believe they have the resources, understand the methods, and do not suffer too much from a cost reduction attitude. But they feel they need improvement on the innovative economic environment and a reduction of the underdog mentality. They believe that innovation is insufficiently rewarded, both in product and financial markets. They also feel negative about the influence of the government. In summary, they believe they can innovate but require the general environment to improve. They are, in some ways, the opposite of the first group. In one sense they are convinced they should and can innovate but blame the environment for creating hurdles. They are like a strong truck that can and wants to move but is somewhat stuck in the mud of the environment. Therefore we will call this group *stuck in the muck*.

Once again, we have analysed whether these clusters are influenced by the composition of the sample and once again we found that there was no influence on the belonging to a group dependent on whether the respondent came from a company with an Asian or non-Asian headquarters.

7.5 What Do We Do with These Results?

To summarize the results of this study:

- We can derive a set of factors that are specific to Asia and that influence the implementation of innovation management in Asia.
- Not all of our respondents have a similar opinion and there are ten consolidated factors along which managers in Asia differ in their opinion about innovation management.
- Contrary to what we expected in the interpretation of these factors there are only minor differences between managers from Asian and non-Asian companies; we admit that our prior expectation was that managers from Asian and non-Asian companies would have a different view on management of innovation. It turns out that the differences are minimal, and, in general, managers from Asian companies are slightly more positive about the environment and about the capabilities of their staff.
- Not all companies/respondents see the importance of the factors specific to Asia in the same way and we were able to determine a typology of four groups of companies/respondents: cluster 1 – the innovation starters; cluster 2 – the tradition fighters; cluster 3 – the poor in knowledge resources; and cluster 4 – the stuck in the muck.

Different attitudes towards the difficulties of managing innovation require different solutions. For management educators and policy-makers it may be worthwhile to understand that the four groups require different types of support. The first group does not blame the environment, but does not know yet very well how to innovate. This group probably needs more basic management education on innovation and project management. The second group feels the burden of the traditional Asian heritage. They need to be able to escape this tradition and perhaps the infusion of new employees coming from different environments can help them. The third group needs access to knowledge resources. They need engineers, designers, managers and knowledge. They may benefit from initiatives by the government or private organizations that enable technology and people transfer. The fourth group thinks they can innovate but feel the environment is not right. They are the ones that may request changes in government policies that enable innovative behaviour.

Notes

1. This chapter is based to a large extent on De Meyer and Garg (2005), Chapter 3.
2. On purpose we leave Japan out of this analysis. Japan is long since an industrialized nation with a strong track record in innovation management and thus very different from the other Asian nations.

References

APO (Asian Productivity Organization), 'Entrepreneurship and innovation in the knowledge-based economy: challenges and strategies', APO, TAIPEI, Republic of China, 2003.

Balfour, F., 'Fakes!', *Business Week*, February 7 (2005), 44–51.

Carney, M. and E. Gedajlovic, 'East Asian Financial Systems and the Transition from Investment-driven to Innovation-driven Economic Development', *International Journal of Innovation Management*, 4(3) (2000), 253–76.

Clark, K. B. and T. Fujimoto, *Product Development Performance, Strategy, Organisation and Management in the World Auto Industry* (Boston: HBS Press, 1991).

Clarke, T., 'Pacific Paradigms', *Creativity and Innovation Management*, 8(1) (1999), 1–7.

Couchman, P. K., R. Badham and M. Zanko, 'Improving Product Innovation Processes: Moving Beyond Universalistic Prescription to Encompass Diversity', *Creativity and Innovation Management*, 8(1) (1999), 28–36.

De Meyer, A. and S. Bhardwaj, 'Pinoy2Pinoy', INSEAD case study, Fontainebleau (2003a).

De Meyer, A. and S. Bhardwaj, Biocon, INSEAD case study, Fontainebleau (2003b).

De Meyer, A. and C. H. Chua, 'MyWeb.com: Bringing the Internet to the Living Room (A1)', INSEAD case study, Singapore (2000).

De Meyer, A. and S. Garg, 'Innovation Management in Asia: Some Preliminary Findings', in S. Albe (ed.), *Cross Functional Innovation Management: Perspectives from Different Disciplines* (Munich: Gabler, 2004a).

De Meyer, A. and S. Garg, 'What makes the implementation of Innovation Management in Asia Different?', INSEAD working paper 2004/81/ABCM/TM (2004b).

De Meyer, A. and S. Garg, *Inspire to Innovate: Management and Innovation in Asia*, (London: Palgrave Macmillan, 2005).

De Meyer, A., P. Mar, F. J. Richter and P. Williamson, *Global Future: The Next Challenge for Asian Business* (New York: Wiley, 2005).

De Meyer, A., P. Williamson and C. H. Chua, 'Banyan Tree Resorts and Hotels: Building an International brand from an Asian Base', INSEAD case study, Singapore (2003).

Hsu, C. W. and H. H. Chen, 'The Taiwan Innovation System', in L. V. Shavinina (ed.), *The International Handbook on Innovation* (Oxford: Elsevier Science, 2003), 976–99.

Kim, W. C. and R. Mauborgne, 'Value Innovation: the Strategic Logic of High Growth', *Harvard Business Review*, 78(1) (1997), 102–13.

Klein, J. and R. Ettenson, 'Branded by the Past', *Harvard Business Review*, 78(6) (2000), 28.

Krugman, P., 'The Myth of Asia's Miracle', *Foreign Affairs*, 73 (1994), 62–78.

Lingle, C., *The Rise and Decline of the Asian Century* (Hong Kong: Asia 2000, 1997).

Nakamura, L., 'Intangibles: What Put the New in the New Economy?', *Federal Reserve Bank of Philadelphia Business Review*, July–August (1999), 3–17.

Nonaka, I. and H. Takeuchi, 'The New New Product Development Game', *Harvard Business Review*, 64(1) (1986).

Plafker, T., 'Can Chinese make the big leap onto the world stage of design?', *International Herald Tribune*, 12 October (2004), 14.

Redding, S. G., *The Spirit of Chinese Capitalism*, (New York: De Gruyter, 1990).

Rothwell, R., C. Freeman, A Harlsley, V. T. P. Jarvis, A. B. Robertson and J. Townsend, 'SAPPHO Updated – Project SAPPHO phase II', *Research Policy*, 3 (1974), 258–91.

Shavinina, L. V. (ed.) *The International Handbook on Innovation* (Oxford: Elsevier Science, 2003).

Singh, A., 'Savings, Investment and the Corporation in the East Asian Miracle', *The Journal of Development Studies*, 34(6) (1998), 112–38.

Tang, H. K. and Yeo K. T., 'Innovation under Constraints: The Case of Singapore', in L. V. Shavinina (ed.), *The International Handbook on Innovation* (Oxford: Elsevier Science, 2003), 873–81.

Wolff, M. F. and P. G. Yoshida, 'Asian Economies Striving to Enhance Innovation Capabilities', *Research Technology Management*, 44(1) (2001), 2–7.

World Bank, *World Development Indicators*, (2002), World Bank, 932.

Zain, M. M., 'Innovation Implementation in Malaysian Firms: process, problems, critical success factors and working climate', *Technovation*, 15 (1995), 375–85.

Zain, M. M., S. Richardson and M. N. Khan Adam, 'The Implementation of Innovation by a Multinational Operating in Two Different Environments: a Comparative Study', *Creativity and Innovation Management*, 11(2) (2002), 98–106.

8
How Do the Speed, Science Linkage, Focus and New Entry Matter in IT Inventions?

Sadao Nagaoka

8.1 Introduction

This paper examines the speed, science linkage and focus of corporate R&D, as well as new entry matter, as the determinants of R&D performance of the IT (information technology) sector,[1] and discusses the recent R&D performance of US, Japanese and European firms from this perspective. We use the number of (forward) patent citations per patent and the number of patents as the performance measures of R&D, both based on US patents. Past studies suggest that the patent citation provides very useful information on the value of patents.[2] In particular, citation per patent of a firm is significantly correlated with its market value (Deng *et al.*, 1999; Hall *et al.*, 2000; Hirschey and Richardson, 2001, 2004; and Nagaoka, 2005). Given the extreme heterogeneity of the value of patents (see, for example, Scherer and Harhoff, 2000), it is important to use both quality and quantity measures of patents in assessing the R&D performance of a firm. The R&D performance of US firms in the IT sector improved significantly relative to the rest of the world in the 1990s in both of these two respects. The average citation per patent of the US firms is 28 per cent higher than that of the Japanese firms for the patents granted for the 1983–7 period, but it is 73 per cent higher than that of the Japanese firms for the patents granted for the 1993–7 period (see Figure 8.1).[3] The patent share of the US firms also increased in the 1990s, reversing the declining trend of the 1980s.

There are several (complementary) factors or hypotheses which may explain the above improved R&D performance of US firms. One is improved management practices and organizations by US firms, which would include more emphasis on the speed of doing business (including R&D), in the face of tougher market competition. For example,

Rosenbloom and Spencer (1996) give a detailed account of the reforms of the corporate research system in US firms, making corporate research more integrated into the value chain of a firm and making efficient use of external research resources, among others. Many US firms also have chosen to focus their business in the widespread trend for vertical disintegration in such industries as computers, semiconductors and telecommunications. Another important development would be an increasing dependence of IT industry innovation on scientific research. Increasing dependency of industrial innovation on scientific progress has clearly played an important role in the biotechnology industry, but it may also have been an important factor in the IT industry, especially in the area of software, as illustrated by the growth of such university-based firms as Qualcomm and Rambus. Given the stronger research capabilities of US universities and stronger linkage between industry and universities in the US, such change in the nature of innovation might have contributed to the better performance of R&D by US firms. A closely related factor is the entry of many new technology firms in the US. The contribution of small firms to the aggregate R&D expanded significantly in the US in the 1990s.[4]

In this paper, I attempt quantitatively to assess the significance and the contribution of the above four factors as the determinants of R&D performance, building on my earlier work (Nagaoka, 2004). Patent information provides important verifiable and comparable facts on the management of R&D, the data of which are often inaccessible through the other means. The time lag between a patent and its prior patent literature, which is referred to as technology cycle time by CHI research, indicates how long a firm takes to assimilate prior technological information and to undertake its inventions. Thus, we can use it as a measure of the speed of R&D, which would be one of the most important factors determining the R&D performance of a firm. The frequency of the references by a patent to scientific journals would provide very crude but important information on the absorptive capability of firms to exploit knowledge published in the scientific community, since a firm with high capability of this nature would utilize possible inventions, using extensively the knowledge disclosed in scientific journals. The degree of the concentration of the patent portfolio of a firm could be used to measure how much a firm focuses its research.

This paper introduces three new dimensions into analysis, compared to my earlier work (Nagaoka, 2004), while focusing on IT technologies. First, it assesses how new entrants have performed relative to incumbents. New entrants in this paper are defined as the firms which are the major patentees in the recent period (1998–2002) but which do not have patents granted in the earlier periods of our database. As pointed out in the above, such firms seem to have played a major role in IT innovations, especially in the USA. Second, it assesses the impacts of R&D management on both the quality and the number of patents. Third, it assesses how the effects of the above key variables differ, depending on whether a firm is a producer of IT products or its user.

The patent data we use for our analysis are from the firm-level US patent data as constructed by CHI research (see Section 8.4 for more details).[5] IT patents in this paper consist of the patents in the following four technology areas: computers and peripherals, semiconductors and electronics, office equipment and cameras, and telecommunications (see Table 8.A1 for technology classification).[6] Japanese and US firms account for 80 per cent of the total IT patents in the database, while the European firms account for 10 per cent of the total patents. Given the general nature of IT inventions, firms with a variety of industry classifications engage in IT inventions. I classify them into the following three sectors: the IT core sector, whose main business is the R&D and production focusing on the above IT products; IT-incorporating machinery firms; and other IT-using firms. In particular, the IT core sector covers firms in the computer, semiconductor, electronic and telecommunications industries, which engage in the production of hardware, 'such as semiconductors, computers and communication equipment,' and software (see Table 8.A1 for industry classification). The share of IT patents in the total number of the patents of each of these four industry sectors exceed 60 per cent. The IT-incorporating machinery sector covers the firms in electrical machinery, general machinery and the instruments and optical industry, which extensively incorporate IT products in their fields. The remaining IT-using firms cover all other firms that use IT either for process or product, excluding universities, government agencies and other organizations with no single industry classification (see Table 8.A1). The IT core firms, IT-incorporating machinery firms and the other IT-using firms account for 68 per cent, 22 per cent and 9 per cent respectively of the IT patents granted in the database (see Figure 8.2).

A major issue in the evaluation of the performance of R&D management is the endogeneity of the measures in practice. For example, in those technology areas in which technical progress is rapid or demand growth is high, many citations will be made to the existing patents, due to the emergence of a larger number of potentially cited patents. Simultaneously, the R&D speed of a firm would be high in those technology areas. We extensively control such endogeneity by introducing as independent variables the numbers of potentially cited patents (total patents as well as own patents) and technology by time period dummies (1983–7, 1988–92, 1993–7 and 1998–2002), as well as by using fixed effects estimation.

The organization of the paper is as follows. In section 8.2, I present a summary picture of the R&D performance by the nationality of firms as well as by the four major determinants of R&D performance (speed of R&D, science linkage, focusing versus diversification in research, and new entry). In section 8.3, I describe econometric specification and in section 8.4 I present the estimation results. In section 8.5 I discusses the R&D performance of national firms and section 8.6 concludes.

8.2 Overview of the Firm-level R&D Performance and its Determinants

Performance of firms by three regions

Let us look at the overall performance of Japanese, US and European firms in IT inventions for the last two decades. Figure 8.1 summarizes the performances of these firms in terms of the number of citations per patent and the number of patents granted. According to the first measure (citations per patent until the end of 2002 relative to the global average), the performance of the Japanese firms deteriorated over time, while that of US firms improved, with the exception of the most recent period (note that there is a substantial bias towards mean for the index in the most recent period, due to the truncation of the citing period). That of the European firms remained roughly constant. According to the second measure (the share of the patents in the global totals), the US share followed the U-shape pattern and increased from 42.1 per cent to 43.0 per cent in the entire period, while the Japanese share followed the inverted U-shape and decreased from 38.9 per cent to 36.4 per cent in the entire period.[7] The share of European firms declined. Thus, the patenting performance of the US firms relative to the Japanese firms looks to have improved in both quantity and quality in IT areas.

Let us turn to the IT invention performance of three types of inventing firms. As shown in Figure 8.2, IT core firms have the highest average forward citations per patent. Such advantage of IT core firms seem to have increased (note again that the truncation reduces the variation across sectors for the last period). In addition, the patent share of IT core firms has expanded significantly over the last 20 years, from 52 per cent to 73 per cent. On the other hand, the share of IT-incorporating machinery

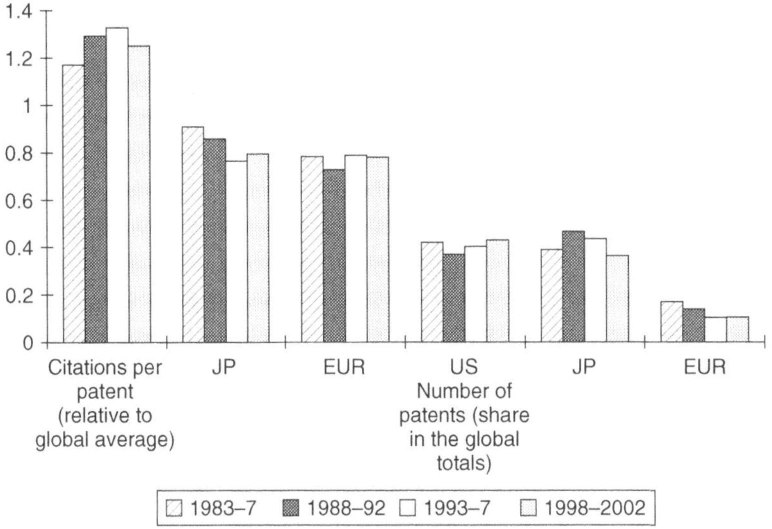

Figure 8.1 Performance of US, Japanese and European firms in IT

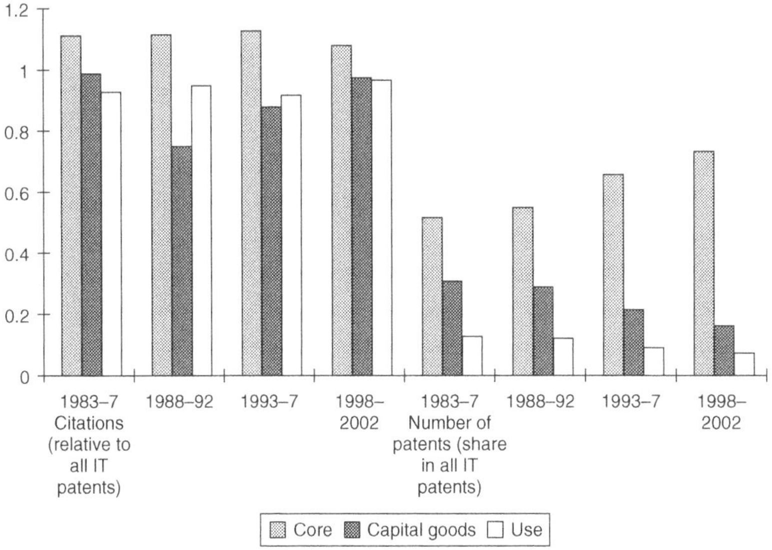

Figure 8.2 Performance of the core, capital goods and the other user industry in IT patents

sector (capital goods sector) declined significantly over time from 31 per cent to 16 per cent. Thus, it seems that there has been more specialization of IT inventions towards the IT core sector.

Speed of R&D and absorptive capability of a firm to use scientific knowledge

I expect that a firm with higher R&D speed will be able to obtain not only more patents but also higher quality patents, since a priority rule governs the patent race. Under the priority rule, only the firm which is the first in invention can obtain a patent and the scope of its patent right is bounded by the prior state of art, which is available when the patent is filed for. I use the average citation lag of the patents granted to a firm in a given period (technology cycle time) as the measure of the speed of R&D of such firm. It is the average median age in grant years of the US patent references cited on the front page of the company's patents. As shown in Figure 8.3, a firm with short technology cycle time (that is, a firm fast in R&D) tends to have higher quality patents, irrespective of whether it has high science linkage or low science linkage.

I also expect that a firm with stronger capability to utilize scientific knowledge would be able to obtain patents with higher quality. The firm which has strong absorptive capacity with respect to science would enjoy the first mover advantage in R&D competition, enabling a firm

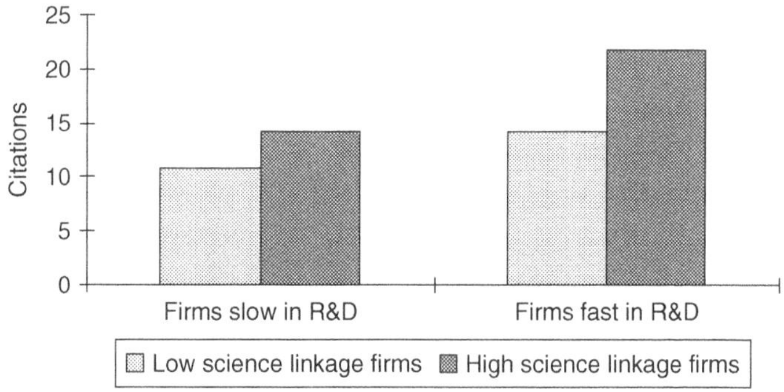

Figure 8.3 Speed, science linkage and quality of IT patents

Notes

(1) The firms fast in R&D belong to the top 25% in terms of the shortness of technology cycle time, and high science linkage firms belong to the top 25% in science linkage.

(2) Quality is measured by the forward citation per patent up to the end of 2002.

(3) US patents granted for 1988–92, excluding government agencies and universities.

to claim larger scope of its patent right. In addition, it may be able to produce more inventions exploiting the broad reach of scientific discovery. I use the average number of (backward) citations of science papers per patent with respect to the patents granted to the firms (science linkage indicator constructed by CHI research) as a measure of such capability.[8] Although the citation of science papers by a patent does not indicate the direct dependence of the patent on the referred science papers in invention process,[9] it would indicate the capability of a firm to engage in research where science is relevant. As shown in Figure 8.3, a firm with more science linkage tends to have higher quality patents irrespective of whether it is fast in R&D or slow in R&D.

Focus in research portfolio and new entrants

How broad a firm should make its research portfolio is a very important issue in R&D strategy. If the synergy among researches of different technology areas within a firm is important, the diversification of R&D portfolio may increase research productivity (for example, see Henderson and Cockburn (1996) for such evidence in the pharmaceutical industry). In addition, a firm may expand its R&D portfolio even if there is no direct synergy in R&D since there is a transaction cost advantage of owning complementary intellectual property rights within a firm. I measure the degree of the diversification of the research portfolio by the HHI (Hirshman-Herfindahl Index) of the patent portfolio of a firm. That is, it is the sum of the squared shares of the numbers of patents in each technology area in the total patents granted to a firm for a given period (see Table 8.A1 for technology classification). As shown in Figure 8.4, a firm with high focus tends to have high quality patents, both for the incumbent firms and for the new entrants in the period from 1988 to 1992. The incumbent firm have the patents granted in the 1983–7 period.

New entrants are often superior innovators, partly due to the selection reason that their successful entries and survival depend significantly on their technological advantage. In addition, many of the start-up firms in the USA are based on inventions in universities or on the use of tacit knowledge embodied in professors. Furthermore, start-up firms tend to have high-powered incentives such as a high proportion of management ownership, so that they have strong drive for efficiently pursuing R&D. Our database confirms these characteristics of new entrants. In this paper we define a new entrant as the firm which has become a major patentee by the 1998–2002 period, but does not have patents granted in earlier periods. As shown in Figure 8.5, the new entrants have

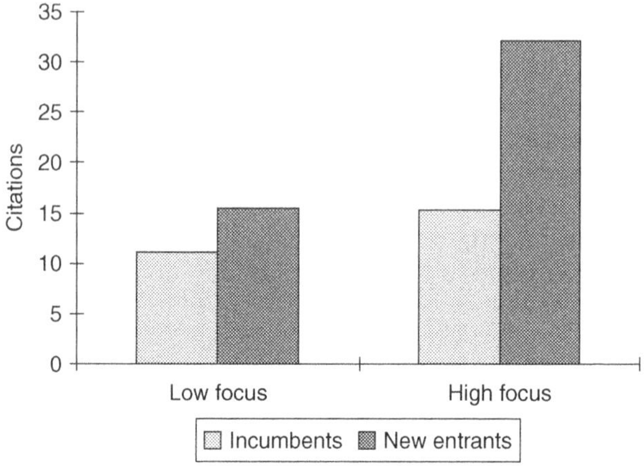

Figure 8.4 Focus, new entrants and quality of IT patents

Notes

(1) High-focus firms belong to the top 25% in terms of the HHI of the patent portfolio of a firm. New entrants are those firms which started to be granted patents in the period from 1988–92.

(2) Quality is measured by forward citation per patent up to the end of 2002.

(3) US patents granted for 1988–92, excluding government agencies and universities.

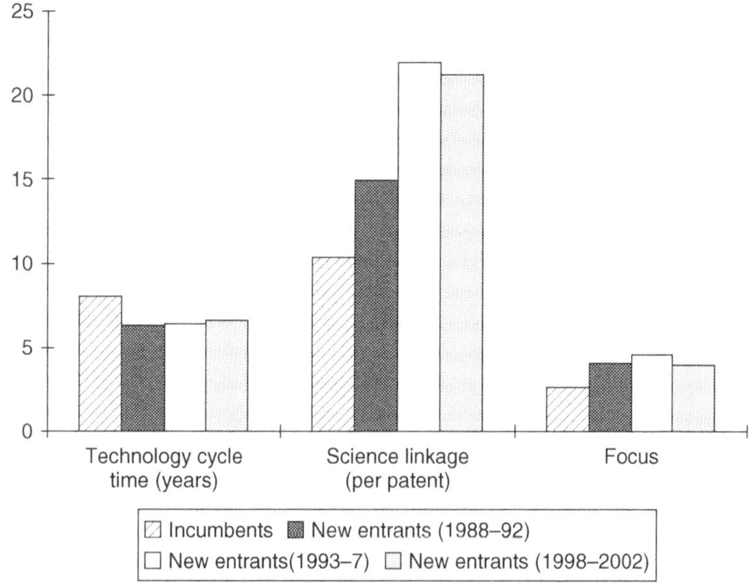

Figure 8.5 New entrants versus incumbents in IT inventions

Notes

(1) Patents granted during the 1988–2002 period.

(2) Science linkage is multiplied by 10 and focus is 1,000th of HHI in percentage.

significantly shorter technological cycle time, significantly higher science linkage and are significantly more focused than incumbents. As shown in Figure 8.4, a new entrant tends to have high quality patents, especially when they have strong focus.

Although the above figures seem to strongly suggest that the speed of R&D, science linkage, focusing of a firm and new entry do matter significantly in R&D performance, there is a possibility that they represent only spurious correlations, reflecting the effects of sector- or firm-level variables, which they do not control. The following sections examine whether these relationships survive, controlling sector- or firm-level missing variables, in particular, the firm-level fixed effects, which would include the firm size and the distinction between new entrants and incumbents.

8.3 Econometric Specification and Data

Econometric specification

I use the average number of citations received per patent until the end of 2002 (*cit*) and the number of patents granted (*pats*) as dependent variables. More specifically, the citation variable $cit_{i,k,t}$ indicates the average citations received per patent by the patents granted to firm *i* in technology area *k* in period *t*. It reflects not only the quality of the patents ($\theta_{i,k,t}$) but also the number of patents which potentially cite the patents through a citation function. I control the latter effect by including the number of the firm's patents (as well as the aggregate number of the patents of all firms) granted in technology area *k* in period *t* and thereafter.[10] I assume that the patent quality depends on the technology cycle time ($tct_{i,k,t}$) and the science linkage ($sci_{i,k,t}$) of firm *i* in technology area *k* in period *t* and on the degree of research focusing of firm *i* in period *t* ($focus_{i,t}$). In addition, I introduce the dummies ($dummies_{entrants,i}$) for the new entrants of the period *i* ($2 \leq i \leq 4$), which can control the sample selection bias when we use firm random-effects estimation. When we use firm fixed-effects estimation, we can avoid the bias of the estimations due to the correlation between firm-level missing variables and the independent variables, although the coefficients of these dummies of new entrants cannot be estimated. Similarly, I assume that the number of patents $pats_{i,k,t}$ granted to firm *i* in technology area *k* in period *t* depends on the speed, science linkage and focus variables of a firm.

I postulate the following functional form for the citation per patent of a firm.

$$\ln(1 + cit_{i,k,t}) = \alpha_1 \ln(1 + tct_{i,k,t}) + \alpha_2 \ln(1 + sci_{i,k,t})$$
$$+ \alpha_3 \ln(focusi_{i,k,t}) + \textstyle\sum_{l=1\sim 3}\alpha_{3+l}\, dummies_{entrants_l}$$
$$+ \textstyle\sum_l \beta_l \ln(1 + patsl_{i,k,t}) + \sum_l \delta_l \ln(1 + tpatsl_{k,t})$$
$$+ \gamma_1 dummies_{tech \times period} + \mu_{i,k}\,(or + \rho_{i,t}\, or + u_i) + \epsilon_{i,j,t} \quad (1)$$

This specification has the following three sets of control variables. First, it has a set of the variables which indicate the number of potentially citing patents. $patsl_{i,j,t}$ is the number of patents of firms i in technology area k which potentially cite its own patents granted in period t and which are granted to firm i in area k in period $(t + l)$. Similarly, $tpatsl_{k,t}$ is the total number of patents in technology area k which are granted in period $t + l$ and which potentially cite the patents of firm i in period k granted in period t. It aggregates the patents granted to all firms in the database in technology area k in period t. I expect that $patsl_{i,k,t}$ and $tpatl_{k,t}$ have positive signs. These variables can also control the truncation bias that more recently granted patents receive fewer citations due to the truncation of the citing period.

Second, I introduce the dummies for the changes of technology and market characteristics over time (that is, technology by period dummies: $dummies_{tech \times period}$). Sector-level technology and demand-side changes or variations favourable to corporate R&D would increase the R&D speed and the science linkage of the firms in that sector. They could also increase the citations received by such firms, since more R&D will be done and more patents will be granted in that sector. The technology by time dummies, together with the numbers of potentially citing patents, would help us to control the potential estimation biases due to these effects.

Third, I introduce three alternative firm-level fixed effects: firm by technology-fixed effects ($\eta_{i,k}$), firm by year-fixed effects ($\rho_{i,t}$) or firm-fixed effects (u_i). Firm by technology-fixed effects ($\eta_{i,k}$) represents the factors specific to each combination of firm and technology, which can control the missing variables specific to each technology area of a firm. In this case the coefficients estimated depend purely on the variation of the firm variables across four periods in four IT technology areas. Firm by period-fixed effects ($\rho_{i,t}$) controls the variation over time of the firm-specific factors, which can control the effects of firm-level missing variables which may change over time. In this case our coefficient estimation depends only on the variation of the firm variables across four IT technology areas. The firm-fixed effects (u_i) represent firm-specific missing variables constant over time, which may affect the quality of patent and may also have a correlation with the explanatory variables such as the technology cycle time and the science linkage of a firm. When I introduce firm-fixed effects, our coefficient estimation depends on the (within) variation of the firm variables over time and across four IT technology areas.

Let us turn the quantity equation. R&D expenditure clearly affects the number of patents granted and may have the correlations with science linkage and the other explanatory variables. Since I do not have R&D data for each sector of each firm, I control the potential bias due to the correlation between the firm-level missing variables including R&D expenditure and independent variables by using the above three fixed-effects estimations. Fixed-effects estimation prevents us from estimating the coefficients of new entry dummies in the quantity equation:

$$\begin{aligned} \ln(pats_{i,k,t}) = {} & \delta_1 tct_{i,k,t} + \delta_2 \ln(1 + sci_{i,k,t}) + \delta_3 \ln(focusi_{i,k,t}) \\ & + \gamma_1 dummies_{tech \times period} + \textstyle\sum_l \beta_l \ln(1 + patsl_{i,k,t}) \\ & + \textstyle\sum_l \delta_l \ln(1 + tpatsl_{k,t}) + \gamma_1 dummies_{tech \times period} \\ & + \eta_{i,k}(or + \rho_{i,t}\, or + u_i) + \varepsilon_{i,j,t} \end{aligned} \tag{2}$$

Dataset

All figures are from the firm-level US patent portfolio data as constructed by CHI research. There are 30 technology areas (see Table 8.A1 for the classification) and I focus on the patents in four IT-related areas (computers and peripherals, semiconductors and electronics, office equipment and cameras, and telecommunications). The database covers 1,484 major patentees belonging to 26 industrial sectors (see Table 8.A1 for the classification), although I exclude universities and government agencies from the sample for estimation. These firms are from 26 countries and account for 65 per cent of all US patents granted. Of these firms, 1,187 have IT patents. I use the data which are aggregated to the following four periods with five-year duration: 1983–7, 1988–92, 1993–7 and 1998–2002. See Table 8.A2 for the sample statistics used for estimations.

8.4 Estimation Results

Quality of patents (forward citations per patent)

Table 8.1 shows four estimation results, which control the effects of firm-level missing variables in a different manner and degree: firm by time-fixed effects, firm by technology-fixed effects, firm-fixed effects and no controls by firm-level-fixed effects except for new entrant dummies. Let us start with estimations 1 and 2, which are, respectively, based on the variation across technology areas and the variation across time. The coefficient estimates for technology cycle time and science linkage are very similar between these two estimations and highly significant (1 per cent level) in both estimations. That is, the results of estimation 1, which controls firm by time-fixed effects (such as the variation of R&D expenditures over time), suggests that a firm is able to obtain a higher quality patent in the technology area where it has a stronger advantage in terms of either higher speed of R&D (shorter technology cycle time) or stronger science linkage. Estimation 2, which controls firm by technology-fixed effects (such as the variation of R&D expenditures across technology areas), suggests that a firm which has strengthened such advantage over time has been successful in enhancing patent quality. Both estimations suggest that 10 per cent improvement of each indicator results in around 2 per cent more forward citations per patent for large values of technology cycle time and science linkage. Thus, both higher speed of R&D (smaller technology cycle time) and stronger science linkage help a firm to obtain patents with higher quality.

Let us turn to the effect of focus. Estimation 1 controlling firm by time-fixed effects is not able to identify such effect, since either variation across firms or variation over time is necessary for estimation. Estimation 2 estimates the coefficient of focusing, based purely on the variation over time. The estimated coefficient is positive but insignificant. Thus, focusing does not seem to have a strong effect on patent quality on the average for all sample firms (later I will present the results of estimations by sectors).

Let us move to estimations 3 and 4. Estimation 3 controls only firm-fixed effects and estimation 4 assumes random-firm effects. The last estimation allows us to evaluate the differentials for entrants relative to incumbents. The coefficients of technology cycle time and the science linkage in estimations 3 and 4 are highly significant and very similar to those for estimations 1 and 2, although we may not claim that the coefficients of these estimations are statistically identical.[11] Estimation 3 estimates the effect of focusing, using the variation across technology areas in addition to variation over time. Different from the results of estimation 2, the focus variable is positive and significant at 5 per cent level. Since the focus variable has the same value for all technology areas for a given firm and for a given period where a firm has at least one granted patent, what this estimation shows is that patent quality is higher in

Table 8.1 Estimation of patent quality equations for IT patents

	Estimation 1		Estimation 2		Estimation 3		Estimation 4	
	Firm by time-fixed effects		Firm by technology-fixed effects		Firm-fixed effects		Firm-random effects	
ln1cit	Coef.	Std err.	Coef.	Std err.	Coef.	Std err.	Coef.	Std err.
ln1tct	−0.179	0.020***	−0.182	0.021***	−0.181	0.017***	−0.179	0.016***
ln1sci	0.181	0.017***	0.155	0.018***	0.167	0.015***	0.180	0.013***
lnfocus			0.005	0.031	0.069	0.030**	0.112	0.019***
tentry2							0.163	0.049***
tentry3							0.127	0.063**
tentry4							−0.262	0.106**
ln1pats l0	0.087	0.009***	−0.027	0.012**	0.059	0.007***	0.063	0.007***
ln1pats l1	0.037	0.012***	0.022	0.008***	0.048	0.007***	0.053	0.007***
ln1pats l2	0.033	0.014**	0.000	0.008	0.020	0.008**	0.021	0.008***
ln1pats l3	−0.045	0.018**	−0.029	0.009***	−0.014	0.009	−0.012	0.009
ln1tpats l0			(dropped)		(dropped)		0.021	0.015
ln1tpats l1			0.086	0.005***	0.081	0.005***	0.071	0.005***
ln1tpats l2			0.045	0.004***	0.045	0.004***	0.046	0.003***
ln1tpats l3			0.024	0.004***	0.024	0.004***	0.023	0.004***
Technical areas by periods dummies	yes		yes		yes		yes	
	Number of observations 9,351 Number of groups 3,625		Number of observations 9,351 Number of groups 3,625		Number of observations 9,351 Number of groups 1,187		Number of observations 9,351 Number of groups 1,187	
	R-sq: within = 0.1248 between = 0.2112 overall = 0.1980 sigma_u = 0.834 sigma e = 0.546		R-sq: within = 0.6507 between = 0.3261 overall = 0.4725 sigma_u = 0.624 sigma e = 0.545		R-sq: within = 0.5816 between = 0.4365 overall = 0.5409 sigma_u = 0.471 sigma e = 0.583		R-sq: within = 0.5813 between = 0.4525 overall = 0.5461 sigma_u = 0.349 sigma e = 0.583	

Notes: *** significant at 1%; ** significant at 5%; * significant at 10%.

those sectors where there are more focused firms among the firms with non-negative number of patents. Estimation 4 shows that once we use cross firm variation, the focus variable becomes highly significant. The estimated coefficient is 0.16, implying that a firm with a single technology domain has 11 per cent higher quality than a firm with two technology domains. However, given the above finding that the variation over time (i.e., pure within estimation) does not yield a significant coefficient for the focus variable, we may not interpret such positive cross-section correlation to represent a causal relationship. It is more likely to represent the influences of the other firm-level missing variables, such as the size of complementary assets on patent quality and their positive correlation with the focus variable.

Let us examine the fixed effects of new entrants in terms of patent quality, using estimation 4. We have to bear in mind that the estimated coefficients may be somewhat biased, given the difference between the coefficients between estimation 2 and 4. The dummies for the entrants (*tentry2* and *tentry3*) in the second period (1988–92) and in the third period (1993–7) have highly significant positive coefficients. The negative coefficient of the dummy for the entrants in the final period (*tentry4*) is not surprising, since some of them started to be granted patents only in the midst of the period. These results indicate that new entrants have around 14 per cent higher citations per patent on average, controlling the effects of their higher level of R&D speed, their higher science linkage and their stronger focus (see Figure 8.4). Thus, a new entrant may have a significant technological advantage, on top of its higher speed of R&D and higher science linkage.

Table 8.2 reports the estimations in which the coefficients of the technology cycle time, science linkage and focusing are allowed to vary by types of IT-related firms. It uses the machinery sector, which incorporates IT products into machinery, as a benchmark. The most important finding is that the focus variable has a positive and highly significant coefficient only for the IT core sector,[12] even if we use only the variation over time for estimation. This implies that a firm which has chosen to narrow its focus in the IT core sector has been able to enhance the R&D quality significantly. The negative estimated coefficient of the focus variable for the other sectors may not be surprising, since a firm whose main business is not IT would have to undertake substantial R&D investments for IT in order to produce competitive inventions, on top of its R&D for its main business. Estimation 7, which uses cross-section variation across firms in addition to variation over time, shows a larger coefficient for the estimated effect of focusing in the IT core sector.

Table 8.2 Estimation of patent quality equations for IT patents by types of IT-related sectors

	Estimation 5		Estimation 6		Estimation 7	
	Firm by time-fixed effects		Firm by technology-fixed effects		Firm-fixed effects	
ln1cit	Coef.	Std err.	Coef.	Std err.	Coef.	Std err.
ln1tct	−0.179	0.047***	−0.118	0.053**	−0.142	0.041***
+ for IT core	−0.055	0.063	−0.131	0.069*	−0.102	0.054*
+ for IT use	0.061	0.055	−0.032	0.060	−0.006	0.047
ln1sci	0.242	0.046***	0.211	0.052***	0.234	0.041***
+ for IT core	−0.053	0.055	−0.112	0.061*	−0.072	0.048
+ for IT use	−0.052	0.052	−0.024	0.057	−0.060	0.045
lnfocus			−0.117	0.076	−0.100	0.076
+ for IT core			0.250	0.089***	0.327	0.089***
+ for IT use			0.054	0.093	0.075	0.093
ln1pats l0	0.088	0.010***	−0.030	0.012**	0.056	0.008***
ln1pats l1	0.037	0.012***	0.027	0.008***	0.052	0.007***
ln1pats l2	0.027	0.015*	−0.005	0.009	0.018	0.008**
ln1pats l3	−0.042	0.018**	−0.023	0.010**	−0.008	0.009
ln1tpats l0			(dropped)		(dropped)	
ln1tpats l1			0.084	0.005***	0.081	0.005***
ln1tpats l2			0.050	0.005***	0.047	0.004***
ln1tpats l3			0.020	0.004***	0.022	0.004***
Technical areas by periods dummies	yes		yes		yes	
	Number of observations 8,572		Number of observations 8,572		Number of observations 8,572	
	Number of groups 3,356		Number of groups 3,331		Number of groups 1,091	
	R-sq: within = 0.1253		R-sq: within = 0.6556		R-sq: within = 0.5871	
	between = 0.0897		between = 0.2049		between = 0.2156	
	overall = 0.1065		overall = 0.3484		overall = 0.2857	
	sigma_u = 0.8780		sigma_u = 0.807		sigma_u = 0.938	
	sigma e = 0.545		sigma e = 0.543		sigma e = 0.581	

Notes: *** significant at 1%; ** significant at 5%; * significant at 10%.

The second important finding is that the coefficient of the technology cycle time tends to be larger for the IT core sector, while that of science linkage tends to be smaller for the IT core sector. The difference is significant in estimation 6, although it is not significant in estimation 5. In summary, focusing looks to matter in the IT core sector and speed may also be significantly more important in this sector.

Number of patents

Table 8.3 shows three estimation results, which control firm by time missing variables, firm by technology missing variables or firm-level fixed effects. Since the size of a firm is a basic determinant of the number of patents granted and is very likely to be correlated with the rest of the explanatory variables, such as the focus of a firm, I did not use the random effects estimation. The coefficient estimates for technology cycle time and the science linkage of a firm are highly significant in all estimations. The estimated coefficients are relatively stable across estimations. Higher speed of R&D (smaller technology cycle time) and stronger science linkage help a firm to obtain more patents, irrespective of whether such variation is across technologies or across time. One-year reduction of technology cycle time results in 2 per cent more patents, while 10 per cent more science linkage results in around 3 per cent more patents for large values of science linkage. Thus, both higher speed and more science linkage improve the R&D performance in both quality and quantity.

On the other hand, the coefficient of focus is significantly negative in estimation 2 and 3 (1 per cent level). Thus, focusing looks to cause a smaller number of patents. This finding, together with the finding for patent quality, suggests the existence of a trade-off between quality and quantity in the choice of the scope of R&D by a firm.[13] If diversification affects the R&D efficiency, we may not observe the trade-off between the quantity and the quality of inventions. On the other hand, the appropriability advantage of diversification can explain such a trade-off. A diversified firm has broad business assets, which provide the advantage for appropriating returns from inventions. Thus, such a firm will seek a patent for a relatively low quality patent. That is, diversification causes a firm to patent lower quality inventions.

Table 8.4 reports the estimations which allow the coefficients of the technology cycle time, science linkage and focusing to vary by the types of IT-related firms, with the machinery sector incorporating IT as a benchmark, as in Table 8.2. These estimations show that technology cycle time and science linkage have significantly large coefficients for

Table 8.3 Estimation of patent quantity equations for IT patents

	Estimation 1		Estimation 2		Estimation 3	
	Firm by time-fixed effects		Firm by technology-fixed effects		Firm-fixed effects	
lnpats	Coef.	Std err.	Coef.	Std err.	Coef.	Std err.
tct	−0.015	0.004***	−0.018	0.003***	−0.015	0.003***
ln1sci	0.322	0.034***	0.231	0.026***	0.293	0.027***
lnfocus			−0.564	0.044***	−0.389	0.055***
Technical areas by periods dummies	yes		yes		yes	
	Number of observations 9,315		Number of observations 9,351		Number of observations 9,351	
	Number of groups 3,637		Number of groups 3,625		Number of groups 1,187	
	R-sq: within = 0.0290		R-sq: within = 0.2685		R-sq: within = 0.1093	
	between = 0.0603		between = 0.0117		between = 0.0163	
	overall = 0.0538		overall = 0.0509		overall = 0.0564	
	sigma_u = 1.366		sigma_u = 1.496		sigma_u = 1.240	
	sigma e = 1.104		sigma e = 0.7968		sigma e = 1.065	

Notes: *** significant at 1%; ** significant at 5%; * significant at 10%.

Table 8.4 Estimation of patent quantity equations for IT patents by types of IT-related sectors

	Estimation 4		Estimation 5		Estimation 6	
	Firm by time-fixed effects		Firm by technology-fixed effects		Firm-fixed effects	
lnpats	Coef.	Std. err.	Coef.	Std err.	Coef.	Std err.
tct	0.027	0.010***	−0.019	0.008**	0.007	0.008
+ for IT core	−0.082	0.013***	−0.018	0.010*	−0.066	0.010***
+ for IT use	−0.037	0.011***	0.006	0.009	−0.017	0.008**
ln1sci	0.126	0.094	0.114	0.076	0.071	0.075
+ for IT core	0.504	0.113***	0.428	0.089***	0.579	0.089***
+ for IT use	0.050	0.107	0.007	0.084	0.082	0.084
lnfocus			−0.480	0.111***	−0.374	0.140***
+ for IT core			−0.112	0.130	−0.010	0.163
+ for IT use			−0.110	0.137	−0.065	0.171
Technical areas by periods dummies	yes		yes		yes	
	Number of observations 8,572		Number of observations 8,572		Number of observations 8,572	
	Number of groups 3,356		Number of groups 3,331		Number of groups 1,091	
	R-sq: within = 0.0430		R-sq: within = 0.2845		R-sq: within = 0.1279	
	between = 0.0206		between = 0.0093		between = 0.0827	
	overall = 0.0265		overall = 0.0466		overall = 0.1088	
	sigma_u = 1.409		sigma_u = 1.547		sigma_u = 1.208	
	sigma e = 1.115		sigma e = 0.795		sigma e = 1.068	

Notes: *** significant at 1%; ** significant at 5%; * significant at 10%.

the IT core sector. The coefficient of focus for the IT core sector is larger but the difference is not significant. Thus, both speed and science linkage are most important in the IT core sector in generating patents.

8.5 Evaluation of the Sources of the Invention Performance of Firms by Regions

Then, let us turn to Figures 8.6 and 8.7 to see how the four determinants of invention performance have evolved for the firms in three regions. First, the advantage of the Japanese firms in the speed of R&D as measured by technology cycle time diminished substantially over the last two decades and has almost vanished relative to the US firms. The Japanese firms used to have substantially shorter technology cycle time in the 1983–7 period (6.2 years for the Japanese firms versus 7.6 years for the US firms and 7.9 years for European firms). However, the advantage of the Japanese firms relative to the US firms vanished completely by the 1998–2002 period (6.0 years for both Japanese and US firms and 6.4 years for European firms).

Second, the science linkage of the Japanese firms has remained the lowest by a substantial margin. Although the science linkage of the Japanese firms has strengthened over time, the gap between the Japanese firms and the US or the European firms remains large. Although the science linkage in the IT area is not high, compared to the biotechnology and pharmaceutical areas, it still matters significantly in determining the patent quality and quantity as shown in the above sections.

Third, the US and European firms in the IT core sector focused their research significantly in 1990s, and only slight focusing occurred in the case of the Japanese firms (see Figure 8.7). The average HHI for 1983–7 was 1,900 for both Japanese and European firms and was 2,200 for the US firms. The HHI for 1998–2002 was 2,200 for the Japanese firms, 3,600 for the US firms and 3,400 for the European firms. According to the finding in the above section (Tables 8.2 and 8.4), focusing by the US and European firms in the IT core sector should have resulted in the improvement of patent quality, although focusing also has the effect of reducing the patenting propensity.

Fourth, there have been substantially more entries of new firms in the US and Europe than in Japan. The new entrants for these two decades accounted for 8.1 per cent of the total patents of major US patentees and 6.2 per cent of that of the major European patentees in the most recent period. However, it accounted for only 0.25 per cent in Japan. Thus, the contribution of new entrants has been very small in Japan.

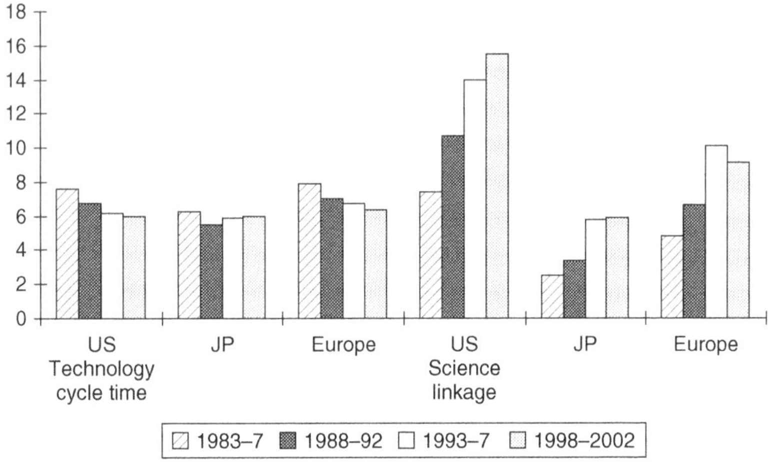

Figure 8.6 Performance of US, Japanese and European firms in technology cycle time and science linkage in generating IT

Note: Science linkage is multiplied by 10.

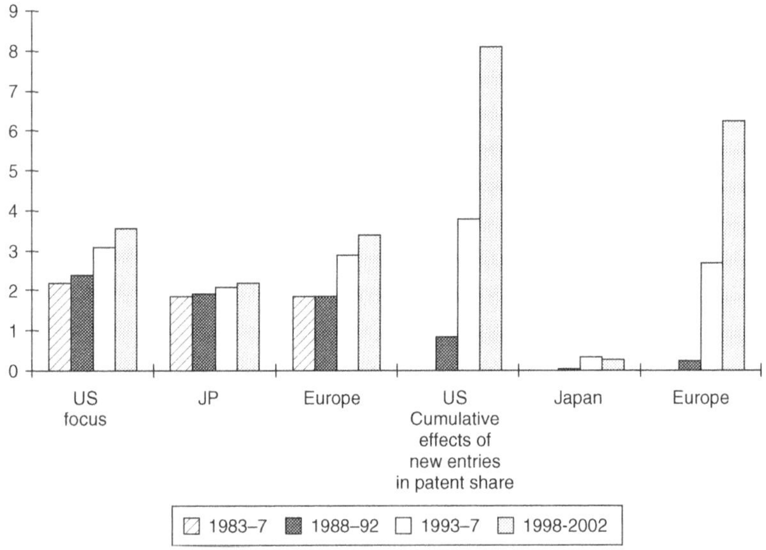

Figure 8.7 Focus of the IT core sector and the cumulative effects of new entrants

Note: A new entrant does not have the patents granted as of the period from 1983–8, but has become a major patentee by 2002. The vertical axis has a unit of 1,000 for focus and % for the entry effect. The entry effect is measured by the contribution of new entrants to the total number of the US patents to the firms in three regions.

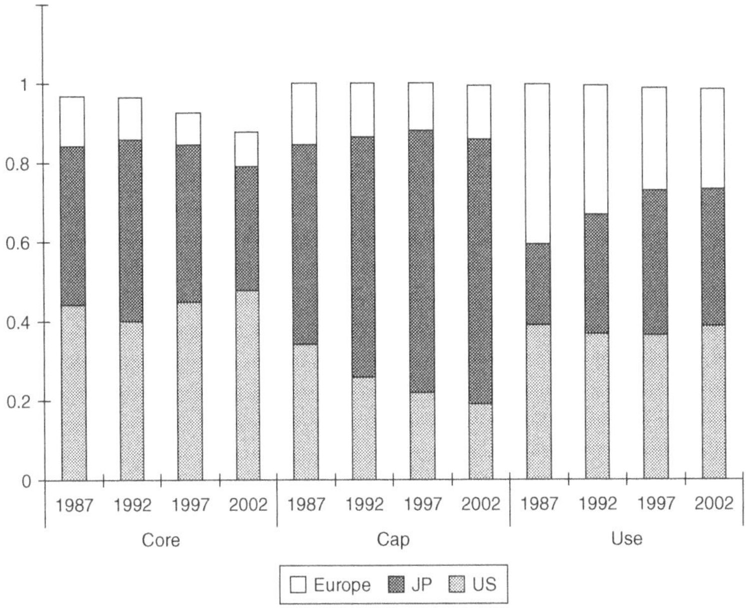

Figure 8.8 The shares of US, Japanese and European firms of IT patents

Finally, let us look at the share of national firms by three sectors: the IT core sector, the IT-incorporating machinery sector and the remaining IT-using sector. As shown in Figure 8.8, the Japanese firms have the largest IT patent share produced in the capital goods sector, and its share has increased. The US firms have expanded their share in the core sector since the beginning of the 1990s. The European firms have relatively large share in the share of IT patents generated by the other IT-using sector. This pattern suggests the possibility that the change of the division of innovation labours between these sectors, in particular, the shift of advantage of IT inventions towards the IT core sector is another reason for the relative decline of the performance of Japanese firms.

8.6 Conclusions

In this paper I have evaluated how the speed, science linkage and focus of corporate R&D as well as new entry matters as the determinants of R&D performance in IT (information technology) and explored their implications for the R&D performance of Japanese, US and European firms. Major findings are the following. First, there is fairly strong evidence for positive effects of speed and science linkage on research productivity. That is, both higher speed of R&D measured by citation lag and stronger science base of a firm measured by its science linkage improve R&D performance in both the quality and the number of the patents granted. Furthermore, speed matters more in the IT core sector, whose main business is the production of IT products. Focusing tends to improve patent quality in the IT core sector, although it might not be due to the improvement of R&D efficiency, and new entrants have higher patent quality than incumbents, only part of which can be explained by their higher speed and higher science linkage on the average.

The US firms have improved their R&D performance relative to the Japanese and European firms since the 1990s in both quality and quantity of the US patents granted. The above findings suggest that such gain reflects their acceleration of R&D speed, their intensification of science linkage and substantially more new entries in the US. It is to be noted that most of the changes in these competitive variables occurred in the US firms. This result is consistent with the conclusion by Kortum and Lerner (1999), who suggested (only by a process of elimination) that the increase in patenting in the US has been driven by changes in the management of innovation of US firms, which brought a real burst of innovation. The performance differential also seems to reflect the change of the division of innovation labours between sectors, in particular, a larger role of the IT core sector in IT inventions.

There are several important limitations and a number of research issues to be further pursued. First, although our results on the R&D speed and science linkage are not affected strongly by the different choices of firm-level fixed effects (firm by technology-fixed effects versus firm by time-fixed effects), this paper does not fully control the endogeneity of explanatory variables. Introducing more firm-level variables, such as R&D expenditures, would help us control the problems, especially with respect to evaluating the effects of focusing. This work is under way by another author. Second, our analysis indicates the possibility that the change of the division of innovation labours between the IT-producing sector and the IT-using sector has taken place. This possibility, as well as its causes, would warrant a further study.

Acknowledgements

I would like to thank Arnoud De Meyer, Charles Baden-Fuller, Hiroyuki Itami, Jaeyong Song, Bruno van Pottelsberghe de la Potterie, Kenneth

Flamm, Shigeru Asaba and other participants in the AEA Conference on Innovation and Intellectual Property in Singapore, the 2003 IT Innovation Conference and the International Conference of the Hitotsubashi COE Programme on 'Knowledge, Innovation and the Japanese Corporate System', both at Hitotsubashi University, for their very valuable comments. I would like to thank (for financial support) NEDO (04B53008) and the COE programme of Japan.

Appendix

Table 8.A1 Technology and industry classifications

Technology	IT
1 Agriculture	
2 Oil and gas, mining	
3 Power generation and distribution	
4 Food and tobacco	
5 Textiles and apparel	
6 Wood and paper	
7 Chemicals	
8 Pharmaceuticals	
9 Biotechnology	
10 Medical equipment	
11 Medical electronics	
12 Plastics, polymers and rubber	
13 Glass, clay and cement	
14 Primary metals	
15 Fabricated metals	
16 Industrial machinery and tools	
17 Industrial process equipment	
18 Office equipment and cameras	•
19 Heating, ventilation and refrigeration	
20 Miscellaneous machinery	
21 Computers and peripherals	•
22 Telecommunications	•
23 Semiconductors and electronics	•
24 Measurement and control equipment	
25 Electrical appliances and components	
26 Motor vehicles and parts	
27 Aerospace and parts	
28 Other transport	
29 Miscellaneous manufacturing	
30 Other	

Continued

Table 8.A1 Continued

	Industry	Types with respect to IT	Share of IT patents in the total patents in each sector
1	Computers	core	0.792
2	Electronics	core	0.603
3	Semiconductors	core	0.777
4	Telecommunications	core	0.755
5	Electrical	capital (incorporating)	0.370
6	Instrument and optical	capital (incorporating)	0.551
7	Machinery	capital (incorporating)	0.115
8	Aerospace	use	0.241
9	Automotive	use	0.088
10	Biotechnology	use	0.010
11	Chemicals	use	0.050
12	Consumer products	use	0.103
13	Energy	use	0.094
14	Engineering and Oil Field Services	use	0.040
15	Food, beverages and tobacco	use	0.024
16	Forest and paper products	use	0.111
17	Health care	use	0.028
18	Materials	use	0.143
19	Metals	use	0.115
20	Pharmaceuticals	use	0.008
21	Textiles	use	0.044
22	Conglomerates	other	0.041
23	Miscellaneous companies	other	0.161
24	Government agencies	other	0.254
25	Research institutes	other	0.131
26	University	other	0.148

Table 8.A2 Summary statistics

						Types of firms			Correlation												
Variable	Obs	Mean	Std dev.	Min	Max	Core	Cap	Use	numpats	cit	tct	scilink	focus	ln1pats_10	ln1pats_11	ln1pats_12	ln1pats_13	ln1tpats_10	ln1tpats_11	ln1tpats_12
numpats	9,351	48.43	208.57	1	8263	99.60	56.79	10.93	1											
cit	9,351	8.27	11.82	0	289	10.56	7.03	7.16	−0.027	1										
tct	9,351	7.94	4.56	0	50.25	6.75	8.02	8.76	−0.094	−0.104	1									
scilink	9,351	0.90	3.23	0	195.5	0.93	0.52	0.89	−0.006	0.046	−0.031	1								
focus	9,351	2704	1693	638	10000	3468	2652	2324	−0.025	0.120	−0.058	0.015	1							
ln1pats 10	9,351	2.17	1.51	0.69	9.02	2.85	2.23	1.65	0.570	−0.028	−0.203	0.008	−0.082	1						
ln1pats 11	9,351	1.53	1.78	0	9.02	2.11	1.57	1.07	0.195	0.290	−0.135	−0.022	−0.063	0.495	1					
ln1pats 12	9,351	0.97	1.66	0	9.02	1.34	1.01	0.69	0.076	0.315	−0.057	−0.061	−0.079	0.269	0.586	1				
ln1pats 13	9,351	0.46	1.29	0	9.02	0.64	0.51	0.32	0.020	0.203	0.006	−0.052	−0.055	0.122	0.332	0.550	1			
ln1tpats 10	9,351	10.20	0.59	9.22	11.24	10.26	10.17	10.17	0.096	−0.335	−0.111	0.095	0.118	0.118	−0.423	−0.551	−0.514	1		
ln1tpats 11	9,351	7.13	4.84	0	11.24	6.90	7.24	7.23	−0.079	0.368	0.018	−0.046	−0.071	−0.097	0.583	0.357	0.202	−0.742	1	
ln1tpats 12	9,351	4.41	5.24	0	11.24	4.03	4.64	4.62	−0.070	0.332	0.056	−0.092	−0.110	−0.091	0.280	0.693	0.402	−0.797	0.515	1
ln1tpats 13	9,351	1.98	4.20	0	11.24	1.79	2.22	2.03	−0.049	0.202	0.073	−0.071	−0.068	−0.071	0.161	0.369	0.762	−0.676	0.265	0.528
obs						3,042	1,704	3,826												

Notes

1. We define information technology broadly in this paper, covering computers and peripherals, semiconductors and electronics, office equipment and cameras, and telecommunications, consistent with the OECD definition of ICT (information and communication technology). According to OECD (1998), the manufacturing ICT industries must be intended to fulfil the function of information processing and communication, including transmission and display, or must use electronic processing to detect, measure and/or record physical phenomena or control a physical process. It covers 3000 – Office, accounting and computing machinery; 3130 – Insulated wire and cable; 3210 – Electronic valves and tubes and other electronic components; 3220 – Television and radio transmitters and apparatus for line telephony and line telegraphy; 3230 – Television and radio receivers, sound or video recording or reproducing apparatus and associated goods; 3312 – Instruments and appliances for measuring, checking, testing, navigating and other purposes, except industrial process equipment; 3313 – Industrial process equipment.
2. See Harhoff *et al.* (2003), Jaffe *et al.* (2002) and Trajtenberg (1990).
3. The number of citations is up to the end of 2002.
4. According to the *Economic Report of the President* (Council of Economic Advisors, 2001), 'Between 1993 and 1998, real spending on R&D by firms with more than 25,000 employees increased by 8 percent, but R&D conducted by firms with fewer than 500 employees nearly doubled ... More than 40 percent of all privately employed scientific researchers now work in these small firms.'
5. See Narin (2000) for details. We thank CHI research for customized data construction.
6. This definition follows broadly the OECD definition of ICT (information and communication technology) industry (see note 1).
7. See Branstetter and Nakamura (2003) for a recent analysis of the innovative capacity of Japanese firms, focusing on patent production.
8. See Branstetter (2003) for a recent empirical assessment of this linkage, which has a finding consistent with this paper.
9. The case studies of Meyer (2000) illustrate several different meanings of science linkage. Science papers may serve as background information for citing patents; they may be used to attack, restrict or modify claims. He concludes that citation link connects patent and science paper insofar as it tells that the patent is granted where a scientist published something relevant.
10. See Caballero and Jaffe (1993), Jaffe and Trajtenberg (1996) and Branstetter (2003) for good expositions of the citation function.
11. The Hausman tests do not support the hypotheses that they are the same between estimations.
12. The *t*-test strongly (at 1 per cent level) rejects the hypothesis that the sum of the base coefficient (−0.117) and that for the IT core sector (0.250) is zero.
13. Since this result is based on variation over time and we do not control the variation of R&D over time, there is a possibility that this effect may reflect the correlation between the focusing by a firm and the reduction of its R&D budget over time. However, the effect of R&D budget is partially controlled in our estimation by the number of patents which are introduced to control the number of potentially self-citing patents.

References

Branstetter, L., 'Is Academic Science Driving a Surge in Industrial Innovation? Evidence from Patent Citations', NBER Working Paper 9438 (2003).

Branstetter, L. and Y. Nakamura, 'Is Japan's Innovative Capacity in Decline?', mimeo (2003).

Caballero, R. J. and A. B. Jaffe, 'How High are the Giants' Shoulders: An Empirical Assessment of Knowledge Spillover and Creative Destruction in a Model of Economic Growth', in O. Blanchard and S. Fischer (eds), *National Bureau of Economic Research Macroeconomics Manual*, Vol. 8 (Cambridge: MIT Press, 1993).

Council of Economic Advisors, *Economic Report of the President* (Washington, DC: Government Printing Office, 2001).

Deng, Z., B. Lev and F. Narin, 'Science and Technology as Predictors of Stock Performance', *Financial Analysts Journal*, 55 (3) (1999), 20–32.

Hall, B. H., A. Jaffe and M. Trajtenberg, 'Market Value and Patent Citations: A First Look', NBER Working Paper 7741 (2000).

Harhoff, D., F. M. Scherer and K. Vopel, 'Citations, Family Size, Opposition and the Value of Patent Rights', *Research Policy*, 32 (8) (2003), 1343–63.

Henderson, R. and I. Cockburn, 'Scale, Scope and Spillovers: The Determinants of Research Productivity in Drug Discovery', *RAND Journal of Economics*, 27 (1) (1996), 32–59.

Hirschey, M. and V. J. Richardson, 'Valuation Effects of Patent Quality: A Comparison for Japanese and US firms', *Pacific-Basin Finance Journal*, 9 (2001), 65–82.

Hirschey, M. and V. J. Richardson, 'Are Scientific Indicators of Patent Quality Useful to Investors?', *Journal of Empirical Finance*, 11 (2004), 91–107.

Jaffe, A. B. and M. Trajtenberg, 'Flows of Knowledge from Universities and Federal Labs: Modeling the Flow of Patent Citations over Time and across Institutional and Geographic Boundaries', NBER Working Paper 5712 (1996).

Jaffe, A. B., M. Trajtenberg and M. S. Fogarty, 'The Meaning of Patent Citations: Report on the NBER/Case-Western Reserve Survey of Patentees', in A. B. Jaffe and M. Trajtenberg (eds), *Patents, Citations, and Innovations: A Window on the Knowledge Economy* (Cambridge: MIT Press, 2002).

Kortum, S. and J. Lerner, 'What is Behind the Recent Surge in Patenting?', *Research Policy*, 28 (1999), 1–22.

Meyer, M., 'Does Science Push Technology? Patents Citing Scientific Literature', *Research Policy*, 29 (2000), 409–34.

Nagaoka, S., 'Assessing the R&D Management of Firms by Patent Citation: Evidence from the US Patents', IIR Working Paper WP#04–10, Institute of Innovation Research, Hitotsubashi University (2004).

Nagaoka, S., 'Patent Quality, Cumulative Innovation and Market Value: Evidence from Japanese Firm Level Panel Data', IIR Working Paper 05–06, Institute of Innovation Research, Hitotsubashi University (2005).

Narin, F., 'Tech-Line Background Paper', in J. Tidd (ed.), *From Knowledge Management to Strategic Competence*, Series on Technology Management, Vol. 3 (London: Imperial College Press, 2000), 155–95.

OECD, 'Science, Technology and Industry Scoreboard 2001 – Towards a Knowledge-Based Economy' (OECD, 1998).

Rosenbloom, R. S. and W. J. Spencer, *Engines of Innovation: US Industrial Research at the End of an Era* (Boston: Harvard Business School Press, 1996).
Scherer, F. M. and D. Harhoff, 'Technology Policy for a World of Skew-Distributed Outcomes', *Research Policy*, 29 (2000), 559–66.
Trajtenberg, M., 'A Penny for Your Quotes: Patent Citations and the Value of Innovation', *RAND Journal of Economics* (1990), 172–87.

9
Complex Innovation Strategies and Patenting Behaviour

Carine Peeters and Bruno van Pottelsberghe de la Potterie

9.1 Introduction

In the last decades, with the rise of innovation as the engine of growth for firms, sectors and nations, patents have gained a central place in business and policy debates. The primary objective of a patent is to provide a legally enforceable protection against imitation to any invention that can demonstrate a sufficient innovative step and that satisfies the criteria of non-obviousness and industrial application. In that sense, the observation of a patent obviously witnesses the presence of some kind of innovation. But patents do not only serve as a protection mechanism. They are also highly valuable strategic tools for firms seeking to develop strong technological positions and build competitive advantage. Patents as defenders of a firm's innovation rents, and patents as builders of a firm's technological and competitive position, both perspectives justify the interest in deepening our understanding of what determines a firm's patenting behaviour.

Seeking to contribute to this research question, this chapter investigates the influence that different innovation strategies pursued by firms exert on the likelihood that they build a portfolio of patents, and on the size of this portfolio. Four dimensions of an innovation strategy are addressed. The first one is whether some kind of R&D activity is undertaken or not. The second dimension refers to the relative importance of basic and applied research on the one hand, and of development work on the other hand, in the total R&D budget of a firm. The third one concerns the use of R&D partnerships as a way to access external knowledge and to develop new knowledge. The last dimension captures the orientation of a firm's innovation efforts towards the development of new products, new processes, or both.

The theoretical framework underlying this study suggests that a firm's patenting behaviour is also influenced by its perception of the limitations and inefficiencies of the patent system. Finally, it is argued that the development of patent portfolios may be limited by the barriers a firm perceives as hindering its innovation activities.

The present study uses original survey data on 148 large firms that operated in Belgium in 2001, in either manufacturing or service sectors. It departs from existing empirical studies on patents' determinants by going beyond the traditional factors related to firm size, market power, technological opportunity and research efforts, and explicitly taking into account differences in firms' innovation strategies. It also differs from previous studies in the indicator of patenting behaviour used. While the existing literature on patents' determinants has mainly focused on the number of yearly patent applications made by firms, this research uses data on the number of patents firms have accumulated over time in their patent portfolio, and for which they still pay renewal fees. This approach enables control for contextual effects that may affect the patenting behaviour of a firm in a given period without necessarily reflecting its general attitude towards patenting.

Two empirical models are built to assess several potential determinants of a firm's patenting behaviour. A binary logit model estimates the probability for a firm to have at least one patent, and a negative binomial model estimates the number of active patents a firm has in its portfolio. The results show that the introduction of innovation strategy variables sharply reduces the significance of traditional determinants related to firm and sector characteristics. Entering into R&D partnerships with scientific institutions and competitors is associated with a significantly more active patenting behaviour. This witnesses the need for strong IP protection resulting from mutual access to the partners' knowledge bases. Product-innovators possess the largest patent portfolios. Innovators that pursue a complex strategy giving high importance to both the development of new products and the development of new processes tend to build patent portfolios of an intermediate size. The patenting behaviour of process-innovators does not significantly differ from the patenting behaviour of firms that do not pursue strong innovation goals, neither product- nor process-oriented.

Section 9.2 of this chapter reviews the main determinants of patent activity studied in the existing literature. Section 9.3 presents the theoretical framework that underlies this empirical study and tested hypotheses. The survey data, empirical model and variables are described in section 9.4. The results are discussed in section 5 and section 6 provides a few concluding remarks.

9.2 Literature Background

Pioneer work in the field of patents probably started with the contributions of Schmookler (1957), Nelson (1959), Arrow (1962) and Scherer (1965). Since then, academic research has increasingly tackled various aspects of patents, from the theoretical analysis of patent systems (see, for instance, Baumol, 2002), to the use of patent data to measure innovation performance and knowledge spillovers (see for instance Griliches, 1990). With the development of extensive and accessible patent databases, several authors have also analysed the microdeterminants of innovation using patent indicators as a measure of innovative output (see, for instance, Crépon *et al.*, 1996, 1998; Duguet and Kabla, 1998; Cohen *et al.*, 2000). Most of these studies focus on traditional determinants of patenting behaviour, such as firm size, market power, market and technological opportunities, and R&D efforts.

The impact of firm size on patenting activity is always taken into account in the existing literature. This originates from the famous Schumpeterian hypothesis that large firms are more innovative than smaller ones (Schumpeter, 1942). The advantage of being large results from three main factors, summarized by Cohen and Levin (1989). First, large firms can benefit from economies of scale and scope that make them more competitive in comparison to their smaller competitors. Second, large firms can take advantage of complementarities and spillovers between different departments. Finally, large firms are favoured by capital markets for the financing of risky innovation projects. Although the empirical evidence seems to tilt towards a validation of the Schumpeterian hypothesis, some authors argue that the relationship is not straightforward. For instance, Baldwin *et al.* (2002) find that the effect of firm size depends on the innovation indicator used, with a weaker relationship when relying on patent data than when relying on the percentage of innovative sales. According to van Ophem *et al.* (2002) the effect of firm size on patent applications is debatable. Large firms can more easily rely on market lead to secure their innovation rents, and hence are less likely to need patent protection. However, they are better able to set up a patent department and to face potential litigations. Their econometric analysis shows a positive effect of firm size on the number of patent applications. Other authors find no significant impact of the size variable when it is controlled for other factors like industry effects, differences in access to external know-how and appropriability conditions (Duguet and Kabla, 1998; Crépon *et al.*, 1998; Cassiman *et al.*, 2001). Brouwer and Kleinknecht (1999) shed some light on this debate by using two different patent indicators. They find that the probability of having at least one patent application increases more than proportionately with the number of employees, while the number of patent applications increases less than proportionately. This means that small firms that do apply for patents do it proportionately more, probably to compensate for disadvantages in terms of market share and brand name.

Another determinant of patenting activity that is quite controversial is the intensity of competition. It is measured either by the firm market share or by an index of industry concentration. The debate originates from Schumpeter's hypothesis that firms with a strong market power are more innovative than firms with weak market power (Schumpeter, 1942). This hypothesis has since been challenged by several authors. Two effects work, indeed, in opposite directions. On the one hand, there is the replacement effect resulting in less innovation investments by firms with more power on the market because the gains they would get would only replace current gains (Arrow, 1962). On the other hand, the efficiency effect suggests that firms with a high market power invest more in innovation because they do not face competition for the exploitation of their inventions (Gilbert and Newberry, 1982). The impact of this variable varies quite importantly according to the innovation indicator and competition indicator used. Cohen and Levin (1989) show in their literature review on the relationship between R&D and market power that even results of studies using the same innovation indicator are often contradictory. Regarding the number of patent applications, Duguet and Kabla (1998) and Nielsen (2001) find a positive influence of firm market power. In their studies the efficiency effect seems to dominate the replacement effect.

Two variables that are also traditionally included in innovation and patent equations are market and technological opportunities. Market opportunity reflects the existence of some market in demand of novelty. Technological opportunity is generally measured at the industry level. It is defined by Levin *et al.* (1987) as the extent to which an industry relies on science-based research. Demand-pull variables are expected to have a stronger impact on innovation output indicators than on R&D investments because output measures are more directly linked to the market. In this respect, the status of patent indicators is controversial. A patent can be viewed as an intermediate indicator reflecting the output of research activities but not necessarily implying the commercialization of an invention. Firms in high technological opportunity sectors are found to patent more than other firms (Crépon *et al.*, 1996, 1998; Brouwer and Kleinknecht, 1999) but the difference is not always significant (Duguet and Kabla, 1998; Baldwin *et al.*, 2002). Concerning market opportunity factors, Crépon *et al.* (1996) find that they have a positive and significant impact on patent applications, but the effect is generally found insignificant (Duguet and Kabla, 1998; Crépon *et al.*, 1998; Cassiman *et al.*, 2001).

Another issue that has largely been studied in the literature is the relationship between R&D and patents (see, for instance, Bound *et al.*, 1984). Scherer (1965) considers patents as an indicator of R&D success. In this perspective R&D precedes patent applications and the causality goes from R&D to patents, with R&D being eventually lagged in the equations. More recently, Hall *et al.* (1986) have argued that there is a strong contemporaneous effect between R&D and patenting and that it is difficult to find the adequate lag structure between R&D and patents. Most studies including an R&D indicator in patent equations find a positive and significant relationship (Duguet and Kabla, 1998; Crépon *et al.*, 1998; Brouwer and Kleinknecht, 1999). Actually, the relationship between R&D and patents can be seen as a virtuous cycle. The former induces the later, which in turn requires further development costs in order to reach the market.

9.3 Theoretical Framework

Existing studies on determinants of firms' patenting behaviour use patent applications data and consider patents as an indicator of innovation. The underlying hypothesis is that patenting is a mechanism firms use to protect their innovation rents. As a consequence, the observation of a patent application reflects the existence of an innovation. However, not all innovations are patented. The relevance of using patent-based indicators of innovation has therefore been subject to a wide debate (see, for instance, Griliches, 1990) that can be summarized in three main points. First, not all innovations are patentable since the three conditions of non-obviousness, inventive step and industrial application must be satisfied in order to get a patent granted. Second, the propensity to patent 'patentable' inventions varies considerably across firms, time and industry (see, for instance, Scherer, 1983; Hall *et al.*, 1986; Arora, 1997). Third, in some sectors patent protection is relatively inefficient and secrecy is favoured as a mechanism to secure the rents resulting from an invention. The importance of various protection mechanisms varies indeed across industries and patenting is very important for only a few of them, mainly chemicals and pharmaceuticals (Mansfield, 1986; Levin *et al.*, 1987). Nevertheless, despite their widely recognized limitations, when interpreted with caution patent statistics have a lot to reveal (Schmookler, 1966).

Moreover, even though patents may be imperfect indicators of innovation, other aspects make them worthwhile to study. Applying for a patent is a strategic decision that is not only driven by the desire to protect innovation rents (Teece, 1998; Rivette and Kline, 2000; Sherry and Teece, 2004). A patent is also a highly valuable tool for technological negotiations with competitors or with potential collaborators, for the exclusion of rivals from a particular technological area, for licensing agreements and attraction of capital, for avoiding being blocked by competitors' patents and for building competitive advantage (see, for instance, Parr and Sullivan, 1996; Teece, 1998; Glazier, 2000; Reitzig, 2004).

Beside the traditional determinants related to firm and sector characteristics widely discussed in the literature this paper explicitly takes into account the effect that different innovation strategies may have on the patenting behaviour of firms. Variables that reflect the perception firms have of certain barriers to innovation and to the use of the patent system are introduced as well. Different firms pursuing similar innovation strategies may indeed have different attitudes towards patenting because they differ in their perception of limitations of the patent system. Differences in observed patent portfolios may also reflect a lower innovativeness resulting from higher perceived barriers to innovations. Both effects will be controlled for in the regressions.

Contrarily to most existing studies that use the number of patent applications in a given period as dependent variable, the present work looks at firms' patent portfolio. Three reasons justify this choice. First, the patents in a firm's portfolio are 'active' patents in the sense that renewal fees have been paid. In the case of older patents this guarantees that the innovation rents they are supposed to protect are actually still protected. Second, these patents bear in themselves an element of 'quality' that patent applications lack. These patents have indeed been granted, which means that the inventive step and industrial applicability of the underlying technology have been recognized by a competent institution. As a result, studying patent portfolios instead of patent applications guarantees that the patents that are looked at can actually be used both as a protection mechanism and as strategic tools to build a firm's technological and competitive position. The third reason is that a patent portfolio is built over time. It is therefore a more adequate indicator of a firm's patenting behaviour since it is less subject to particular events that may affect the number of patents a firm applies for in a given year. A firm may be a recurrent innovator with a strong preference for patent protection but no patent application in the particular time-frame a study is interested in. Another firm may happen to apply for one or

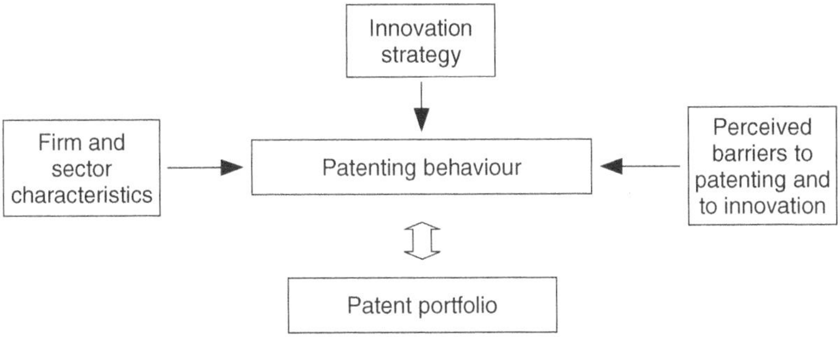

Figure 9.1 Theoretical framework of the determinants of firms' patent portfolios

more patents because of a significant technological invention that would eventually be made during the studied period. This may, however, be highly contextual and not reflect a general strong patenting behaviour. Looking at the patent portfolio a firm builds over time enables these potential contextual biases to be reduced and provides a more stable indicator of patenting behaviour.

The theoretical framework underlying this study is sketched in Figure 9.1. It suggests that a firm's portfolio of active patents is determined by three types of factors. The first ones are firm and sector characteristics that most existing studies already consider: firm size, market concentration and opportunities, and technological opportunity. The two others are less traditional and refer to the type of innovation strategy a firm pursues, and the barriers to the use of the patent system and to innovation it perceives.

Four variables are used to characterize the innovation strategy. The first one differentiates R&D active firms from non-R&D active firms. The second one relates to the kind of R&D activities undertaken and, more particularly, the importance of basic and applied research in the total R&D budget of firms. If the positive relationship between the relative effort in R&D and patenting has been widely illustrated, there is little evidence so far about the content of R&D (see, for instance, Hall *et al.*, 1986; Duguet and Kabla, 1998; Crépon *et al.*, 1998; Brouwer and Kleinknecht, 1999). Since patents are by definition the codification of an invention, they might be the outcome of basic and applied research, as opposed to development activities. The latter would surely be associated with patenting (development of inventions), but provided a sufficient share of total R&D is devoted to basic and applied research.

A firm's innovation strategy can also be characterized as more or less outward-oriented. One way to assess this is to look at the propensity of firms to enter into research partnerships with other institutions like competitors, vertical partners, universities, consultants, complementary firms and other firms in the same group. These institutions form an external stock of knowledge that might prove useful for a firm's own innovation activities (see, for instance, Tether, 2002; Ritter and Gemünden, 2003), as it might reduce their cost and their risk. Since a research collaboration agreement often implies a mutual access to the partners' knowledge bases, partnering firms are likely to seek patent protection for their inventions. In addition, a piece of technology protected by a patent becomes a tradable asset that can prove very useful when negotiating future collaborative agreements. Brouwer and Kleinknecht (1999) and van Ophem *et al.* (2002) show that firms participating in research partnerships apply for more patents than firms that focus on internal research.

The last dimension of a firm's innovation strategy that this study takes into account is its orientation towards the development of new products, new processes, or both. It is traditionally found that process innovations are less likely to be patented (Arundel and Kabla, 1998; Brouwer and Kleinknecht, 1999), as secrecy might prove a more appropriate protection mechanism for this type of innovation (Cohen *et al.*, 2000). The publication of technical information a patent requires might indeed be less recommended for process innovations, for which infringement is difficult to detect. In that case, firms might opt for a non-legal protection mechanism such as secrecy. Conversely, product innovations might be easier to imitate through reverse-engineering and a legally enforceable protection might prove to be useful. Furthermore, it could be argued that firms following complex innovation strategies involving high levels of both new products and new processes patent more than any other firms. First, these firms give the highest importance to innovation and are therefore more likely to come up with patentable inventions. Second, complex innovation strategies are more likely to result in major innovations with potential applications well beyond the business of a particular firm. The innovative firm is therefore likely to be very cautious about securing the high potential revenues resulting from its innovation efforts. Patenting might be the best solution for these major innovations since the technology would be protected from imitation, innovators could envision earning licensing revenues, and it would provide a valuable asset for technological negotiations.

The discussion on the dimensions of an innovation strategy that can determine a firm's patenting behaviour is formalized into five hypotheses to be tested empirically:

- Hypothesis 1: Firms that undertake R&D activities patent more than firms that have no R&D activity.
- Hypothesis 2: A larger relative share of basic and applied research in the total R&D budget of a firm is associated with a more active patenting behaviour.
- Hypothesis 3: Firms that enter into R&D partnerships patent more than other firms.
- Hypothesis 4: Firms that focus on developing new products patent more than firms that focus on developing new processes.
- Hypothesis 5: A complex innovation strategy targeting high levels of both product and process innovation is associated with a more active patenting behaviour than any other orientation of an innovation strategy.

The patenting behaviour of firms is also likely to be influenced by the barriers to innovation they perceive. Some authors use innovation survey data to test the effect of potential barriers to innovation on firms' innovation activities (see, for instance, Lööf and Heshmati, 2002; Veugelers and Cassiman, 1999). They generally find that a lack of interest from customers, a lack of technological information and a lack of qualified personnel have a negative impact on firms' innovation performance. Barriers to innovation are also likely to have an impact on firms' patent portfolios, as indicator of innovation involvement and R&D success. Cassiman *et al.* (2001) find that high innovation costs and lack of financing have a positive effect on firms' propensity to patent. This counter-intuitive positive effect highlights a recurrent problem in measuring barriers to innovation. It is indeed often difficult to discern firms' perception of barriers from the barriers that actually hinder their innovation efforts.

The perception firms have of the effectiveness and cost of the patent system might influence their patenting behaviour as well. Actually, the advantage for a firm to patent an invention is not always clear since a patent offers protection to its holder at the high indirect cost of revealing important technical information. Applying for a patent does not seem to be the most popular protection mechanism for manufacturing firms, which often favour secrecy and lead time over competition (see, for instance, Levin *et al.*, 1987; Brouwer and Kleinknecht, 1999; Cohen *et al.*, 2000; Arundel, 2001). The risk of having competitors 'inventing around' and the disclosure of critical information are the most important reasons why patents are not always considered as an effective protection mechanism of innovation rents (Levin *et al.*, 1987; Scotchmer and Green, 1990; Cohen *et al.*, 2000). Everything else equal, firms that perceive important limitations to the patent system are therefore likely to patent less than other firms.

9.4 Empirical Implementation

The dataset used in the present empirical study comes from an original firm-level survey on innovation realized in Belgium in 2001. The questionnaire was sent to the CEOs of 1,301 large firms active in either manufacturing or service sector in Belgium. An extensive statistical analysis of the survey results can be found in Peeters and van Pottelsberghe (2003a). A total of 148 questionnaires were filed and sent back.

Empirical model

Two econometric models are used in order to identify the determinants of firms' patenting behaviour. The first one focuses on whether firms have a patent portfolio or not, that is, the probability for a firm to have at least one patent. The second one intends to explain the size of this portfolio, which is the number of active patents a firm has in its patent portfolio. Authors like Crépon *et al.* (1996) and Brouwer and Kleinknecht (1999) have already adopted this dual approach using data on the number of yearly patent applications by firms.

A binary logit model is used to estimate the equation related to the probability for a firm to have at least one patent.[1] It is written as follows:

$$y_i = \begin{cases} 1 & if\, y_i^* \geq 0 \\ 0 & if\, y_i^* < 0 \end{cases} \qquad with\; y_i^* = \alpha + \beta^t X_i + \varepsilon_i \quad (i = 1,\ldots,n)$$

where the errors ε_i follow a logistic distribution $F(t) = \frac{1}{1+e^{-t}}$, and $\beta^t = (\beta_1\, \beta_2, \ldots, \beta_p)$ is the vector of the p parameters associated with the vector of the p explicative variables $X_i^t = (x_{i1}\, x_{i2},\ldots, x_{ip})$. y_i^* is the latent dependent variable that represents some decision criteria. If y_i^* is positive the firm has a patent portfolio with at least one patent. If y_i^* is negative the firm does not have a patent portfolio.

A negative binomial model is used to estimate the equation related to the size of the patent portfolio. This method has been chosen for four main reasons. First, as a count model it accounts for the non-negativity and discreteness of the data. Second, as opposed to the poisson model it allows the conditional mean and variance of the dependent variable to be different. Third, the coefficients can be estimated using the pseudo-maximum likelihood approach that yields robust estimates even if the distribution is not correctly specified. Finally, it enables correction for possible heteroscedasticity without loosing too much efficiency. The negative binomial model can be written as follows:

$$Z/X_i \sim NB\left(\frac{\theta(\lambda_i + 1)}{\theta + 1}, \frac{\theta}{\theta + 1}\right) \quad (i = 1,\dots,n)$$

where $X_i^t = (x_{i1}\, x_{i2},\dots,x_{ip})$ is the vector of explicative variables, $\lambda_i = e^{\beta' xi}$ is the conditional mean of the dependent variable, and θ a parameter that enables the introduction of some heterogeneity in the model (if $\theta = 0$, the poisson and the negative binomial model are equivalent).

Estimates of both models are corrected for potential heteroscedasticity using the procedure of White. The explicative variables are classified into three categories: firm and sector characteristics, innovation strategy variables and barriers perception variables.

Firm and sector characteristics

As in most existing studies estimations are controlled for firm and sector characteristics. The present model includes the firm size and degree of internationalization, and the sector concentration and technological opportunity. The *firm size* is measured by the total number of employees in 2000. This information is retrieved from the BelFirst database, a database comprising the annual reports of most firms operating in Belgium. A positive relationship with firms' patent portfolios is expected. The *degree of internationalization* is measured as the number of countries a firm is operating in. A firm is considered to operate in a country if it has customer contacts in this country. Firms operating in a large number of countries are expected to patent more for two main reasons. First, they face a larger potential market than firms operating only in their local or regional market. The number of countries in which a firm operates would therefore reflect some kind of market opportunity effect. Second, these firms face more international competition, which is likely to increase the need for innovation rents protection because the number of potential imitators increases and infringement is more difficult to detect. Both effects might translate into higher patenting on a global scale.

The *sector concentration* is proxied by a C4 concentration ratio, computed as the total sales of the four largest firms in a firm's main sector of operation (in terms of sales) divided by the total sales of that sector.[2] The sector of activity is determined using the 4 digits Nace-bel code. The C4 concentration ratio is an imperfect indicator of market concentration since it is measured at the Belgian level, while many firms face international competition. Moreover, it is based on firms operating in a same kind of activity and does not necessarily reflect a firm's direct competitors.

Finally, the sector *technological opportunity* variable is proxied by five dummy variables depending on whether the firm belongs to a hi-tech (HT), medium hi-tech (MH), medium low-tech (ML), low-tech (LT), or service sector.[3] The service sector dummy is not included in the regressions and is therefore considered as the reference group. In line with the existing literature, firms in higher technological opportunity sectors are expected to patent more than others.

Innovation strategy variables

The first innovation strategy variable is a dummy variable that reflects whether or not a firm has undertaken some kind of *R&D* activity in 2000. In line with existing studies, a positive effect on firm's patent portfolio is expected for that R&D variable. The second variable is the percentage of *basic and applied research*, as opposed to development activities, in total R&D budget in 2000. The expectation is for this type of research to be associated with more patents than development activities. Firms that give low importance to basic and applied research and high importance to development work are comparatively more likely to come up with improvement innovations, which are less likely to be patented.

Involvement in *R&D partnerships* is accounted for by two variables. They are based on a factorial analysis of the survey questions related to the existence of collaboration agreements with different types of partners in the last three years preceding the survey.[4] The first variable (factorial axis) reflects the extent of collaborations with universities, research institutes and public labs. The second one reflects partnerships with competitors and negatively relates to the use of consultants, customers and suppliers as R&D partners. Both variables are expected to have a positive impact on firms' patent portfolios. The main reason for a positive effect in case of scientific collaborations is the basic nature of academic research that is more likely to result in patentable inventions. Moreover, collaborating with external partners implies reciprocal openness and access to the firms' knowledge bases. In case of partnerships with competitors, patent protection could therefore prove particularly worthwhile.

The *importance of developing new products and new processes* for a firm's innovation strategy is proxied by four dummy variables. The first one takes the value of 1 if the firm has answered 4 or 5, on a Likert scale from 1 to 5, to the importance of new product development only. The second one equals 1 if the firm has answered 4 or 5 to the importance of new process development only. The third one takes the value of 1 if the firm has answered 4 or 5 to both the importance of new product and new process development. The last one takes the value of 1 if the firm has rated both types of innovation 3 or lower. The four modalities are mutually exclusive and sum to 1. Therefore, the last modality (low importance of both types of innovation) is removed and considered as the reference group. All coefficients are expected to be positive since they compare firms that give low importance to innovation in general to firms that rate high at least one type of innovation: product, process, or both. In line with previous studies in the field a product-oriented innovation strategy is expected to result in more patents than a process-oriented strategy. A complex strategy that combines both product and process innovation is expected to drive the largest patent portfolios because the likelihood of major innovations with wide potential applications is higher and firms are likely to be willing to secure these sources of potentially high revenues.

Barriers perception variables

The perception firms have of several *barriers* that might hinder their *innovation* efforts is accounted for by three variables. They are the firms' coordinates on the first three factorial axes resulting from the factor analysis of the scores firms have attributed to a series of potential barriers proposed in the survey. The first variable reflects a high score of internal barriers related to a firm's organizational rigidities, lack of qualification, employees' resistance to change, poor internal communication, and lack of leadership. The second variable accounts for the high economic risks and high costs associated with innovation projects, and the lack of financial resources. The last type of barrier is external, resulting from rigidities and lack of reaction of customers, lack of access to competent suppliers, and inappropriate regulations. These factors are likely to limit a firm's innovation efforts or hinder their successful implementation. As a result, they are likely to negatively affect the patenting possibilities of firms, and hence their patent portfolio.

The variable that accounts for the perceived limitations of the patent system also comes from a factor analysis of the 1 to 5 scores firms have attributed to various potential drawbacks proposed in the survey: the cost of fees and protection, the lack of efficacy and preference for secrecy or market lead strategies, the disclosure of critical information and the risk of copy. The first factorial axis adequately summarizes all perceived limitations of the patent system. The coordinates of firms on this axis are therefore used as an explicative variable of differences in firms' patenting behaviour. Firms that perceive high limitations of the patent system are expected to patent less than other firms.

Basic statistics

Table 9.1 displays basic statistics on firms' patent portfolios, firm and sector characteristics, and innovation strategy variables used in the econometric study. The first column provides the variables' names followed by their respective unit of measure. The second column shows the number of firms for which the particular information is available. The third column presents the percentage of responding firms that score 1

Table 9.1 Basic statistics on dependent and explicative variables

Variables	N	% of 'yes'	Mean	Std dev.
Patents (0/1)	134	44		
Patents (number)	134		34	127
Number of employees	144		921	1774
Number of countries	132		27	30.56
Sector concentration (%)	147		61.58	25.30
Hi-tech (0/1)	148	10		
Medium hi-tech (0/1)	148	26		
Medium low-tech (0/1)	148	20		
Low-tech (0/1)	148	16		
Service (0/1)	148	28		
R&D (0/1)	144	80		
Basic and applied research (%)	139		35.79	27.86
R&D collaborations (0/1)	144	88		
Product innovation (0/1)	142	21		
Process innovation (0/1)	142	13		
Complex strategy (0/1)	142	47		
Nor product nor process (0/1)	142	19		

Source: Own survey, Belgium, 2001.

on a binary variable. The mean and standard deviation of quantitative variables are provided in the last two columns.

It appears that 44 per cent of respondents have at least one patent and that their patent portfolio comprises on average 34 patents. It should, however, be noticed that the standard deviation of the size of the patent portfolio is high, witnessing a high dispersion in the distribution of this variable. There are indeed many companies with no or only one patent, and a few companies with large patent portfolios. The average company in the database employs 921 persons. The standard deviation of this variable is also high since there are few very large companies in the database. All firms that participated in the survey have, however, been selected because they were among the largest in their respective industries. They are thus all significant players in their industry. The average firm is active in 27 countries. The last two observations are representative of the small open Belgian economy. The four largest firms in a sector represent, on average, 62 per cent of the sector's total sales. Two sector categories are slightly under-represented in the respondents' sample, with only 10 per cent of hi-tech companies and 16 per cent of low-tech companies.

An average of 80 per cent of firms in the database declared some kind of R&D activity in 2000. Approximately 36 per cent of their R&D budget was allocated to basic and applied research, leaving 64 per cent to development activities. It should be noted that the largest share of these, 36 per cent, accounts for applied research (see Peeters and van Pottelsberghe, 2003a). Most respondents have entered in at least one R&D collaboration agreement during the last three years preceding the survey. They significantly differ in their choice of partners, which will be taken into account in the estimations (see Peeters and van Pottelsberghe, 2003a). Finally, 21 per cent of firms have answered 4 or 5 only to the question relative to the importance of product innovation, 13 per cent of firms target almost exclusively the development of new processes, and 47 per cent of firms pursue a complex innovation strategy with a high importance of both product and process innovation. An average of 19 per cent of firms has rated both product and product innovation 3 or lower on the 1 to 5 likert scale.

9.5 Empirical Results

Table 9.2 presents the estimation results when only firm and sector characteristics are introduced as explicative variables of the probability for a firm to have a patent portfolio and of the size of this portfolio. The first

Table 9.2 Patent portfolio and firm and sector characteristics

	Binary logit prob (no. of patents > 0)	**Negative binomial no. of patents in portfolio**
Firm and sector characteristics		
Firm size	0.0002	0.0004***
	(0.0002)	*(0.0001)*
Degree of internationalization	0.0283***	0.0207**
	(0.0089)	*(0.0092)*
Sector concentration	0.0273***	0.0558***
	(0.0089)	*(0.0101)*
Hi-tech	1.4723	2.9343***
	(0.8980)	*(1.1289)*
Medium hi-tech	2.0912***	4.2322***
	(0.8100)	*(1.0197)*
Medium low-tech	2.2836***	3.0754***
	(0.8104)	*(0.8955)*
Low-tech	2.6135***	2.4717**
	(0.8310)	*(1.0460)*
Constant	−4.5984***	−5.4486***
	(0.9271)	*(1.2384)*
N	116	116
Pseudo log-likelihood	−55.5184	−239.6987
Pseudo R-squared	0.2943	0.1107

Notes: Robust logit and negative binomial estimates. Significance levels: * 10%, ** 5%, *** 1%; standard errors in parentheses.

Source: Own survey, Belgium, 2001.

column displays the explicative variables. The second one displays the estimated coefficients of the binary logit model related to the probability for a firm to have at least one patent. The third column displays the estimation results of the negative binomial model that estimates the number of active patents in the portfolio. The traditional determinants of patenting activity related to firm and sector characteristics turn out to exercise a significant effect, with the estimated coefficients showing expected signs.

Estimation results when the innovation strategy and perceived barriers variables are introduced in the equations are displayed in Table 9.3. A first general observation is that the introduction of explicative variables related to the kind of innovation strategy pursued by a firm sharply reduces the significance of traditional determinants related to firm size, sector concentration and market and technological

Table 9.3 Patent portfolio, innovation strategy and perceived barriers

	Binary logit prob (no. of patents > 0)	**Negative binomial** no. of patents in portfolio
Firm and sector characteristics		
Firm size	0.0007	0.0004***
	(0.0008)	*(0.0001)*
Degree of internationalisation	0.0225	−0.0012
	(0.0240)	*(0.0078)*
Sector concentration	0.0421**	0.0161
	(0.0212)	*(0.0123)*
Hi-tech	−0.8188	1.6331*
	(1.6440)	*(0.9184)*
Medium hi-tech	1.7659*	2.8168***
	(0.9629)	*(0.7985)*
Medium low-tech	0.1327	2.2128***
	(1.3309)	*(0.7851)*
Low-tech	4.0584**	1.5436
	(1.7516)	*(1.1938)*
Innovation strategy		
R&D	1.5093	1.8902*
	(1.1824)	*(1.1334)*
Share of basic and applied research	0.0555**	−0.0018
	(0.0263)	*(0.0138)*
R&D collaborations:		
Scientific institutions	3.0866***	2.5145***
	(0.9228)	*(0.6000)*
Competitors >< vertical partners and consultants	4.0539***	1.9529**
	(1.3672)	*(0.7911)*
Product innovation	0.1054	2.7402***
	(1.1447)	*(0.5850)*
Process innovation	−1.4998	0.1250
	(2.2131)	*(2.8580)*
Product and process innovation	−1.7258	1.2216**
	(1.2248)	*(0.5997)*
Perceived barriers		
Limitations of patent system	0.2518	0.2215
	(0.1714)	*(0.1444)*
Barriers to innovation:		
Internal	−0.0182	−0.2315
	(0.3179)	*(0.1973)*
Risks and costs	−0.8487**	−0.5204**
	(0.3727)	*(0.2049)*
External	−1.2871***	−0.1581
	(0.4229)	*(0.1605)*
Constant	−7.7345***	−5.6830***
	(2.2782)	*(1.4692)*
N	97	97
Pseudo log-likelihood	−22.9891	−193.7456
Pseudo R-squared	0.6559	0.2115

Notes: Robust logit and negative binomial estimates. Significance levels: * 10%, ** 5%, *** 1%; standard errors in parentheses.

Source: Own survey, Belgium, 2001.

opportunities. In the same time, better pseudo R-squared and log-likelihoods witness an increased quality of the models.

From the first row of results it appears that large firms are not more likely to patent but when they do they have larger patent portfolios than smaller firms, which is not surprising. A more unexpected result is the high probability for low-tech companies to have at least one patent. However, these firms do not have significantly larger patent portfolios than other firms. This result is probably due to a slight over-representation of low-tech firms with at least one patent in the sample of respondents. It turns out from the estimation of the patent portfolios' size that hi-tech, medium hi-tech and medium low-tech manufacturing firms have larger patent portfolios than low-tech firms and service companies. The estimated coefficients associated with the three significant sector technological opportunity variables (1.6331 for hi-tech, 2.8168 for medium hi-tech and 2.2128 for medium low-tech) are, however, not significantly different from each other at a 5 per cent probability level.

The middle part of Table 9.3 displays the estimated coefficients of the innovation strategy variables. As many studies have pointed out, doing R&D leads firms to patent more than non-R&D firms (see, for instance, Duguet and Kabla, 1998; Crépon *et al.*, 1998; Brouwer and Kleinknecht, 1999). But also the kind of R&D activities seems to drive different patenting behaviours. In particular, firms that are relatively more active in basic and applied research have a higher probability to have a patent portfolio than firms focusing relatively more on development work. The orientation of R&D activities has, however, no significant impact on the size of the patent portfolio.

Pursuing R&D projects in collaboration with scientific institutions and/or competitors has a highly significant positive influence on both the probability to have a patent portfolio and the size of this portfolio. Two main reasons can explain this finding. First, joint R&D projects with scientific institutions are usually science-based and likely to concern fundamental knowledge that a single firm cannot afford to develop alone, for technical or economical reasons. Such fundamental knowledge has often potential applications beyond the specific field of activity of a particular firm. The inventor is therefore more likely to seek patent protection since a patent helps prevent imitation and can drive revenues through licensing agreements (Parr and Sullivan, 1996). Second, firms that collaborate on R&D may want to patent more than other firms because a partnership implies opening, at least to some extent, their knowledge base to their partner(s). Accessing knowledge is an important driver of strategic alliances (see, for instance, Grant and

Baden-Fuller, 2004), and while sharing some of its knowledge, a firm may want to protect other valuable pieces of knowledge. This suggests that the mutual access to partners' knowledge bases requires a strong IP strategy, especially in case of partnerships with competitors.

The type of innovation a firm seeks to develop influences its patenting behaviour as well. In that respect, present results clearly confirm findings of previous studies that show that product innovations are more likely to be patented than process innovations (see, for instance, Arundel and Kabla, 1998; Brouwer and Kleinknecht, 1999). An innovation strategy targeted towards the development of new products appears indeed to be associated with larger patent portfolios than the patent portfolios of process-innovators. This validates hypothesis 4. A complex innovation strategy combining a high importance of both new products and new processes also positively impacts the number of patents a firm has in its patent portfolio. However, the positive coefficient associated with the product innovation variable turns out to be significantly higher than the coefficient associated with the complex innovation strategy variable, which refutes hypothesis 5. Firms that target process innovations do not show significantly different patenting behaviours with respect to firms that do not give a high importance to innovation, be it product or process. In terms of size of patent portfolio, it appears, therefore, that firms with an innovation strategy exclusively targeted towards the development of new products possess the largest patent portfolios, followed by firms with a complex innovation strategy pursuing both high product and process objectives. Finally, process innovators do not seem to patent more than non-innovators. Noticeably, the kind of innovation targeted by a firm is not found to influence significantly its probability to have a patent portfolio. Only the size of the portfolio is affected.

The limitations of the patent system perceived by firms do not seem to significantly impact their patenting behaviour. These results suggest that if patenting is a relevant strategy because a firm wants to protect its innovation rents through a legally enforceable mechanism, or because it seeks licensing revenues, inventions will be patented even if the system presents some drawbacks and inefficiencies.

Regarding perceived barriers to innovation, high risks and costs are found negatively to influence both the existence and the size of firms' patent portfolios. This probably results from a negative effect on firms' innovation efforts. A negative effect on the probability to have a patent portfolio is also found for the barriers to innovation coming from a firm's external environment, including customers, suppliers and public regulations.

9.6 Concluding Remarks

The objective of this study was to shed new light on the determinants of a firm's patenting behaviour. Two models have been estimated in order to assess the impact of several potential determinants on both the probability for a firm to have a patent portfolio, and on the size of this patent portfolio. In addition to traditional determinants related to firm and sector characteristics, this study investigates the potential impact of different types of innovation strategies on the patenting behaviour of firms. It is also suggested that a firm's patent portfolio can be influenced by the limitations of the patent system it perceives. Finally, it is tested whether a lower patenting activity can partly result from the perception of more barriers hindering innovation efforts.

Three major findings emerge from this study. First, even after controlling for firm and sector characteristics, the kind of innovation strategy followed by a firm significantly influences its patenting behaviour. Actually, the explanatory power of traditional determinants, such as market and technological opportunities, drops sharply after the introduction of innovation strategy variables. This introduction also significantly improves the general quality of estimations.

A second major finding is the highly significant impact of collaborating with universities, research institutes and public labs on a firm's patenting behaviour, probably because these joint R&D projects are science-based and more likely to result into patentable inventions. Moreover, the mutual access to partners' knowledge bases implied by R&D partnerships results in higher need for a strong IP strategy. This last point is likely to drive more particularly the positive effect of R&D partnerships with competitors on a firm's patenting behaviour.

The last major finding concerns the type of innovation sought by a firm. It appears that the largest patent portfolios are those of firms focusing almost exclusively on developing new products. Firms pursuing a complex strategy directed towards both product and process innovation show also larger patent portfolios than firms giving low importance to any kind of innovation. However, their patent portfolios are on average smaller than what is observed for product innovators. Finally, process innovators do not patent more than firms for which innovation is not a major strategic objective.

As it has been sketched in the theoretical section of this paper, an active patenting behaviour from part of a firm can reflect both a high innovativeness and a willingness to build a strong technological position vis-à-vis competitors. Being able to disentangle these two effects would provide a significant advance to the existing knowledge about patents. As in most previous empirical studies, this work is, however, not able to differentiate between these two perspectives on patents. This certainly constitutes a meaningful issue for further research. Moreover, it would be worthwhile to validate the present findings using larger databases of companies.

Acknowledgement

Dr Carine Peeters gratefully acknowledges a post-doctoral fellowship from the Belgian American Educational Foundation (BAEF).

Notes

1. A probit model would have been adequate as well. Both models lead generally to similar results (see Greene, 1993, 874–5 for a discussion), but only the logit model enables interpretion of the estimated coefficients as variations in the odds ratios thanks to a simple transformation: $e^{\hat{\beta}} = \Delta(P(Y = 1)/P(Y = 0))$.
2. Sales data come from the BelFirst database.
3. The categorization is based on the OECD classification of manufacturing firms into four classes: hi-tech, medium-high, medium-low and low-tech firms: HT = aeronautic construction, desks and computing machines, pharmaceuticals products, radio, TV and telecommunication machines; MH = professional equipment, motorcar vehicles, electric machines, chemical industries, other transport equipment, non-electric machines; ML = rubber and plastic materials, naval construction, other industrial sectors, non-iron metals, non-metallic mineral products, metallic works, petroleum and coal, steel industry; LT= paper, printing and editing, textile industry, clothing and leather, food, drinks and tobacco, wood and furniture. A category for all service companies is added: commerce, hotels and restaurants, transports, posts and telecommunications, insurances, financial services, real estate activities, computer activities.
4. A detailed description of factor analyses realized on the survey data is provided in Peeters and van Pottelsberghe (2003b).

References

Arora, A., 'Patents, Licensing, and Market Structure in Chemicals', *Research Policy*, 26 (4–5) (1997), 391–403.

Arrow, K., 'Economic Welfare and the Allocation of Resources for Invention', in R. R. Nelson (ed.), *The Rate and Direction of Inventive Activity* (Princeton: Princeton University Press, 1962), 609–25.

Arundel, A., 'The Relative Effectiveness of Patents and Secrecy for Appropriation', *Research Policy*, 30 (4) (2001), 611–24.

Arundel, A. and I. Kabla, 'What Percentage of Innovations is Patented?', *Research Policy*, 27 (2) (1998), 127–41.

Baldwin, J. R., P. Hanel and D. Sabourin, 'Determinants of Innovative Activity in Canadian Manufacturing Firms', in A. Kleinknecht and P. Mohnen (eds), *Innovation and Firm Performance: Econometric Explorations of Survey Data* (New York: Palgrave, 2002).

Baumol, W. J., *The Free Market Innovation Machine* (Princeton: Princeton University Press, 2002).

Bound, J., C. Cummings, Z. Griliches, B. H. Hall and A. B. Jaffe, 'Who Does R&D and Who Patents?', in Z. Griliches (ed.), *R&D, Patents and Productivity* (Chicago: University of Chicago Press, 1984), 21–54.

Brouwer, E. and A. Kleinknecht, 'Innovative Output and a Firm Propensity to Patent. An Exploration of CIS Micro Data', *Research Policy*, 28 (6) (1999), 615–24.

Cassiman, B., D. Pérez-Castrillo and R. Veugelers, 'Endogenizing Know-How Flows through the Nature of R&D Investments', *International Journal of Industrial Organization*, 20 (6) (2001), 775–99.

Cohen, W. M. and R. C. Levin, 'Empirical Studies of Innovation and Market Structure', in R. Schmalensee and R. D. Willig (eds), *Handbook of Industrial Organization* (Amsterdam: North-Holland, 1989).

Cohen, W. M., R. R. Nelson and J. P. Walsh, 'Protecting their Intellectual Assets: Appropriability Conditions and Why US Manufacturing Firms Patent (or not)', NBER Working Paper 7552 (2000).

Crépon, B., E. Duguet and I. Kabla, 'Schumpeterian Conjectures: A Moderate Support from Various Innovation Measures', in A. Kleinknecht (ed.), *Determinants of Innovation – The Message from New Indicators* (New York: Palgrave, 1996).

Crépon, B., E. Duguet and J. Mairesse, 'Research, Innovation, and Productivity: An Econometric Analysis at the Firm Level', *Economics of Innovation and New Technology*, 7 (2) (1998), 115–58.

Duguet, E. and I. Kabla, 'Appropriation Strategy and the Motivations to use the Patent System: an Econometric Analysis at the Firm Level in French Manufacturing', *Annales d'Economie et de Statistique*, 49/50 (1998), 289–327.

Gilbert, R. and D. Newberry, 'Preemptive Patenting and the Persistence of Monopoly', *American Economic Review*, 72 (3) (1982), 514–26.

Glazier, S. C. *Patent Strategies for Business* (L B I Law & Business Institute, 2000).

Grant, R. M. and C. Baden-Fuller, 'A Knowledge Accessing Theory of Strategic Alliances', *Journal of Management Studies*, 41 (1) (2004), 61–84.

Greene, W. H., *Econometric Analysis* (New Jersey: Prentice Hall, 1993).

Griliches, Z., 'Patent Statistics as Economic Indicators: A Survey', *Journal of Economic Literature*, 28 (4) (1990), 1661–707.

Hall, B. H., Z. Griliches and J. A. Hausman, 'Patents and R and D: Is There a Lag?', *International Economic Review*, 27 (2) (1986), 265–83.

Levin, R. C., A. K. Klerovick, R. R. Nelson and S. G. Winter, 'Appropriating the Returns from Industrial Research and Development', *Brookings Papers on Economic Activity*, 3 (1987) 783–831, printed in E. Mansfield and E. Mansfield (eds), The *Economics of Technical Change* (Vermont: Edward Elgar, 1993).

Lööf, H. and A. Heshmati, 'Knowledge Capital and Performance Heterogeneity: An Innovation Study at Firm Level', *International Journal of Production Economics*, 76 (1) (2002), 61–85.

Mansfield, E., 'Patents and Innovation: An Empirical Study', *Management Science*, 32 (2) (1986), 173–81.

Nelson, R. R., 'The Simple Economics of Basic Scientific Research', *Journal of Political Economy*, 67 (3) (1959), 297–306.

Nielsen, A. O., 'Patenting, R&D and Market Structure: Manufacturing Firms in Denmark', *Technological Forecasting and Social Change*, 66 (1) (2001), 47–58.

Parr, R. L. and P. H. Sullivan, *Technology Licensing* (New York: John Wiley & Sons, 1996).

Peeters, C. and B. van Pottelsberghe, 'Measuring Innovation Competencies and Performances – A Survey of Large Firms in Belgium', IIR Working Paper 03–16, Institute of Innovation Research, Hitotsubashi University (2003a).

Peeters, C. and B. van Pottelsberghe, 'Organizational Competencies and Innovation Performances – The Case of Large Firms in Belgium', IIR Working Paper 03–19, Institute of Innovation Research, Hitotsubashi University (2003b).

Reitzig, M., 'Strategic Management of Intellectual Property', *Sloan Management Review*, 45 (3) (2004), 35–40.

Ritter, T. and H. G. Gemünden, 'Network Competence: Its Impact on Innovation Success and its Antecedents', *Journal of Business Research*, 56 (9) (2003), 745–55.

Rivette, K. G. and D. Kline, *Rembrandts in the Attic* (Boston: Harvard Business School Press, 2000).

Scherer, F. M., 'Firm Size, Market Structure, Opportunity, and the Output of Patented Inventions', *American Economic Review*, 55 (5) (1965), 1097–125.

Scherer, F. M., 'The Propensity to Patent', *International Journal of Industrial Organization*, 1 (1) (1983), 107–28.

Schmookler, J., 'Inventors Past and Present', *The Review of Economics and Statistics*, 39 (3) (1957), 321–33.

Schmookler, J., *Invention and Economic Growth* (Cambridge: Harvard University Press, 1966).

Schumpeter, J. A., *Capitalism, Socialism and Democracy* (New York: Harper, 1942).

Scotchmer, S. and J. Green, 'Novelty and Disclosure in Patent Law', *RAND Journal of Economics*, 21 (1) (1990), 131–46.

Sherry, E. F. and D. J. Teece, 'Royalties, Evolving Patent Rights, and the Value of Innovation', *Research Policy*, 33 (2) (2004), 179–91.

Teece, D. J., 'Capturing Value from Knowledge Assets: The New Economy, Markets for Know-How, and Intangibles Assets', *California Management Review*, 40 (3) (1998), 55–79.

Tether, B. S., 'Who Co-operates for Innovation, and Why – An Empirical Analysis', *Research Policy*, 31 (6) (2002), 947–67.

van Ophem, H., E. Brouwer, A. Kleinknecht and P. Mohnen, 'The Mutual Relation between Patents and R&D', in A. Kleinknecht and P. Mohnen (eds), *Innovation and Firm Performance: Econometric Explorations of Survey Data* (New York: Palgrave, 2002).

Veugelers, R. and B. Cassiman, 'Make and Buy in Innovation Strategies: Evidence from Belgian Manufacturing Firms', *Research Policy*, 28 (1) (1999), 63–80.

10
On the Relationship Between Patents and Venture Capital

Astrid Romain and Bruno van Pottelsberghe de la Potterie

10.1 Introduction

Venture capital (VC) is a financial intermediary that aims at meeting innovative start-ups' needs. These firms are generally associated with large growth potentials and high levels of uncertainty. A growing number of scholars have documented the positive impact that venture funds have on the probability of success of start-ups, as well as on the growth of their sales and employees. Most government bodies in industrialized countries now recognize the importance of VC as a factor underlying firm creation and sustainable growth.[1] Despite this wide recognition of venture funds as key players underlying economic performances, there are huge differences across industrialized countries in the relative amounts of VC. It is relatively high in the USA and Canada for instance, whereas it is very low in Japan. The diversity of national financial systems is undoubtedly one important factor underlying these international differences (see, for example, Black and Gilson, 1998). Other factors also play an important role, as shown by Gompers and Lerner (1998) and Jeng and Wells (2000). With a panel dataset of 21 countries, Jeng and Wells show that labour market rigidities, the level of initial public offerings (IPO), government programmes for entrepreneurship, and bankruptcy procedures explain a significant share of cross-country variations in VC intensity. Gompers and Lerner focus exclusively on the US market and identify several factors influencing the level of VC.

The objective of this chapter is to contribute to this recent stream of research. Our central hypothesis is that two broad factors, unheard of in the existing empirical literature, might also contribute to explain the heterogeneity of VC intensity across countries. These factors are related to the entrepreneurial environment and to technological opportunity – in particular to intellectual property rights. We first develop a theoretical model which takes into account the factors that affect the demand and supply of VC. They include the growth of GDP, short-term and long-term interest rates, several indicators of technological opportunity (the business R&D expenditures growth rate, the level of business R&D capital stock and the number of triadic patents) and indicators of entrepreneurial environment. In order to evaluate the parameters of the theoretical model we exploit a panel dataset composed of 16 countries over an 11-year period.

The results show that GDP growth, technological opportunity and interest rates significantly influence VC intensity. The number of patents plays an important role as it stimulates the level of VC intensity. Higher levels of entrepreneurship – that is, the percentage of people being involved in the creation of nascent firms – induce a positive and significant relation between the R&D capital stock and VC intensity.

10.2 Literature Review

Four main streams of research have identified various determinants of venture capital intensity. The first one focuses mainly on differences in financial systems. For instance, Black and Gilson (1998) provide evidence that an active stock market is crucial for the development of strong venture capital market because of the potential for VC exit through an initial public offering. A second stream of research analyses the historical and socioeconomic context influencing the development of a VC industry (see, for example, Feldman, 2001; Kenney and von Burg, 1999; Kenney, 2001; Avnimelech *et al.*, 2005). The third one is more interested on behavioural analyses at the microeconomic level. Few articles have so far focused on the determinants of VC performance (Hege *et al.*, 2003; Manigart *et al.*, 2002). For Gompers and Lerner (1998) the individual firm performance and reputation, measured with the firm age and size, positively impact the capacity to raise larger funds. Hellmann and Puri (2000) use a probit model to show that the strategy of a company is one of the determinants of VC investment when controlling for the age of the company and its industrial sector. If the strategy is an innovative one it has a higher probability to benefit from VC compared to companies that follow an imitation strategy.

In this paper the focus is more on the fourth stream of research – that is the macroeconomic determinants of VC. To the best of our knowledge, only a few articles have attempted so far to evaluate quantitatively the macroeconomic determinants of VC. Jeng and Wells (2000) develop

Table 10.1 Potential determinants of VC

Potential determinants	Gompers and Lerner (1998) US, 1972–94	Jeng and Wells (2000) 21 countries, 1986–95
Initial public offering	(Market value of IPO) No effect at aggregate Level	+ Except for early stage funds
Gross domestic product	+	Not significant
Stock market opportunities[a]	+	Not significant
Finance reporting standards	n.a.	–
Labour market rigidities	n.a.	Not significant for total VC investment but – for early stage funds
Private pension funds	(Dummy for changes in ERISA's prudent man rule) +	(Level and growth of pension funds) + Over time but not across countries
Capital gains tax rate	–	Not significant
Level of interest rate	+ At aggregate level and – at state level	n.a.
Industrial and academic R&D	(Expenditures) +	n.a.
Number of patents	n.a.	n.a.

Note: [a] This variable is proxied by an indicator of market capitalization growth by Jeng and Wells (not significant, but probably correlated with GDP and IPO) and by an indicator of equity market return by Gompers and Lerner (positive and significant).

a model aiming at identifying the determinants of VC and test it on a cross-section of 21 countries over a period of ten years. Gompers and Lerner (1998) focus on the US economy over the period 1969–94. Their results are summarized in Table 10.1.

IPO is the strongest driver of VC according to Jeng and Wells (2000), because it reflects the potential return to VC funds. Gompers and Lerner (1998) take it as a proxy for fund performance but cannot find any significant effect in their empirical estimates. It seems that the IPO variable is strongly correlated with the expected return on alternative investments and with the gross domestic product (GDP), which might also be considered as a proxy for exit opportunities. GDP and market capitalization growth (MCG) are part of the impact of IPOs and therefore turn out to be not significant for Jeng and Wells (2000). However, the reverse is true for Gompers and Lerner (1998), who find a positive and significant impact of equity market return and GDP on VC but no impact of IPO. Higher GDP growth implies higher attractive opportunities for entrepreneurs, which lead to a higher need for venture funds.

For Jeng and Wells (2000), getting the basic legal and tax structures into place appears to be an important factor influencing VC. Gompers and Lerner (1998) also recognize the importance of government decisions on the private equity funds. The labour market legislation is typically put in place to protect employees from arbitrary, unfair or discriminatory actions by employers. Some authors argue that venture financing can suffer from the rigidity of the labour market in Europe (e.g., Ramón and Marti, 2001). Jeng and Wells (2000) show that it does not significantly influence total VC but affects negatively the early stage of VC investment.

With the clarification of the Employee Retirement Income Security Act (ERISA) 'prudent man' rule of 1979, the share of money invested by pension funds had risen to more than 50 per cent. Jeng and Wells (2000) find that the level of investment by private pension funds in VC is a significant determinant of VC over time but not across countries. Gompers and Lerner (1998) use a proxy for the amendment of the 'prudent man' rule to show the impact of pension regulation and reach a similar conclusion. After 1979, the additional capital provided by pension funds led to a dramatic shift in commitments to VC.

The capital gains tax rate (CGTR) on VC activity is often considered a potential determinant of VC itself. Gompers and Lerner (1998) show that a decrease in CGTR has a positive and important impact on commitment to new VC funds. In fact, they confirm the result of Poterba (1989), who built a model of the decision to become an entrepreneur. He found that decreases in CGTR might increase the raising of VC funds not through stimulation of the supply side (that is, the potential fund providers) but rather on the demand side. Indeed, decreases in CGTR often encourage entrepreneurship and thus the desire of people to create their own firm and to engage in R&D activities. Anand (1996) also highlights the fact that the level and composition of investments appear to be negatively affected by increases in the CGTR but investments in one industry may be affected by myriad other factors like technology shifts, tastes and so on.

Interest rates might also be an important factor influencing VC. Although Jeng and Wells (2000) do not take this factor into account into their cross-country investigation, Gompers and Lerner (1998) show that it affects positively the demand for VC funds in the United States. Economic theory would suggest a reverse relationship: if interest rates rise, the level of investment should fall. The positive impact estimated by Gompers and Lerner is probably due to the fact that they use a short-term interest rate. If short-term interest rates increase, the attractiveness of venture financing versus credit through usual financial institutions increases from the entrepreneur's viewpoint.

Both industrial and academic R&D expenditures are significantly related to venture capital activity at the state level in the model of Gompers and Lerner (1998). For them, the growth of VC fundraising in the mid-1990s may be due to increases in technological opportunities. But neither Gompers and Lerner (1998) nor Jeng and Wells (2000) test the impact of intellectual property rights on the level of VC funds.

10.3 Modelling the Amount of Venture Capital

As Poterba (1989) and Gompers and Lerner (1998), we argue that changes in the level of VC funds come from changes either in the supply or the demand of VC. The demand comes from the entrepreneurs willing to set up an innovative start-up. The supply of VC corresponds to the share of risk capital provided by private investors, pension funds and banks. The actual amount of VC invested represents the equilibrium between the demand and the supply of VC.

The demand and supply of VC can be modelled through equations (1) and (2) that characterize the demand price of VC, P^d, and the supply price of VC, P^s, respectively. The supply price of VC is assumed to be a positive function of the available VC funds, the interest rate (r) and the corporate tax rate (TAX). The more VC is available on the market, the higher will be the supply price of VC, due to increasing marginal costs ($a_{vc} > 0$). If interest rates increase we can expect the fund providers to increase their return requirement ($a_r > 0$; otherwise they would opt for alternative investment opportunities). Similarly, an increase in the corporate income tax rate would increase the return requirements ($a_{tax} > 0$):

$$P^s_{VC} = a_C + a_{vc}\, VC + a_{tax}\, TAX + a_r\, r \tag{1}$$
$$P^d_{VC} = b_C + b_{vc}\, VC + b_{\hat{Y}}\, \hat{Y} + b_{to}\, TO + b_{en}\, EN + b_{tax}\, TAX + b_r\, r \tag{2}$$

The equation of the demand price of VC reflects the entrepreneurs' viewpoint. Decreasing marginal returns to VC is assumed (the projects with the largest expected returns are selected first). The more VC is available the lower is the demand price of VC ($b_{vc} < 0$). The other factors that are assumed to influence the demand of VC are the GDP growth (Y), technological opportunities (TO), entrepreneurial culture (EN), the level of corporate income tax rate (TAX) and interest rates (r). The countries with a high GDP growth, large technological opportunities and a strong entrepreneurial culture are more likely to be associated with a strong demand for VC (and hence positive effects on the demand price of VC: $b_Y > 0$; $b_{TO} > 0$; $b_{EN} > 0$). The general level of taxation will probably reduce the rate of entrepreneurship (the demand for VC and therefore $b_{tax} < 0$). Concerning interest rates, we consider that innovative start-ups need important amounts of money in the short term. Therefore, if the cost of capital increases entrepreneurs are more likely to switch from the banking sector to the venture fund providers ($b_r > 0$).

Equations (3) and (4) show the equilibrium level of VC that equalizes the supply and demand of VC:

$$(a_{vc} - b_{vc})VC = (b_C - a_C) + b_{\hat{Y}}\,\hat{Y} + b_{to}\,TO + b_{en}\,EN + (b_{tax} - a_{tax})\,TAX_{it} + (b_r - a_r)r \tag{3}$$

$$\text{where} \quad \begin{cases} a_{vc} > 0 \rightarrow \text{increasing marginal cost of VC investment} \\ b_{vc} < 0 \rightarrow \text{decreasing marginal return} \\ (a_{vc} - b_{vc}) \rightarrow \text{always positive} \end{cases}$$

$$VC = \left[\frac{(b_C - a_C)}{(a_{vc} - b_{vc})}\right] + \left[\frac{(b_{\hat{Y}}}{(a_{vc} - b_{vc})}\right]\hat{Y} + \left[\frac{b_{to}}{(a_{vc} - b_{vc})}\right]TO + \left[\frac{b_{en}}{(a_{vc} - b_{vc})}\right]EN + \left[\frac{(b_{tax} - a_{tax})}{(a_{vc} - b_{vc})}\right]TAX + \left[\frac{(b_r - a_r)}{(a_{vc} - b_{vc})}\right]r \tag{4}$$

Since the denominator is always positive, the numerator provides the expected sign of the parameters between brackets. All the right-hand-side variables, except the level of taxation and the interest rate, are expected to have a positive impact on VC. For the interest rate (r), the impact is either negative or positive, depending on the difference between the demand-price effect and the supply-price effect. If the demand-price effect of a high interest rate is larger than its supply-price effect, then the overall impact of interest rates on VC should be positive. The effect of the level of corporate income tax rate on the equilibrium level of VC will always be negative since ($b_{tax} - a_{tax}$) is always negative.

The empirical implementation of equation (4) is presented in equations (5) and (6). The growth rate of GDP allows testing the cyclicality of VC. Regarding interest rate, we suspect that short-term and long-term interest rates could affect differently the venture fund providers and the 'hi-tech' entrepreneurs. We therefore plan to use a short-term interest rate (one year, r^{ST}), a long-term interest rate (ten years, r^{LT}) and the spread (difference between short term and long term) in the empirical model. Technological opportunity is proxied by three variables, the growth rate of business R&D outlays, the business R&D capital stock and the number of triadic patents. The growth rate of business R&D expenditures represents the research dynamics of a country. The business R&D capital stock is an indicator of the available stock of knowledge (or of the cumulated innovative efforts). The number of triadic patents is an indicator of innovative output. It measures the number of highly valuable inventions invented in each country (it is counted by country of inventor and by priority year).

The entrepreneurial environment can be measured with two variables: the level of taxation and the level of entrepreneurial activity. Other factors like shareholder rights, labour market rigidities, legal protection and accounting standards could also be taken into account to measure the entrepreneurial environment. The level of taxation is measured with the corporate income tax rate (CITR). The measure of entrepreneurial activity (TEA) is an index available for one year in our database. We therefore introduce it in interaction with another variable. For instance, we test whether TEA would affect the impact of the business R&D capital stock on the intensity of VC. This is equivalent to testing whether the impact of the available stock of knowledge, (SBRD) on VC intensity is composed of a fixed component ($\beta^c\Delta_{sbrd}$) and a component that varies across countries according to the level of entrepreneurship (that is, $\beta\Delta_{sbrd} = \beta^c\Delta_{sbrdp} + \beta_{tea}SBRD$). That interaction is illustrated in equation (6).

Model with no interaction

$$VC_{it} = \beta_{\Delta gdp}\Delta GDP_{it} + \beta_r r_{it} + \beta_{\Delta brd}\Delta BRD_{it-1} + \beta_{sbrd}SBRD_{it-1} + \beta_{pat}LPAT_{it-2} + \beta_{citr}CITR_{it} + \sigma_G G + \phi_i + \varphi_t + \mu_{it} \quad (5)$$

Model with interactions with TEA

$$VC_{it} = \beta_{\Delta gdp}\Delta GDP_{it} + \beta_r r_{it} + \beta_{sbrd}SBRD_{it-1}\beta_{citr}CITR_{it} + \beta_{tea}(SBRD^{*}_{it-1}\,TEA_i) + \sigma_G G + \phi_i + \varphi_t + \mu_{it} \quad (6)$$

where Δ represents the first logarithmic difference and L the natural logarithm. In this equation, the parameters that are to be estimated are assumed to be constant across countries and over time; they are defined as follows (the expected signs are presented between parentheses):

$\beta_{\Delta gdp}$ The impact of GDP growth (+)
β_r The impact of interest rate (?)

$\beta\Delta_{brd}$ The impact of business R&D expenditures growth rate (+)
β_{sbrd} The impact of the level of business R&D capital stock (+)
β_{pat} The impact of the number of triadic patents (+)
β_{tea} The impact of the level of entrepreneurship on β_{sbrd} (+)
β_{citr} The impact of the CITR (−)

A range of control variables is included in all the regressions.

G is a dummy equal to 1 for Germany in 1991, and 0 otherwise; in order to take into account the exogenous shock of the German unification
ϕ_i are country dummies which take into account country-specific framework conditions that might affect VC intensity
φ_t are time dummies which take into account exogenous shocks that are common to several countries, such as changes in exchange rates

The variables (for country *i* and time *t*) are defined as follows:

VC is the venture capital intensity, that is, the VC funds divided by GDP (*sources*: EVCA and OECD)[2]
GDP is the gross domestic product (*source*: OECD, *Main Science and Technology Indicators*)
r is the one-year national deposit interest rate (*source*: IMF) or the long-term national interest rate (ten years, *source*: OECD)
BRD is the business R&D expenditures (*source*: OECD, *Main Science and Technology Indicators*)
SBRD is the business R&D capital stock. It has been computed using the perpetual inventory method from total intramural business R&D expenditures, in constant 1990 GDP prices and US PPPs. The depreciation rate is 15 per cent. Sensitivity analysis show that the results of the regressions do not change significantly with the chosen depreciation rate (Guellec and van Pottelsberghe, 2001, 2004) (*source*: OECD, *Main Science and Technology Indicators*)
PAT is the number of triadic patents. These patents have been applied at the USPTO, the Japanese Patent Office and the European Patent Office. We can therefore assume that they reflect patents with a very high value (*source*: OECD, *Main Science and Technology Indicators*)
TEA is the total entrepreneurship activity (TEA)-index computed by adding the proportion of adults involved in the creation of nascent firms and the proportion involved in new firms (*source*: Global

Entrepreneurship Monitor, 2001). The variable is a ranking from 1 to 20. This measure of entrepreneurial activity can be meaningfully used for international comparisons. Since the indicator is fixed over time, it is introduced in interaction with SBRD

CITR is the corporate income tax rate (*source*: Office of Tax Policy Research OTPR)

The estimates are performed with a panel dataset of 16 OECD countries over the period 1990–2000. These 16 countries are Australia, Belgium, Canada, Denmark, Finland, France, Germany, Ireland, Italy, Japan, the Netherlands, Norway, Spain, Sweden, the United Kingdom and the United States. The period can vary across countries based on availability of information. Descriptive statistics of all the variables are presented in Table 10.2. The average value of the dependent variable (VC intensity) varies from 0.02 per cent in Denmark and Japan, to 0.18 per cent in Canada, as shown in the last column.

10.4 Empirical Results

Table 10.3 presents the results of the estimates. All variables have the expected impact as far as their sign and significance are concerned except for the business R&D investment growth rate and the corporate income tax rate (CITR).

Columns 1 to 3 present the model described in equation (5), with different indicators for the interest rates. Results concerning the growth rate of GDP are in line with those of Gompers and Lerner (1998). In column 1, the GDP growth is significant, whereas in column 2, it is less significant, probably due to the simultaneous introduction of the long-term interest rate in the model. The difference between short-term and long-term interest rates has a significant and negative impact (column 3). It seems, therefore, that the short-term and long-term cost of capital and their difference play an important role in explaining the intensity of VC. These results witness a stronger influence of the cost of capital on the demand side (entrepreneurs) than on the supply side (investors). However, the larger the difference between long-term and short-term interest rates, the lower the VC intensity, suggesting a stronger influence of the spread on the supply side of VC.

The variables representing research efforts and number of patents play a significant role in determining VC intensity. The strong and positive impact of the business R&D capital stock and the number of triadic patents show that the demand of VC is sensitive to the available stock of

Table 10.2 Descriptive statistics (%)

		Yearly average growth rates (in %)				Average		% shares
Country	**Period**	**GDP**	**Business R&D invest.**	**Business R&D capital stock**	**Number of patents***	**Corporate income tax rate**	**Level of enterpreneurship**	**VC intensity (GDP)**
Australia	1995–8	3.47	−4.64	5.79	6.87	0.35	15.2	0.09
Belgium	1990–8	1.68	5.28	3.72	6.77	0.39	4.5	0.06
Canada	1995–9	3.49	3.83	4.93	10.47	0.38	12.2	0.18
Denmark	1990–9	2.25	6.95	7.18	7.11	0.36	7.6	0.02
Finland	1990–2000	2.44	9.84	8.33	12.36	0.26	12.5	0.06
France	1990–2000	1.88	1.37	2.70	0.89	0.34	5.0	0.07
Germany	1990–9	2.87	0.59	1.52	4.23	0.41	6.9	0.05
Ireland	1990–2000	7.42	14.21	14.37	5.99	0.37	9.1	0.08
Italy	1990–2000	1.74	0.62	2.35	1.20	0.36	8.1	0.04
Japan	1994–8	0.94	4.86	3.55	5.83	0.38	5.7	0.02
Netherlands	1990–2000	3.21	3.01	2.26	3.63	0.35	6.4	0.15
Norway	1990–9	3.10	3.50	3.31	10.41	0.28	10.9	0.07
Spain	1990–9	2.37	1.23	4.16	4.83	0.35	6.6	0.04
Sweden	1990–2000	1.93	8.21	6.33	10.11	0.30	6.6	0.07
United Kingdom	1990–2000	2.42	0.12	0.97	2.99	0.33	6.9	0.13
United States	1990–9	3.11	3.71	2.96	3.05	0.35	16.7	0.12

Note: * The data 'Number of triadic patents' are not available after 1998.

Sources: OECD, MSTI (Major Science and Technology Indicators), EVCA and own calculations.

Table 10.3 Estimation results of the VC intensity, complete model and interactions

		Dependent variable: VC intensity (VC/GDP)			
Regressions		GLS 1	GLS 2	GLS 3	GLS 4
Economic variables					
GDP growth rate	ΔGDP_{it}	0.002*	0.002	0.002*	0.002**
		(1.67)	*(1.50)*	*(1.64)*	*(2.46)*
One-year interest rate	r_{it}	0.00004**			0.00005***
		(2.35)			*(3.54)*
Long-term interest rate	r_{it}		0.00007***		
(10 years)		*(2.95)*			
Log [r10/r1]	r_{it}			−0.0001***	
			(−2.49)		
Technological opportunity					
Business R&D investment	ΔBRD_{it-1}	0.0006*	0.0005	0.0005	
growth rate (t − 1)		*(1.68)*	*(1.39)*	*(1.48)*	
Business R&D capital stock	$SBRD_{it-1}$	1.43***	1.32***	1.44***	−1.42**
(t − 1) (*10^{-14})		*(4.47)*	*(4.05)*	*(4.69)*	*(−2.40)*
Log Number of triadic	$LPAT_{it-2}$	0.0003**	0.0004***	0.0003***	
Patents (t − 2)		*(2.31)*	*(2.93)*	*(2.52)*	
Entrepreneurial environment					
Corporate income tax rate	$CITR_{it}$	−0.0002	0.0004	−0.0002	−0.0002
		(−0.50)	*(1.19)*	*(−0.75)*	*(−0.60)*
Level of entrepreneurship	$SBRD_{it-1}$				1.70***
(*10^{-15})	$xTEA_i$				*(3.90)*
Control variables					
German reunification dummy (t)		Yes	Yes	Yes	Yes
Country-specific intercept		Yes	Yes	Yes	Yes
Time dummies		Yes	Yes	Yes	Yes
Adjusted R-squared		0.939	0.927	0.930	0.933

Notes: Panel data, 16 OECD countries, 1990–2000, 154 observations. * indicates the parameters that are significant at a 10% probability threshold; ** 5% probability threshold; *** 1% probability threshold. The econometric method is GLS.

knowledge and to the level of innovation output, as proxied by the number of high-value patents. This result about triadic patents is consistent with the results of Kortum and Lerner (1998) or Tykvova (2000), who show that a surge of patents may increase the VC fundraising. In other words, the property of highly valued intellectual assets (triadic patents are associated with a much higher value than the patents applied only in one country or region) seems to stimulate the demand for VC.

The remaining column tests the specification described in equation (6), with the interaction variable representing a country's entrepreneurial environment. The level of entrepreneurship is interacted with the stock of available knowledge (the R&D capital stock, in column 4). The estimated parameters indicate that the impact of the R&D capital stock on the VC intensity is composed of a fixed negative component and a country-specific component that depends on the relative level of entrepreneurship (TEA): the higher the level of entrepreneurship, the stronger the impact of the business R&D capital stock on VC intensity. In order to have a positive impact of the available stock of knowledge on VC performances, a minimum level of entrepreneurship is required. The estimated parameters suggest that the impact of the business R&D capital stock on the VC intensity becomes positive and significant above a threshold of 8.4 in the TEA index (level of entrepreneurship).

Table 10.4 summarizes the main findings of our empirical investigation and compares them with the results obtained by Jeng and Wells (2000) and Gompers and Lerner (1998). The cyclicality of VC with respect to GDP growth confirms both our expectation and the results of Gompers and Lerner (1998). Jeng and Wells (2000) did not find any significant effect partly because of the structure of their dataset (cross-section of countries) and partly because of the use of the IPO variable.

Concerning the cost of capital, we confirm the positive impact of the short-term interest rate obtained by Gompers and Lerner (1998) at the aggregate level. We also show that the difference between the long-term interest rate and the short-term interest rate has a negative and significant impact on the VC intensity.

A strong entrepreneurial culture and more intense technological opportunities improve the positive effect of the stock of knowledge on the VC intensity. Moreover, the property of highly valued intellectual assets seems to stimulate the demand for VC.

10.5 Concluding Remarks

This paper aims to contribute to the literature on the determinants of VC intensity. Our contribution consists of (1) developing a theoretical model that takes into account the supply-side and demand-side variables to explain VC intensity; and (2) introducing simultaneously traditional determinants of VC and new potential determinants like the cost of capital, the level of entrepreneurship, and novel proxies aiming at measuring technological opportunity, especially the number of triadic patents. The empirical results can be summarized as follows.

Table 10.4 Comparison of our results with the state of the art

	Jeng and Wells (2000), 21 countries, panel data and cross-section	**Gompers and Lerner (1998) US industry aggregate data**	**Our analysis 16 countries, panel data**
Macroeconomic conditions			
Gross domestic product	0	+	+
Interest rate 1 year		+ at aggregate level – at state level	+
Interest rate 10 years			+
Difference between 10-year and 1-year interest rate			–
Private pension funds funds	+ over time 0 across countries	+ over time	
Entrepreneurial environment			
Taxation rate	0	–	0
Labour market rigidities	– at the early stage 0 at expansion stage		
Initial public offering	0 at early stage across countries + at expansion stage	0	
Stock market opportunities	(market capitalization growth) 0	(equity market return) +	
Level of entrepreneurship			+ increases the impact of R&D on VC
Technological opportunity			
Number of tradic patents			+
Business R&D growth		+	+
Stock of knowledge		+	+

Interest rates have a significant impact on VC intensity. Whereas short-term and long-term interest rates influence positively the relative level of VC via a strong demand-side effect, the difference between long-term and short-term interest rates has the opposite impact, via a stronger supply-side effect.

VC is pro-cyclical. It follows a similar evolution to GDP growth rate. In periods of high growth, the flow of venture capital out-performs the GDP growth rate, and vice versa. We also show that indicators of technological opportunity, such as the available stock of knowledge and the number of high-value patents (triadic patents), influence significantly a country's investment in VC. The positive impact of the stock of knowledge is strongly reinforced in the countries where the rate of entrepreneurship is very high.

One important policy implication that emerges from these results is that in order to stimulate VC in a country, demand-side factors have to be taken into account. The most important factors affecting the demand of VC are the stock of knowledge, innovative outputs proxied by the number of highly valued (triadic) patents, and interest rates. In addition, the level of entrepreneurship does play an important role.

Acknowledgement

Astrid Romain has a research grant provided by the Région de Bruxelles-Capitale.

Notes

1. See OECD (1996), Engel (2002), Hellmann and Puri (2002), Kortum and Lerner (2000) and Romain and van Pottelsberghe (2003) for empirical evidence on the economic impact of VC.
2. Definitions and data collection about VC are different in the USA and in Europe. The European Venture Capital Association included management buy-outs (MBOs) and management buy-ins (MBIs) in the definition of the VC. In the present analysis, in order to have the same definition of VC for each country, venture expenditures include only seed, start-up and early stage capital and do not include replacement capital and buy-out.

References

Anand, B., 'Tax Effects on Venture Capital', *mimeo*, Yale School of Management (1996).

Avnimelech, G., M. Kenney and M. Teubal, 'A Life Cycle Model for the Creation of National Venture Capital Industries – Comparing the US and Israeli Experiences', *mimeo*, UC Davis (2005).

Berger, A. N. and G. F. Udell, 'The Economics of Small Business Finance: The Roles of Private Equity and Debt Markets in the Financial Growth Cycle', *Journal of Banking and Finance*, 22(6–8) (1998), 613–73.

Black, B. S. and R. J. Gilson, 'Venture Capital and the Structure of Capital Markets: Banks versus Stock Markets', *Journal of Financial Economics*, 47 (1998), 243–77.

Engel, D., 'The Impact of Venture Capital in Firm Growth: An Empirical Investigation', ZEW discussion paper 02–02 (2002), 30pp.

Feldman, M., 'The Entrepreneurial Event Revisited: Firm Formation in a Regional Context', *Industrial and Corporate Change*, 10(4) (2001), 861–91.

Global Entrepreneurship Monitor (2001), *Executive Report*.

Gompers, P. and J. Lerner, 'What Drives Venture Fundraising?', *Brookings Papers on Economic Activity*, Microeconomics (1998), 149–92.

Gompers, P. and J. Lerner, 'The Venture Capital Revolution', *Journal of Economic Perspectives*, 15(2) (2001), 145–68.

Guellec, D. and B. van Pottelsberghe, 'R&D and Productivity Growth: Panel Data Analysis of 16 OECD Countries', *OECD Economic Studies*, 33(2) (2001), 103–26.

Guellec, D. and B. van Pottelsberghe, 'From R&D to Productivity Growth: The Sources of Knowledge Spillovers and Their Interaction', *Oxford Bulletin of Economics and Statistics*, 66(3) (2004), 353–76.

Hege, U., F. Palomino and A. Schwienbacher, 'Determinants of Venture Capital Performance: Europe and the United States', RICAFE Working Paper, 001, Risk Capital and the Financing of European Innovative Firms RICAFE (2003).

Hellmann, T. and M. Puri, 'The Interaction between Product Market and Financing Strategy: The Role of Venture Capital', *Review of Financial Studies*, 13 (2000), 959–84.

Hellmann, T. and M. Puri, 'Venture Capital and the Professionalization of Startup Firms: Empirical Evidence', *Journal of Finance*, 57(1) (2002), 169–97.

International Monetary Fund, *International Financial Statistics*, Yearbook 2002, vol. LV (2002).

Jeng, L. A. and P. C. Wells, 'The Determinants of Venture Capital Funding: Evidence Across Countries', *Journal of Corporate Finance*, 6(3) (2000), 241–89.

Kenney, M., 'Regional Clusters, Venture Capital and Entrepreneurship; What Can the Social Sciences Tell Us About Silicon Valley?', *OCDE Proceedings* (2001).

Kenney, M. and U. von Burg, 'Technology, Entrepreneurship and Path Dependence: Industrial Clustering in Silicon Valley and Route 128', *Industrial and Corporate Change*, 8(1) (1999), 67–103.

Kortum, S. and J. Lerner, 'Assessing the Contribution of Venture Capital to Innovation', *RAND Journal of Economics*, 31(4) (2000), 674–92.

Manigart, S. and C. Beuselinck, 'Supply of Venture Capital by European Governments', Working paper 2001/111, Ghent University (2001), 20p.

Manigart, S., P. Desbrières, K. De Waele, M. Wright, K. Robbie, H. Sapienza and A. Beekman, 'Determinants of required return in venture capital investments: A five country study', *Journal of Business Venturing*, 17(4) (2002), 291–312.

OECD, *Jobs Study*, Organisation for Economic Co-operation and Development, Paris (1994a).

OECD, *Employment Outlook*, Organisation for Economic Co-operation and Development, Paris (1994b).

OECD, *Venture Capital and Innovation*, Organisation for Economic Co-operation and Development, Paris (1996).

OECD, OECD statistics: *Main Science and Technology Indicators*, 1, Organisation for Economic Co-operation and Development, Paris (1997, 1999, 2001).

O'Shea, M. and C. Stevens, 'Quand le gouvernement apporte du capital-risque', *L'Observateur de l'OCDE*, 213 (1998), 26–9.

Poterba, J. M., 'Venture Capital and Capital Gains Taxation', NBER Working Paper 2832 (1989).

Ramón, B. M. and J. Marti, 'The Determinants of Private Equity Fundraising in Western Europe', Social Science Research Network Working Paper, presented at the EFMA Lugano Meetings (2001).

Romain, A. and B. van Pottelsberghe, 'The Impact of Venture Capital on Productivity', IIR Working Paper 03–20, Institute of Innovation Research, Hitotsubashi University (2003).

Tykvova, T., 'Venture Capital in Germany and Its Impact on Innovation', Social Science Research Network Working Paper, presented at the 2000 EFMA Conference, Athens (2000).

Ueda, M. and M. Hirukawa, 'Venture Capital and Productivity', *miméo*, University of Wisconsin (2003).

Index

Notes: f = figure; n = note; t = table; **bold** = extended discussion or heading emphasized in main text.

The manufacturer's authorised representative in the EU is Springer Nature Customer Service Centre GmbH, Europaplatz 3, 69115 Heidelberg, Germany. If you have any concerns regarding our products, please contact ProductSafety@springernature.com

Printed and bound by CPI Group (UK) Ltd, Croydon, CR0 4YY
14/10/2026
02233145-0009